VIRGINIA WOOLF
THE INWARD VOYAGE

VIRGINIA WOOLF

The Inward Voyage

By HARVENA RICHTER

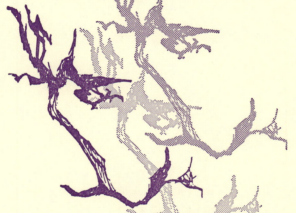

PRINCETON UNIVERSITY PRESS, 1970

COPY 2

Printed in the United States of America
by Princeton University Press

FOR LEON EDEL

who showed me the way

Preface

In 1913, that extraordinary year which saw the appearance of the first two volumes of *Remembrance of Things Past* and the final beginnings of *A Portrait of the Artist*, a young Englishwoman had just finished a novel also exploring the inner world of adolescence and first love.[1] Proust's search for lost time and Joyce's excursion into a young man's consciousness have become landmarks of what we now call the psychological novel. Virginia Woolf's *The Voyage Out*, on the other hand, has generally been dismissed as conventional. But as a glimpse into internal reality and the essence of lived experience, this first fictional voyage, in the narrator's words, went "farther inland than any one's been yet."

This study is of Mrs. Woolf's subjective methods—not only the ways by which her reader is led "inland" to the consciousness of her characters, but also the means by which he senses its very geography and climate. An aura of emotional awareness drawn from the entire being, consciousness is more than a stream of associated ideas and feelings: it is part of a complex synthesis of the individual's total response to life. We may call this a sense of *lived reality*, and the modes by which Virginia Woolf shows it are those by which man himself experiences this reality. Using principles of perception and mind function, she seeks to approximate the actual ways in which man sees, feels, thinks, and experiences time and change. The reader, placed within the mind of the character, becomes to some extent that mind, receiving certain of the emotional stimuli and sharing in its response.

This view of the psycho-physical totality of the self,

[1] Both Virginia Woolf's and James Joyce's novels were published in 1915, Mrs. Woolf's having been delayed because of illness.

and the means by which to express it, was a far cry from earlier experiments in fiction which had tried to externalize certain aspects of the inner and partially unconscious world of the mind, such as the novels of Henry James's major phase or Russian attempts to render dream, hypnagogic, and pathological states. Before *The Voyage Out* was written, no novelist had ever tried to describe exactly how the eye-mind experiences the object, or how the body participates in this experience. Indeed, no one had ever really considered perception and the mental and physical influences which act upon it. In the final chapters of Mrs. Woolf's first novel (and one can note her modes of subjectivity in a rudimentary form in the earliest surviving manuscripts), the contents of Rachel's world, as she lies in the delirium of typhoid fever, are detailed with astonishing accuracy. It is this emphasis on the subject's experience of the object which separates Virginia Woolf most clearly from her contemporaries. The external world in Mrs. Woolf's novels is colored by the character's emotion, distorted by the physical angle of vision at which he sees the object, governed by complex visual processes such as those which abstract line from mass, or color from shape. Mirroring the state of mind of the perceiver, the reality of the object, in psychoanalytical terms, is subsumed in the "projections" of the viewer.

In a parallel manner, the character's inner world is externalized through mental processes which abstract, concretize, or compress feeling into image, metaphor, and symbol, and so explore areas of submerged emotion usually glimpsed only by the dreaming mind. The mind, for example, "abstracts" a sequence of felt emotions into a reverie or dream, or may condense an emotion into one violent image, translate it into myth, change its shape to amplify its meaning.

In later novels Virginia Woolf would experiment with

other psychological techniques which help place the reader in the mind of the character: the discontinuity of thought and its patterns, the simultaneity of perceptual experience, the "scrambled" data of consciousness, the moment of present time.[2] But even these now classic modes of subjectivity, shared with such writers as Joyce and Faulkner, she shaped to her own vision. Time, for example, is seen not merely as the present moment but as dimension, motion, growth. Her interior world is one of constant transformation, for experience is never static. Even the prose rhythms reflect the flux and flow of certain emotional patterns. As the reader becomes caught up in the shifting world of time and motion, of sense and sensibility, in which personality itself is in a constant state of change, he achieves the illusion of the character's very growth and development. Thus, in Virginia Woolf's novels, *the traditional frame of point of view may be said to dissolve in participation; analytical structure into synthetical experience.*

These modes of subjectivity have, to a large extent, been overlooked because, without our being aware of them, we use them constantly ourselves. Like the process of breathing, they exist on the periphery of consciousness—we do not usually think about them, for they interrupt our sense of living. In much the same way, it does not occur to us that a writer would utilize these methods; we have difficulty in perceiving them because they are part of the organic nature of the work. It is difficult, for instance, to define what makes the delirium scenes in *The Voyage Out* so vividly real. What makes them authentic—the distortion of Rachel's angle of vision, the discontinuity of the delirium state with its shifting metamorphoses and symbols, the eerie expansion and contraction of time and space—is the result of a combination of subjective modes.

[2] Leon Edel discusses these modes of subjectivity which stem from point of view in "A Logic of Subjectivity," *The Modern Psychological Novel*, rev. edn. (New York, 1964), pp. 198-201.

Abstraction, reflection, metamorphosis, discontinuity—these and other modes are the means by which Mrs. Woolf brings the reader into the very center of the work. They are not artificial techniques, imposed from without, but the actual processes which, when rendered through the medium of language, tend to make the act of reading approximate the experience itself.

It is this sense of reader participation that makes Virginia Woolf's method so pertinent today. The reader is no longer a passive spectator in a horizontal sequence of events. He is involved actively in the character's total environment—an *enveloppement* in which all the senses, all central and peripheral feelings, are called upon. The response of the reader may vary according to his particular self, but it is a response on a universal or collective level rather than a simply individual one. Virginia Woolf's concept of the "common reader," discussed in the final chapter of this study, is brought into the very fabric of her fiction.

In an early draft of an essay on Percy Lubbock's *The Craft of Fiction*, Mrs. Woolf states that "when we come to judge a novel, we have no tradition to guide us." There is, she continues, "something so personal, so emotional, so unamenable to rules of art in fiction itself, that it is hopeless to judge it by the old stern standards."[3] When certain characteristics of the "time novels" were applied to those of Virginia Woolf, partly under the influence of Wyndham Lewis, partly in the belief that anything to do with time and reality must necessarily reflect Bergson's philosophy, the main factor of Mrs. Woolf's writing—the conveying of emotion with its multiple sources

---

[3] *J. R. Notebook III*, June 11, 1922. This essay, considerably revised, became "On Re-reading Novels" (*The Moment and Other Essays*), *Collected Essays*, II.

—was scanted. There were no standards to judge her work by except those which, however obscurely, she had raised herself. Indeed, it was difficult to find even those standards until two principles were discovered which seemed to lend order to her other ideas about fiction. The first was a seemingly random remark that a book "is not form which you see, but emotion which you feel."[4] The second was implied by her essay "The Moment: Summer's Night" which deals with the myriad flashes of stimuli and response that make up the lived moment of being and shows that not merely visual and audial scorings on consciousness are registered but felt impulses from the body as well. In other words, the multi-dimensional response to the moment included a body-ego, whose presence had never before been taken into account by fiction writers.

It is difficult, when we also consider Mrs. Woolf's concern with the way the subject experiences the object, not to connect her view of emotional reality with certain aspects of Edmund Husserl's phenomenology, an influence which certainly must have operated on G. E. Moore (see Chapter II, ii). Yet there are dangers in linking any writer's method with a specific philosophy or doctrine, and however Bloomsbury may have felt the impress of Husserl, we can only conclude that philosophy in general and psychology in particular had moved away from the mind-matter split of the nineteenth century toward a more complex view of man which would present him, as Virginia Woolf herself did, as a mind-body-feeling gestalt. When, in 1916, Mrs. Woolf wrote of readers looking to contemporary writers to give them the "mind" and "body of our time,"[5] she had not yet encountered Proust's narrator whose body so dominates the opening pages of *Swann's*

[4] "On Re-reading Novels" (*M.*), *Essays*, II, p. 126.
[5] "Hours in a Library" (*Granite and Rainbow*), *Essays*, II, p. 37.

Way. But she had already shown, in Rachel of *The Voyage Out*, the world as seen by what Husserl's disciple, Merleau-Ponty, would later call the "body-subject." And she would refine and develop her concept of the mind-body-feeling gestalt until, in *The Waves*, the different characters would represent its various aspects, with Jinny (" 'little animal that I am' ") personifying a synthesis of physical and sexual attitudes. What began as an urge to communicate life itself—for " 'it's life that matters,' " Virginia Woolf cried out in her diary and in *Night and Day*—developed into a complex and sophisticated method of conveying the many interrelated components of lived experience. Even her concept of inward form, cast in the "dimensions of the human being" (as the final chapters of this study set forth), was the logical outcome of her apprehension of man's mental and physical totality.

As MY research on and analysis of Mrs. Woolf's subjective modes progressed, a new understanding of her novels emerged. Method was seen to fuse with form and, especially in *The Waves* and *The Years*, become its meaning. Because of the complexity of her novelistic vision, this study attempts to present the modes in the sequence in which the principles themselves unfolded. The first chapters present the intellectual milieu which shaped Virginia Woolf and her work and which helped to lead to her understanding of emotion as presented in her essay "The Moment." Following the various aspects of subjectivity which this seminal essay sets forth, the modes appeared to group themselves in four categories. The first deals with the way the character thinks, and comprises the thought patterns, conscious and unconscious, which commitment to the single point of view imposes. The second includes the whole process of perception—the way the character sees the object. The third shows how the character experiences time and includes the modes of personality bound up with memory and the moment. The last category, how the character feels, may be seen in the primitive modes of subjectivity—the shapes of feeling: image, metaphor, and symbol—and in the externalization of feeling as form shown in Chapters XI and XII. Part of the difficulty and challenge of this study lay in the interfusion of Mrs. Woolf's methods which necessitated continual cross-reference in order to present the modes in their completeness. The joy of the study lay in the fact that, as a novelist myself, I was exploring another writer's method, discovering not only Mrs. Woolf's particular techniques but also certain fundamental principles which may be employed by any fiction writer.

Very few novelists have been able to describe the act of writing itself—what we might term the creative process. It is accomplished partly in the unconscious, involuntary as the act of the oyster secreting a pearl.[6] Yet however intuitive Virginia Woolf's method may have been, the results are open to analysis. Mrs. Woolf herself, in her essays and through a number of characters in her fiction (most notably Bernard of *The Waves* and Lily Briscoe of *To the Lighthouse*), described facets of the creative process. For those who may be interested in method and theory, and perhaps in confirming, as I did, some intuitions, I hope this log of her inward voyage may prove of interest. For the "common reader" or student, I hope the journey may not be wearisome but offer some small pleasures along the way.

I WOULD like to express appreciation to the late Leonard Woolf for allowing me to quote extensively from his wife's manuscripts and published works; to the Henry W. and Albert A. Berg Collection at the New York Pub-

[6] *A Writer's Diary* (hereafter called *Diary*), August 7, 1939.

lic Library, Astor, Lenox, and Tilden Foundations, for access to manuscripts of her novels, essays, and reviews, and permission to quote from them, and to Dr. Lola Szladits for her patient help; to the American Association of University Women for a research and writing fellowship; and to the MacDowell Colony for a quiet studio where much of the work was accomplished. My special thanks go to Dr. Henry Elkin, Professor of Psychology at Duquesne University, for reading this volume in manuscript, and to Professor Elkin and Dr. Frederick Baekeland, M.D., for recommending and lending certain research material. Finally, I wish to express my warm gratitude to Professors Emeriti Oscar Cargill and Gay Wilson Allen of New York University for their unflagging interest in and encouragement of my work. To Professor Leon Edel, who suggested this inquiry into Virginia Woolf's subjective methods, my debt is unbounded.

In regard to the footnotes, Virginia Woolf's essays are listed according to both the original book in which they appear and their place in the newly edited four volumes of *Collected Essays*. The abbreviations used for the original essay collections are as follows:

C.D.B.	*The Captain's Death Bed and other Essays*
C.R.I	*The Common Reader* (first series)
C.R.II	*The Common Reader: Second Series*
C.W.	*Contemporary Writers*
D.M.	*The Death of the Moth and other Essays*
G.R.	*Granite and Rainbow*
M.	*The Moment and Other Essays*

Contents

CONTENTS

CONTENTS

of the "act" itself—a summing up of the reader's
role in the subjective modes—Mrs. Woolf's
place today

VIRGINIA WOOLF

THE INWARD VOYAGE

CHAPTER ONE

The Delicate Transaction

IN THE CHAPTER in *Orlando* heralding the approach of the twentieth century, Virginia Woolf speaks of the delicate "transaction between a writer and the spirit of the age." Upon it, she continues, "the whole fortune of his works depends." For the novelist of the early 1900's, the transaction would prove to be difficult indeed, for the spirit of the age was one of change. Not only was there a philosophical shift in man's concept of himself and reality, but change moved on all levels, from the historical to the personal. People felt differently now; the position of the heart itself had changed.[1]

Seemingly more sensitive than her contemporaries to this spirit of her age, Mrs. Woolf shows its effect on fiction in a series of essays which illuminate the problems facing the writer of her time and offer a remarkable prophecy of literary forms to come. "In or about December, 1910, human character changed," she stated somewhat arbitrarily in "Mr. Bennett and Mrs. Brown." The change was due, she explained, to a shift in human relations—"between masters and servants, husbands and wives, parents and children." These shifts were related to or part of a larger complex of changes "in religion, conduct, politics, and literature."[2] The Edwardian novelists, especially Arnold Bennett, Mrs. Woolf charged, had not recognized what had taken place inside the very people with whom their novels were concerned. Seeing the world as a globe which

[1] Review of *Revolving Lights* by Dorothy Richardson (1922), *C.W.*, p. 125.
[2] (*C.D.B.*), *Essays*, I, pp. 320-21.

3

constantly moved and tilted with each successive age, she sought the emotional perspective by which the reality of this new era could be viewed.

The date of December, 1910, was not a random choice. It was sufficiently long after Victoria's death for the changing values in England to show themselves. It was, in general, a period of unrest, of experiment, of growth. Abroad, England was encountering serious challenge. At home, other shifts in power were taking place. Wealth was moving from the aristocracy to the middle class. The socialist movement and Labour Party were growing. There were strikes, agitation for women's rights. But there was also a feeling of expansion, of freedom from restraint, of new things stirring that found its way into artistic and intellectual circles. Not only had human character changed, as Mrs. Woolf said, but also the artist's and philosopher's way of looking at the world.

There is an implicit reference in Mrs. Woolf's remark about December, 1910, to the opening of the Post-Impressionist Exhibition in London, which showed the new way the artists saw reality. It was a world in which time, space, and motion had been split. Human figures were reduced to essence or outline, or given multiple personality; objects were abstracted for values of color and design. It appeared at first a bizarre view of reality. Yet it showed a wholeness of vision, a view of things in the totality of their appearance, which the art critic Roger Fry felt the Impressionists had possessed for the first time.[3]

The desire for a wholeness of vision was to take twentieth-century art, especially that of the novel, into areas where it had never been before, "the dark places of psychology," as Mrs. Woolf phrased it in her essay "Modern

[3] Roger Fry, *Vision and Design* (London, 1920), pp. 11-12, 25, 239. Roger Fry, a close friend of Virginia Woolf, had organized the Post-Impressionist exhibition with Desmond MacCarthy.

4

Fiction," and the philosopher's new world of time/space. It was true that such different nineteenth-century writers as Thomas De Quincey and Lewis Carroll had written of their visions of dreams and the unconscious, but they did not stir the imagination as did the Russian novelists whose works were now being translated into English, or Freud, whose *Interpretation of Dreams* seemed to authenticate the very voices from the underground heard in Dostoevsky's novels. Frazer's final volumes of *The Golden Bough* likewise directed the attention to myth, ritual, and the power of symbols whose hold on the racial or collective unconscious Jung would systematically explore.

This new view of man included more than that of a submerged irrational self. Man was seen to be a complex of consciousness, existing on many levels. He was also seen to be a complex of personalities, consisting not of a single integrated ego but rather of separate states of awareness. This "discontinuity" of personality meant that man was never the same from one moment to the next; his identity changed with each new set of perceptions. The instability of self was echoed in the philosophers' view of time, space, and objects, which were also seen as mental concepts. If objects had a life of their own, it was not one which man could know. Man was alone in his visual universe. Once the special creation of a deity, or at least the controlling center of himself and his surroundings, he was now a floating organism, one among many, attempting to establish his identity in an environment he could not truly comprehend.

This total view of man and his universe, which now seemed to be in fragments, was hardly that of Galsworthy, Bennett, and Wells. What they were doing, Mrs. Woolf said, was "writing against the grain and current of the times."[4] The modern current seemed that of flux and flow,

---

[4] "Mr. Bennett and Mrs. Brown" (*C.D.B.*), *Essays*, I, p. 335.

of the shifting, the discontinuous. It appeared to allow no hold to which the drifting self—or novelist—could cling. It offered no metaphysic save an existential or nihilistic one. Yet this very sense of the fluid, the shifting, the fragmented in life was to become one of the main characteristics of fiction, whether the Edwardians recognized it or not. It was to offer novelists areas of experimentation and possibilities of effect which the nineteenth century could not extend. It was to give them a new range of theme. And it was to force a concentration on the phenomena of life itself, on the moment and its values.

THE TRANSITION from the old to the new, from a stable world dealing in absolutes to one committed to the present moment of feeling, was visualized by Virginia Woolf as "the narrow bridge of art" across which the writer must pass, renouncing old methods and taking with him very few of his former tools.[5] In the essay by the same name, which first appeared in 1927, she takes up the problem of change where she had left it four years earlier in "Mr. Bennett and Mrs. Brown." If human character had changed, so must the form of the novel which would show that character. All around her she found writers who were attempting what they could not achieve, who were forcing the form they used "to contain a meaning strange to it." What the modern novel must do was to take the mould of the modern mind itself.

The difficulties posed seemed enormous. The mind, for Virginia Woolf, was a "queer conglomeration of incongruous things." It was full of "monstrous, hybrid, unmanageable emotions." Yet this emotional world, "tu-

[5] "The Narrow Bridge of Art" (*G.R.*), *Essays*, II, pp. 227-28.

multuous and contradictory," must be ordered in a form which would express it in its totality. For the novel, Mrs. Woolf wrote elsewhere, "is not form which you see, but emotion which you feel."[6] This form, or structure, is necessarily "one of infinite complexity" because it is made up of many kinds of emotion.[7]

One by one she rejected past literary forms which she felt as inadequate to embody these emotions as "a rose leaf to envelop the rugged immensity of a rock." The lyric poem, the poetic play, and, by implication, the past genres of the novel, were discarded. Yet out of the fragments of these old forms the new ones would arise. "That cannibal, the novel, which has destroyed so many forms of art," she wrote, "will by then have devoured even more. We shall be forced to invent new names for the different books which masquerade under this one heading. And it is possible that there will be among the so-called novels one which we shall scarcely know how to christen."

It might be said parenthetically that Mrs. Woolf's own novels followed this pattern of remaking and breaking form. Each new novel was "breaking" the "mould,"[8] for the individual emotional value of a work demanded for Mrs. Woolf a fresh matrix. Yet each of them reflected, in its way, the novel's "cannibalism" in its synthesis of earlier genres. Viewed in this sense, her novels appear to take elements of drama, poetry, or the essay; techniques of fiction genres such as the poetic romance, the "anatomy" (as Northrop Frye puts it),[9] or the essay novel, and fuse

6 "On Re-reading Novels" (*M.*), *Essays*, II, p. 126.
7 *A Room of One's Own* (hereafter called *A Room*), pp. 107-108.
8 *Diary*, July 27, 1934.
9 Northrop Frye, in "Specific Continuous Forms," *Anatomy of Criticism* (Princeton, 1957), sees the anatomy as "a vision of the world in terms of a single intellectual pattern" (p. 310) and shows how it combines elements of satire and phantasy. Seen in this way, *Orlando* and even, to some extent, *Between the Acts*, are "anatomies."

them into a form which continually modifies and adapts itself to its changing subject matter and emotion.

The final shadowy form which Mrs. Woolf foresaw in "The Narrow Bridge of Art" was a synthesis which, in her most complex novel, she herself attained. It was a form, she explained in her essay, which would be dramatic and yet not a play; it would have the "exaltation of poetry, but much of the ordinariness of prose." It would give the outline rather than the detail, observe deeply "but from a different angle." Finally, it would give "the relations of man to nature, to fate; his imagination; his dreams."

It is not difficult to relate this final form to Joyce's *Finnegans Wake* or to Mrs. Woolf's own novel *The Waves*. By the time her essay was written, several early fragments of Joyce's last novel had appeared. Mrs. Woolf herself had just finished writing *To the Lighthouse*, with its central part, "Time Passes," like the moving cinema-screen of the sleeping mind. She was already planning *Orlando* and *The Waves*.[10] *Orlando* can be seen as a dream phantasy, an analogue of the writer's imagination. But it is *The Waves* which may be said to take the shape of her prophecy. Absorbed, like *Finnegans Wake*, in the imaginative dreaming mind, it verbalizes with creative ingenuity what might be called the *stream of unconsciousness*—that stream of "memory, experience, contact and imagination"[11] which runs below our conscious thought and which bears a more direct relation to nature and to fate.

☖ ☖ ☖

IF THE NEW novel's form would express a more total view of man, his mind and his emotions, then the

[10] See *Diary*, November 23, 1926; March 14 and June 18, 1927.
[11] Winifred Holtby, *Virginia Woolf* (London, 1932), p. 189.

"proper stuff of fiction," as Virginia Woolf phrased it in an essay first drafted in 1919, would consist of "every feeling, every thought; every quality of brain and spirit." Ordinary plot, comedy, or catastrophe, which occupied the "materialist" writers (she again takes Bennett, Galsworthy, and Wells to task), would be discarded for the real "life" of the moment, the response of the individual to the "myriad impressions" which constantly assail him, "an incessant shower of innumerable atoms" that "shape themselves into the life of Monday or Tuesday."[12]

Chapter III of this study, which offers Mrs. Woolf's anatomy of the moment, suggests the variety of these impressions whose scope seems to embrace the psycho-physical totality of the self. In the essay "Modern Fiction," quoted above, she is concerned with the process of recording these "atoms as they fall upon the mind in the order in which they fall," with the tracing of the "pattern, however disconnected and incoherent in appearance, which each sight or incident scores upon the consciousness."[13] Casual as this comment appears, there is implicit in it a suggestion of the scientific spirit of inquiry with which she would approach her analysis of the self and its reactions, a commitment to the idea that life, and the moment of feeling which is its essence, is the most important subject of fiction. For life is "a luminous halo, a semi-transparent envelope surrounding us from the beginning of consciousness to the end. Is it not the task of the novelist," she asks, "to convey this varying, this unknown and uncircumscribed spirit, whatever aberration or complexity it may display?"[14]

The phrase "a luminous halo" recalls William James's analytic descriptions of states of thought and feeling in his chapter on the stream of consciousness, most partic-

---

[12] "Modern Fiction" (*C.R.I*), *Essays*, II, pp. 110, 106.
[13] *Ibid.*, p. 107.   [14] *Ibid.*, p. 106.

9

ularly his portrayal of the mental image with its *"halo of relations,"* its *" 'psychic overtone'* or *'fringe.'* "[15] This "halo" or "psychic overtone" is the aura of the moment of feeling in Mrs. Woolf's novels. Some of the light comes from subliminal areas—"the flickerings of that innermost flame which flashes its messages through the brain"[16]— perhaps mere biological memories activated within. Some derives from the immediate response to those myriad impressions which the mind selects from the welter of out- ward stimuli, according to that mind's practical or aes- thetic need.[17] It should be noted that, as the mind itself selects or rejects, so does the novelist as he chooses his data, artfully mimicking the haphazard thrust of the im- pressions of actual life, the patterns of emotional response. The furthest this method was to take a writer is the opening section of William Faulkner's *The Sound and the Fury* when the reader is plunged into the feelings of an idiot, receiving the confused impressions and associations which Benjy's moment brings. Yet Mrs. Woolf continually immerses the reader into just such situations. "What a lark! What a plunge!" Clarissa thinks at the opening of *Mrs. Dalloway*, and one is literally submerged into her consciousness, learning about her life only as she reveals it in seemingly random thoughts. These are well-sifted by the author. The reader, however, is conscious only of things as they are happening at the moment to Mrs. Dallo- way. Much later, after he has finished the novel, he can mentally arrange the horizontal chronicle of her life. In the book he is vertically plunged into it, experiencing it himself.

The problems of this method—and "any method is right," Mrs. Woolf declares, "that expresses what we wish to express, if we are writers"—are several, as she

[15] William James, *Psychology: Briefer Course* (New York, 1892), p. 166.
[16] "Modern Fiction" (*C.R.I*), *Essays*, II, p. 107.
[17] James, *Psychology*, p. 171.

was only too quick to point out. With its emphasis on every perception, with its exclusion of "the alien and external," there is the danger of never venturing "outside itself and beyond." This is the predicament she feels Joyce himself assumed in *Ulysses*. The reader is centered in a self, "in a bright yet narrow room."[18] In "A Letter to a Young Poet," she explains the problems of this self-containment as those of infolding, of creating the "private universe" with no doorway, the set of symbols decipherable to the writer alone.

In other words, what Mrs. Woolf is referring to is the relation of the reader to the work. For the novelist, the problem is one of rendering this new private vision to the public—of contemplating "landscapes and emotions within" and making them "visible to the world at large."[19] For the reader, it is the problem of his own transaction with the spirit of his age. Like the novelist, he must be willing to forsake the old-fashioned "materialist" conceptions of fiction and enter a new subjective world which, familiar as it may be to his own experience, he has never encountered on the printed page. He must submit to a process of self-examination, of exploring unknown, perhaps tabooed, areas of himself; of participating rather than playing the role of the disinterested spectator. This makes great demands on the imagination and patience of the reader. But if he is willing to be creative, as Mrs. Woolf so often insists in her essays he must be, the transaction can be rewarding indeed.

A FINAL PROBLEM, which Mrs. Woolf exposes in her essays on women and fiction, most notably *A Room*

---

[18] "Modern Fiction" (*C.R.I*), *Essays*, II, pp. 106-108.
[19] "A Letter to a Young Poet" (*D.M.*), *Essays*, II, p. 189.

of One's Own and "Professions for Women," concerns the relation of women writers to the spirit of the age. If the subjective novel would explore every atom of sensation, it must enter dark areas which the Victorians had never dared. For the feminine novelist, this offered obstacles; for, as Mrs. Woolf confessed, a woman still has a secret desire to be veiled.[20] It was difficult to tell the truth about her body, to write about certain passions which she images as the largest fish to slumber in "the depths, the dark places" of the pool. If everything was the proper stuff of fiction, that "Angel in the House"—the feminine instinct to be pure, to hide the fact that you have a mind and body of your own—must be killed.[21] It was especially difficult for Virginia Woolf inasmuch as she was the daughter of Leslie Stephen, a man of Victorian morals who regarded Sterne as prurient and Balzac as unwholesome, and who felt that the highest art came from the "healthiest mind."[22]

Yet Virginia Woolf, in her way, managed to follow the general literary revolt of her time. She did not go as far as Joyce or D. H. Lawrence. But her line tangled with the deepest fish in her pool; up from the unconscious she dredged uncommon hates and fears, androgynous tendencies which her father had condemned,[23] aspects of homosexual love, latent or manifest. These are not exploited for their shock value but rather form part of the halo of existence itself, minute reflections, shimmering sometimes at the very edge of consciousness, othertimes beyond the "fringe," suggested through the symbolic association which forms one of Mrs. Woolf's most powerful means. Ephemeral as it seems, this is the method which she felt to be as

[20] *A Room*, p. 76.
[21] "Professions for Women" (*D.M.*), *Essays*, II, pp. 287-88.
[22] Noel Annan, *Leslie Stephen, His Thought and Character in Relation to His Time* (London, 1951), pp. 228, 266-67.
[23] *Ibid.*, p. 224.

12

"clear and composed" as that of earlier novelists, yet "deeper and more suggestive, for conveying not only what people say, but what they leave unsaid; not only what they are, but what life is."[24]

[24] "Jane Austen" (*C.R.I*), *Essays*, I, p. 153.

CHAPTER TWO

"A Little Voyage of Discovery"

THE SHAPE OF Virginia Woolf's novels did not spring solely from the changed character of the times. Two other factors were involved in the search for a method which would attempt to render in fiction the complex world of the mind. The first factor was her own particular temperament. The second was the intellectual milieu—the Stephen household, and later the circle of friends who became known as the Bloomsbury group—in which this temperament matured.

These two factors, which verge on the biographical, can be touched upon only briefly. It is perhaps pertinent, however, to suggest that in a psychological novel, dealing with aspects of the mind and emotion, the relation of the author to the work is particularly close. Regarding the genesis of *To the Lighthouse*, for example, Virginia Woolf mentions in her diary certain emotional urgencies which forced her back to memories of her childhood summers.[1] Her first novel, *The Voyage Out*, can be seen as an attempt to accommodate herself to the reality of her brother's death. In other words, the needs of the novel are frequently those of the author. And form, and the means to achieve it, the "grain of experience once selected" and "put precisely in its place," are reached by a "process which never yields its secrets to the analyst."[2]

[1] November 28, 1928.
[2] "How it Strikes a Contemporary" (*C.R.I*), *Essays*, II, p. 159. Cf. the "vital particle," the "grain" or "virus of suggestion" which Henry James feels orders the growth of the work. Preface to *The Spoils of Poynton* in his *The Art of the Novel: Critical Prefaces*, ed. R. P. Blackmur (New York, 1934), pp. 119-20.

For Virginia Woolf, as for Proust and Joyce, the conjunction of times and temperament seemed particularly fortunate. If the modern mind was suddenly thrown open to analysis, the inward-turning author, freed from old strictures, could make an exploration of his own. For Proust and Joyce, for Dorothy Richardson in her thirteen-volume *Pilgrimage*,[3] and especially for Virginia Woolf the novel became "a little voyage of discovery."[4] And the search, or journey, was always a voyage "in." Orlando, thinking of writing a piece of prose, could feel something opening within her that was "intricate and many-chambered, which one must take a torch to explore."[5] What each of these writers would find, upon the exploration of that maze of mental experience, depended on his or her particular temperament. Joyce was to find a Daedalian labyrinth, Proust a palimpsest of finely engraved memory, stimulus and response. Virginia Woolf seemed fascinated by the curious workings of the mind itself, by "its oddities and its whims, its fancies and its sensibilities," as she herself put it in describing the mind of Laurence Sterne.[6] And she observed herself relentlessly, as her diary so often reveals, to try to discover the hidden modes of her own conscious and unconscious being.[7] For writing, as she expressed it in *Night and Day*, is "that process of self-examination, that perpetual effort to understand one's own feeling and express it . . . in language" (p. 38).

Her self-absorption, like that of Proust and Joyce, was influenced in part by physical factors. Illness in Proust and

[3] The first volume, *Pointed Roofs*, was published the same year as Virginia Woolf's first novel. *Pilgrimage* stays within the consciousness of a single character, Miriam Henderson.

[4] "Jane Austen" (*C.R.I*), *Essays*, I, p. 152.

[5] *Orlando*, p. 159.

[6] "Phases of Fiction" (*G.R.*), *Essays*, II, p. 92.

[7] April 20, 1919; August 15, 1924; undated entry following July 25, 1926; September 30, 1926; March 14, 1927; February 16, 1930; February 7, 1931; September 5, 1935.

near-blindness in Joyce had turned them inward. Virginia Woolf's delicate health as a child and early neurasthenic tendencies likewise affected her outlook and the substance and texture of her work. It is not within the scope of this study to discuss these particular influences on her extraordinary temperament. Leonard Woolf, in the third volume of his autobiography,[8] gives a vivid picture of her struggle between insanity and the urge to live a creative and productive life. Whatever the forces that moulded her—her nervous and brooding father, the early loss of her mother, the difficulties in arriving at her own sense of femininity, as depicted in *Orlando* and elsewhere—they produced a hyper-sensitive and acutely feeling writer who happened to possess the verbal resources which enabled her to project and depersonalize her inner anguish.

Indeed, of the three novelists, Virginia Woolf is perhaps the most inward-searching. Joyce exploited, intellectually, every external aspect of his Dublin, and Proust the French society in which he lived. Virginia Woolf, on the other hand, explicitly avoided the external ("place" figures very little in her novels) and, making capital of the emotions which she knew firsthand, exploited her inner self.

This is not to say that Virginia Woolf's novels are confessional in the usual sense of the term. It is rather to recognize that in her own experience, mental and emotional, she found her most absorbing material. In her essay on De Quincey's autobiography she quotes him as saying that if a writer " 'were really able to pierce the haze which so often envelops, even to himself, his own secret springs of action and reserve, there cannot be a life . . . that would not . . fall within the reach of a deep, solemn, and some-

[8] Leonard Woolf, *Beginning Again: An Autobiography of the Years 1911 to 1918* (New York, 1964). Note especially pp. 75-82.

times . . . thrilling interest.' "[9] These "secret springs of action"—the childhood traumas, conflicts, and emotions,[10] indeed all of the past which impinges on the present moment—is what Virginia Woolf sought to portray, not to show emotion for emotion's sake, but to give validity to experience. Rather than presenting the effect, which is the action, Virginia Woolf showed the cause, tunneling backward and downward into the past and psyche of her character to find the emotions and drives which motivate and give meaning to action. "Beneath it is all dark, it is all spreading, it is unfathomably deep," Mrs. Ramsay thinks in *To the Lighthouse*, "but now and again we rise to the surface and that is what you see us by" (p. 100).

This preoccupation with her family and with the embryo self emerging from it forms part of the shadowy "iceberg" underlying her characters.[11] Monique Nathan observes that her main women characters—Mrs. Dalloway, Isa Oliver, Mrs. Ramsay, Rachel Vinrace, Sara Pargiter— have their original in Virginia Woolf,[12] and her novels may be seen as ways of exploring this unknown element in herself as well as in others. Her own growing years and identity problems, for example, are detailed in *The Voyage Out* and *Night and Day*; her conflict with her family and grief for her mother's death dominate *To the Lighthouse*[13] and *The Years*; concerns with difficult aspects of love and friendship underlie *Mrs. Dalloway*; questions of death and time, rising out of her life-long grief for her brother Thoby, appear in *The Waves* as well as in the earlier *The Voyage*

[9] (*C.R.II*), *Essays*, IV, p. 4.

[10] In *Suspiria De Profundis* De Quincey shows his awareness of how his childhood influenced him. *Confessions of an English Opium-Eater and Suspiria De Profundis* (Boston, 1855), p. 163.

[11] Cf. E. M. Forster's remark in *Aspects of the Novel* (New York, 1927) that "human beings" are "enormous, shadowy and intractable, and three-quarters hidden like an iceberg" (p. 129).

[12] Monique Nathan, *Virginia Woolf*, trans. Herma Briffault (New York and London, 1961), p. 69.

[13] See *Diary*, May 14, 1925.

Out and *Jacob's Room*. These, however, are merely an arbitrary categorizing of the personal and thematic areas which these novels probe; each, in its own way, is the author's attempt to understand her multi-leveled relationship with reality. One might say that each voyage landed her on the same shore—that of herself. It was only the ship, the vehicle of the voyage, that changed.

THIS PREOCCUPATION with emotion and its source suggests the double role which Virginia Woolf as writer would play through her entire life: that of feeling and perceiving simultaneously.[14] This dual capacity seemed to issue from a complex personality whose mental aspect was, to use Virginia Woolf's own term, "androgynous." Masculine in its bent for abstract and logical thought, feminine in its intuitive grasp of emotional relationships and their mythopoeic and metaphoric equivalents, her mind embraced the duality of the creative mind which Mrs. Woolf described in *A Room of One's Own*.[15] In her work as a whole, this duality manifested itself in her alternation between criticism and fiction. In the fiction itself, it appeared in a fluidity of form and feeling combined with an intuitive apprehension of the processes by which both are achieved.

This accuracy of perception may have been a legacy from her father, Sir Leslie Stephen, the noted biographer and essayist, as well as from the rational nineteenth-century atmosphere of the Stephen home in which many of the eminent Victorians were visitors. It was also fostered

[14] Cf. Bernard in *The Waves*: " 'The double capacity to feel, to reason' " (p. 55).
[15] Pp. 145-58. See also my Chapter VIII, iii.

18

by the scientific outlook of the oncoming generation, the friends who became the Bloomsbury group[16] and who, lively and verbal, stirred in the quiet Virginia a sense of masculine competition.[17]

The Bloomsbury "myth"—that of an intellectual set with a fixed doctrine—has largely been exploded. Yet if we are to examine certain artistic and philosophical sympathies of members of this circle, as does J. K. Johnstone in *The Bloomsbury Group*, we find emanating from the cluster of divergent ideas a mental atmosphere or "climate" in which Virginia Woolf's natural impulses and perceptions found direction and shape.[18]

Governed by G. E. Moore's "scientific method," the Bloomsbury attitude was outwardly rational and questioning but also inward-turning, examining philosophical and aesthetic questions from an intuitive or neo-mystical[19] standpoint. Maynard Keynes in his memoirs has described it as a "religion."[20] This term is misleading, but it does suggest the pervasiveness of certain ideas which became not dry doctrine but a mode of living and perceiving reality. What applied to art and philosophy could apply to life. Questions of inward and outward reality, subject and

[16] These included Lytton Strachey, the economist Maynard Keynes, G. E. Moore, the art critic Clive Bell who married Vanessa Stephen, Roger Fry, Duncan Grant, Desmond MacCarthy, and Leonard Woolf.

[17] Duncan Grant describes Virginia Stephen's manner to "most men" at this period as being "a little aloof and even a little fierce." "Virginia Woolf," *Horizon*, III (June 1941), 403-404.

[18] Jean Guiguet, *Virginia Woolf and Her Works*, trans. Jean Stewart (London, 1965), p. 53.

[19] J. K. Johnstone, *The Bloomsbury Group: A Study of E. M. Forster, Lytton Strachey, Virginia Woolf, and their Circle* (London, 1954), pp. 32-38. "Neo-mystical" here would be "the extension of intuition to the unseen," and pertains particularly to the philosophy of G. E. Moore (p. 38).

[20] Leonard Woolf, *Sowing: An Autobiography of the Years 1880 to 1904* (London, 1960), pp. 146-47. Woolf goes on to deny that Moore's doctrine was a "religion" and emphasizes the "clarity, freshness, and common-sense" of Moore's views.

object, conscious and unconscious, or problems of the relationship between the self, art, and the world, were strong Bloomsbury concerns,[21] and they find their echo in the works of Virginia Woolf. A more specific example, perhaps, is that of G. E. Moore's principle of organic unity[22] which widened, especially for Virginia Woolf, and to some extent for E. M. Forster and Roger Fry, into a recognition of the unity between the self and the preceptual world. Roger Fry found its aesthetic correlative in his and Clive Bell's theory of "significant form."[23] Virginia Woolf fused it into a literary gestalt in which feeling and form, theme and content, and aspects of self, time, and reality form a reciprocal and interdependent whole.

J. K. Johnstone points out the influence of the theory of "significant form" on Virginia Woolf and her work. But he neglects a perhaps still more profound influence, that of G. E. Moore's principles of perception, which helped her to see or perceive reality in a way which became intrinsic to her methods of subjectivity.

The cornerstone for these principles is laid in *Principia Ethica* with Moore's emphasis on states of consciousness. But it is in *Philosophical Studies*, which Johnstone by-passes, that Moore sets forth in detail the particular quality of the relationship of consciousness with the external world. Here, in chapters with such titles as "The Nature and Reality of Objects of Perception" or "The Status of Sense-Data," Moore examines the different varieties of

[21] Johnstone, *The Bloomsbury Group*, pp. 54-59.

[22] *Ibid.*, pp. 22-28. Philosophically, this deals with the values of complex wholes as related to the component parts. Since this involves the value judgment of the perceiver, a subject-object relationship occurs which operates between various aspects of self and the universe.

[23] This is Clive Bell's term which Roger Fry adopted and which alludes to "the idea, the state of mind behind a work of art that gives it its significance" (*ibid.*, pp. 56-57). See also my Chapter XII, ii.

sensory experience and the separation of that experience, or consciousness of it, from the object itself. Certain of these ways of perceiving the object Virginia Woolf was to incorporate into her own subjective modes: for example, the importance of the physical *angle of vision* at which an object is seen in determining our subjective experience of it;[24] his distinguishing between individual and universal modes of perception;[25] and his way of presenting complicated abstract ideas as a pictorial diagram.[26] It is here, too, that we find a chapter on William James which grounds Moore's method in that of the earlier philosopher: a combination of accurate observation with absolute clarity of meaning. Virginia Woolf's rendition of the various processes of perception is done with just such accuracy, together with the luminosity and visual force of expression which was characteristic of William James.

A final note on the influence of Moore and, through Moore, James on Virginia Woolf, concerns the term "diaphanous" which Moore uses to describe the quality of a state of mind or consciousness.[27] The term means transparent or translucent, and it is a reworking of William James's image of the "halo" or "penumbra" which surrounds consciousness, with an added suggestion of its fleeting and tenuous quality. Virginia Woolf's description of the moment of being as "a luminous halo, a semi-transparent envelope," presents a similar image of a thin, transparent substance which catches within its net the

[24] G. E. Moore, *Philosophical Studies* (New York, 1922), pp. 185-96. See my Chapter VI for Mrs. Woolf's use of this method.

[25] Moore, *Philosophical Studies*, pp. 31-96. See my Chapter V on different ways of "seeing the object."

[26] Moore, *Philosophical Studies*, pp. 155 and 172-75. Virginia Woolf uses his "black marks on a white ground" in *Night and Day* and elsewhere. See the discussion on abstraction, in my Chapter XI, ii.

[27] Moore, *Philosophical Studies*, p. 20.

"myriad impressions" of the moment.[28] However fleeting the moment, those impressions are never merely "evanescent." Grounded in psycho-physical laws of perception and subjected to the questioning of Bloomsbury, they achieve an authority which raises them above the random and sensuous observations of impressionistic writing.

🪲 🪲 🪲

IF BLOOMSBURY brought Virginia Woolf's attention to theories which would help her codify her own ideas on mental reality and artistic form, it was her father who, in a sense, "permitted" his daughter the direction of her fictional voyages by suggesting new limits to which the novel might go. The influence of Sir Leslie Stephen has been little understood except by the critic James Hafley in his careful examination of Stephen's concepts of art and the novel. These concepts, gleaned from the many essays in *Hours in a Library*,[29] concern the novelist's subject and method as well as the writer's relation to his work, and they are important in a consideration of Virginia Woolf's view of the novel as set forth in Chapter I.

It was perhaps Leslie Stephen's feeling that every writer "exhibits his own character" in his novels through "setting forth the varying phases of his own mind" which helped to liberate Virginia Woolf from the author's traditional position of purely external involvement in his writing. Most of Leslie Stephen's comments in regard to novels

[28] Cf. Henry James's description of sensibility as "a kind of huge spider-web of the finest silken threads suspended in the chamber of consciousness, and catching every air-borne particle in its tissue." *The Art of Fiction and Other Essays* (New York, 1948), pp. 10-11.

[29] I am indebted to James Hafley for pointing out the passages from *Hours in a Library* quoted in this chapter. *The Glass Roof: Virginia Woolf as Novelist* (Berkeley, 1954), p. 24.

tend toward a new freedom which the fiction writer can exercise. He need not be bound to prose or to narrative plot; indeed, he can take on certain prerogatives of the poet and "saturate" his prose with poetry.[30] This implies that, entering the domain of the poet, the novelist can use the poet's concerns (which Stephen says are also those of the philosopher—" 'the nature of man and the world in which he lives' ") as well as the poet's traditional means: "intuitions, thought as emotion, and idea represented as symbol."[31]

This widened the novelist's scope considerably. Not that earlier writers like George Meredith or Emily Brontë had not used poetic methods. But new areas were suggested for the novelist in which he could assume the epic poet's potentially dramatic role by using both macrocosm and microcosm for his stage. This role must have particularly appealed to Virginia Woolf, whose major drive was toward poetry and who dramatized this secret aspect in a phantasy-self she called "Shakespeare's sister."[32] It also liberated her from the Edwardian fidelity to fact which she criticized in her essay "Mr. Bennett and Mrs. Brown."

The novel as poem, the novel as emotion, idea as symbol, characters as aspects of the self: all these were to be characteristics of the new psychological fiction in general and Virginia Woolf's in particular. If one adds to this Leslie Stephen's acute appraisal of De Quincey's style and techniques—the relation of De Quincey's art to music and

[30] *Hours in a Library* (New York, 1904), I, pp. 95, 226, 29, and 89. "A novelist is on the border-line between poetry and prose, and novels should be, as it were, prose saturated with poetry" (p. 29).

[31] Hafley, *Glass Roof*, p. 24. Hafley is here quoting and paraphrasing another edition (unavailable here) of *Hours in a Library*, II (London: Smith, Elder, 1894), pp. 270 ff.

[32] *A Room*, pp. 70-75. *Orlando* nearly pictorializes this "myth" with a poet-writer whose inspiration comes from Shakespeare and who turns into a woman.

his psychological portrayals of time and space[33]—as well as Stephen's sense of the relation of a work of art to its own particular time,[34] one can sense a parental climate of artistic thought congenial to his gifted daughter.

🦌🦌🦌🦌

THESE, THEN, were some of the influences which might be said to have contributed to the nature of Virginia Woolf's work and the direction it would take. Classed by some critics as "psychological," by others as lyrical or even "expressionistic," her fiction tends to elude specific labels of class or genre. Virginia Woolf herself—although in her later essays she was able to describe her exact position on the chart—could not describe her voyage there. "For the methods by which she had reached her present position, seemed to her very strange, and the strangest thing about them was that she had not known where they were leading her. That was the strange thing, that one did not know where one was going, or what one wanted, and followed blindly . . . always unprepared and amazed and knowing nothing; but one thing led to another and by degrees something had formed itself out of nothing . . . things formed themselves into a pattern . . . and in that pattern lay satisfaction and meaning."[35]

This study is the search for method—for the means by which Virginia Woolf permeates this inner world,

---

[33] See "De Quincey," *Hours in a Library*, I, pp. 326-34.

[34] Noel Annan writes that Leslie Stephen "warned the 'pure' critics that to wrench a poem or novel from its social setting is to neglect the fact that a work of art has a life of its own in Time, and is subject to different kinds of perception in each age, in that the communication between author and reader is constantly changing." *Leslie Stephen*, pp. 272-73.

[35] *Voyage*, pp. 384-85.

"the mystery of personality"[36] which, for psychologist and novelist alike, offers the ultimate challenge. The element of mystery, of enigma, lies at the heart of all her novels; as in a tale of ratiocination, the reader searches to understand the genesis of a certain character. Mrs. Ramsay's inexplicable sadness, the bird-like sharpness of Mrs. Dalloway, Sally Pargiter's living Antigone—these and others pose the riddle of human personality which Virginia Woolf attempts to solve by uncovering each character's past and showing its relationship to the immediate present. In her sensitive book about Mrs. Woolf, Winifred Holtby remarks that her characters' lives "are barely indicated . . . yet we know almost everything about them." The subconscious world they inhabit, she continues, one of "unformed thoughts and impulses," is a territory "uncharted and extremely hazardous."[37]

The hazards of these voyages can be guessed from Mrs. Woolf's diary, which keeps a careful log of her novelistic journeys. They can also be glimpsed in a description of Mrs. Ramsay from an early version of *To the Lighthouse* as a stone figure "dredged" from a "sea of bitterness . . . with eyes pearl encrusted,"[38] as if covered with the shimmering glaze of long submergence in emotion. And they can be seen in full and tragic detail in *The Voyage Out*. The word "out" in the title is merely the physical direction of the voyage to South America. The journey is inward, symbolized by the country of Santa Marina to which the travelers go, "marina" suggesting the watery world of emotion and the inner depths. Begun shortly after the death of her brother Thoby from typhoid fever, the novel appears to be an attempt on Virginia Woolf's part to dis-

[36] Guiguet, *Virginia Woolf and Her Works*, p. 21.
[37] Holtby, *Virginia Woolf*, p. 189.
[38] *Lighthouse Notebook I*, p. 25 (March, 1926?).

cover and come to terms with the tragedy. Rachel dies of typhoid; Virginia Woolf herself, after putting the novel through at least seven revisions, suffered a major breakdown. The title of the French translation comes closer to expressing the essence of her work: *La Traversée des Apparences*—the crossing of outward appearance into reality. What Virginia Woolf brought to light in the traversing of this meridian, the very shapes and sources of emotion and inward being, is the concern of the following chapters.

CHAPTER THREE

A Shower of Atoms

ℜ

THE CENTER OR meeting place for experience was, to Virginia Woolf, the *moment*—a cross-section of consciousness in which perceptions and feelings converged and formed for an instant something round and whole. To render these moments of being in their entirety, to describe them so that the reader was placed in the very center of the consciousness experiencing the moment—receiving from all sides the shower of atoms[1] as they fell, those myriad impressions of perception and emotion—was her task as she saw it.

Mrs. Woolf's closest attempt to examine her own subjective methods—and so explain what "an ordinary mind" experiences "on an ordinary day"[2]—occurs in "The Moment: Summer's Night." This essay is a minute and sophisticated examination of a brief measure of time, and it reveals the exact qualities of those impressions—"trivial, fantastic, evanescent, or engraved with the sharpness of steel"—which the mind of the character receives. The moment is nightfall:

> . . . the table in the garden among the trees grew whiter and whiter; and the people round it more indistinct. An owl, blunt, obsolete looking, heavy weighted, crossed the fading sky with a black spot between its claws. The trees murmured. An aeroplane hummed like a piece of plucked wire. There was also, on the roads, the distant explosion of a motor cycle, shooting further and

[1] "Modern Fiction" (*C.R.I*), *Essays*, II, p. 106.
[2] *Ibid.*

further away down the road. Yet what composed the present moment? If you are young, the future lies upon the present, like a piece of glass, making it tremble and quiver. If you are old, the past lies upon the present, like a thick glass, making it waver, distorting it.[3]

These are only the first of the "visual" and "sense impressions" which Virginia Woolf describes as making up the moment, experience screened—it should be noted—through the filter of time future and time past, and indeed through no "ordinary mind": an awareness of change in the shape and color of the immediate surroundings (garden, people); an awareness of perspective and dimension (people, then trees, finally the predatory owl in the sky beyond); an awareness of sounds at close, middle, and far distances. Added to these impressions is a sense of violence (the owl's prey, the explosion of the motor cycle) which is linked subtly with dangers from the nonhuman world of the past (the "obsolete owl") and the mechanical world of the future (the airplane, the motorcycle). Time future and time past, their relation to the human and the nonhuman worlds, are suggested through emotional reactions to sensory stimuli.

Mrs. Woolf continues to note sensory impressions in her essay and the response of the physical being aware of the infinite gradations of time and change: the feeling of coolness on the skin, feet expanding in slippers, different pressure of light and color on the eyelids. The sense of cyclical change in the color of the sky, in lights appearing, affects the emotions in a similar manner. The reader is made to watch the external scene and to participate in it through corresponding reactions in body and mind.[4]

[3] (M.), Essays, II, p. 293.

[4] Note the use of bodily response to cyclic changes in the external scene in To the Lighthouse, p. 36, when Lily Briscoe and William Bankes, watching the bay at evening, feel in their bodies "some sort

But the external scene, she assures us, "is only the wider circumference of the moment," and she contracts it to the center in "a knot of consciousness." Visual impressions coalesce to form an emotion which begins a flight of thought, an instantaneous flash of daydream. Words "explode" with their associative meanings which in turn affect the body. The word "hay," for instance, induces a sneeze, and the sneeze, in turn, affects visual perception: "the whole universe is shaken" as the "head is jerked up, down." The myriad atoms of impression combine and recombine to produce emotion that "shoots through the moment, makes it quiver with malice and amusement." Walled by the outer circumference of sight and sound, Mrs. Woolf's moment finds its center and depth in the meaning of emotion itself.

This is not the end of Virginia Woolf's vertical slice of a summer's night, but it is enough to suggest the complexity of what she felt must be conveyed in order to put the reader inside the consciousness of the character— in other words, to accomplish "point of view." To *view* the world from the vantage *point* of a single character, the reader is asked not only to see, hear, taste, smell, and feel a multitude of impressions *simultaneously*, but also to experience mentally the associational actions of these physical impressions upon his thoughts and their result upon his body. He must be aware of the change, the flux and flow, within the moment itself, which Virginia Woolf never renders as static; of the correspondence with and interaction between himself and the world of objects; and of the relation between the present and both the past and future. He must be aware, too, of the personality of others whose identity tends to merge with or impinge upon his own.

---

of physical relief" as the tide flowed and the bay flooded with sunset.

The governing element of Virginia Woolf's "moment," then, is emotional rather than simply sensual. The sensory perceptions and thought recordings are means, not ends— they are an intricate instrument panel whose buttons, when pressed, govern the entire emotional direction of the machine. The sight of the owl, the sound of the airplane, the reaction of the body to the cooling air, the spoken words and unspoken thoughts—all these quantitative aspects lead to the qualitative aspect of the moment which is *felt*. The falling night, with its metamorphosis of objects and people, its extension into a far racial past and an intuited future, produces a feeling compounded of relief, dread, and fascination which comprises its reality.

THIS CONCEPT of emotional life as reality—of feeling compounded of the synthesized responses of mind and body, acting as a unit, to outside influences—is of foremost importance in understanding the principle underlying Virginia Woolf's fiction: that a novel is "not form which you see, but emotion which you feel."[5] The intention of all novelists may be said to be that of reproducing the illusion of life. The difference between them lies expressly in their view of what life or reality is. Proust is possibly the only writer who approaches Virginia Woolf's absorption in the living moment; however, he is more concerned with character and story values; the "moment" is not the central fact of his fiction. For Mrs. Woolf, the moment of being becomes the emotional unit out of which the larger complex of her fiction is spun. That complex depends on an intricate relationship of emotions: a web of personal feelings radiating from each person and at times

[5] "On Re-reading Novels" (*M.*), *Essays*, II, p. 126.

forming a tangling or intersecting of strands. This criss-crossing forms the conflicts or tensions which affect each character. The patterns of these inner tensions as they shift from changing moment to moment make up the form of her novels.[6]

It is important, at the beginning of an examination of Virginia Woolf's subjective modes, to place her concept of emotion as reality within the modern framework of philosophical and psychological thought. Susanne K. Langer, in her chapter "The Process of Feeling" in *Philosophical Sketches*, posits a definition of feeling which is useful to examine here, for it defines the areas of sensation and emotion Virginia Woolf dealt with in "The Moment." Dr. Langer designates feeling as "anything that may be felt" and continues:

> In this sense it includes both sensation and emotion— the felt responses of our sense organs to the environment, of our proprioceptive mechanisms to internal changes, and of the organism as a whole to its situation as a whole, the so-called "emotive feelings." We feel warmth, pinprick, ache, effort, and relaxation; vision is the way the optic apparatus feels the impingement of light, and hearing is the way the auditory structures feel sound waves; we feel bodily weakness or high tonus, and we feel expectation, frustration, yearning, fear, satisfaction. All these ways of feeling have characteristic forms, and a closer study of their forms shows a striking resemblance between them and the forms of growth, motion, development, and decline familiar to the biologist, the typical forms of vital process.[7]

[6] See Chapter XII, ii.
[7] Susanne K. Langer, *Philosophical Sketches* (Baltimore, 1962), p. 8.

31

These, then, are the raw feelings which must be translated by the novelist into language or verbal images to convey emotion. Dr. Langer goes on to explain that feeling (or nerve impulse) is somehow "felt as thought." The conversion takes place automatically. For the novelist to reproduce emotion as thought is to copy the human process. Moreover, feeling, which seems for Dr. Langer "to be the generic basis of all mental experience—sensation, emotion, imagination, recollection, and reasoning"—is not passive but rather active. To feel "is an activity, not a product," she explains. Thus Mrs. Woolf's emotional moment may be said to be not passive cerebration but the activity which we know as life. It is not limited to the brain but embraces the entire body, for the "mechanisms of felt activity are heightened forms of unfelt vital rhythms, responses, and interactions."[8] Thus the vertical moment of being can be seen to run from the conscious verbalization or awareness of feeling to the unconscious and down to the very processes which make up physical life. These "unfelt vital rhythms"—as Maud Bodkin recognizes in *Archetypal Patterns in Poetry*—raise in the reader "an organic response" which is mainly on the instinctual or unconscious level;[9] and they contribute, as will be seen, to an understanding of Virginia Woolf's concept of feeling as form.

🐉 🐉 🐉

THIS RESPONSE of the reader to the many aspects of the individual moment of being is predicated on the prime subjective mode of the novelist: that of *point of view*. It is the standpoint or position which makes pos-

[8] *Ibid.*, pp. 9 and 11.
[9] Maud Bodkin, *Archetypal Patterns in Poetry* (London, 1934), p. 113.

sible all the other modes of subjectivity, for without the confining of the reader to the consciousness of a single character the atmosphere of the moment could not be conveyed. William James in his discussion of the stream of thought in *Principles of Psychology* emphasizes the personal quality of consciousness, the exclusivity of its thoughts. From this consciousness the mind of the author is absent; the reader likewise sheds his own sense of identity for that of the character and experiences the novel as if it were a drama of his own consciousness.

The first two sections of the chapter attempted, through comparison and definition, to establish the *kind* of experience the reader would undergo when plunged into the consciousness of a character. Now, before examining certain modes of subjectivity which stem from point of view, it is useful to systematize the "shower of atoms" which gives shape or pattern to the moment. As suggested earlier in the chapter, these stimuli originate both inside and outside consciousness and are important not only in their relation to perception and thought but also for their effect within the body which may be termed a secondary level of reaction or response. For clarity, they may be grouped into four divisions: the ways in which the character *feels*, *sees*, *thinks*, and *experiences time*. Although these aspects of consciousness tend to fuse or overlap, they may be found sufficiently distinct to aid in an understanding of the methods which Virginia Woolf uses to show the processes of thought and perception.

How the character feels. By "feeling," we have indicated the sum of psychic, physical, and mental experience. For the purposes of our discussion we shall limit feeling to the aspects of emotion and physical sensation which are not related to conceptual thought. Yet even so, we are faced with a range of response so vague and varied that it is impossible to make adequate distinctions. The easiest way to examine feeling as such is to deal with the *influences* upon feeling which Mrs. Woolf herself gives, leaving them to work upon the reader and produce the desired effect. These influences may be roughly categorized as external/historical, external/physical, internal/physical, and internal/mental.

The external/historical influences can be seen to range from the temper of the times which contributes its attitude and pressures, as in *Jacob's Room* or *The Years*, to the historical past which is part of the present consciousness, as shown in *Orlando*, and even to the evolutionary or racial past of a people preserved in instinct or reaction, as in *Between the Acts*. The external/physical influences, on the other hand, are those of the natural world: the object as it acts upon the subject, the cyclical movements and changes in season, temperature, planets, etc., all of which affect mood and outlook, as shown in "The Moment," *The Waves*, and *To the Lighthouse*. Internal/physical influences are those of the body and its health which so preoccupied Virginia Woolf; of energy tone and bodily cycles and changes which she catalogues in the essay "On Being Ill" and Chapter XXV of *The Voyage Out*. Finally, the internal/mental influences—usually normal, sometimes pathological, and always related to the physical—deal with repressed aspects of the unconscious, such as aggressions, fears, or anxieties.

How the results of these various influences—the feelings themselves—are externalized for the reader by Mrs. Woolf so that he may experience them constitute the modes of subjectivity such as *reflection* or refraction, in which people or objects become mirrors for the moods or anxieties of the character viewing them; *metaphor*, *myth*, and *symbol* (primitive modes of subjectivity) which abstract feeling and are shown in phantasy, dream, or symbolic action;

and the *kinetic mode*, the tempo or speed at which the character experiences a situation. Thus the way a character "feels" may be seen to affect, and be affected by, the ways in which he sees, thinks, and experiences time.

How the character sees. A character's perception of the external world, then, is influenced by his emotions or feelings. Two other factors, however, also come under consideration, and those are the way in which the eye organically sees and the influence of the mind (as opposed to the influence of the emotions) on visual perception. Organic perception, Mrs. Woolf seems to have realized, is not the simple action of the camera with its shutter lens. The eye does not record objective reality; it is a visual organ which scans (like certain electronic devices, such as that used with television), selects, even arranges what it "sees" into a pattern.[10] Thus the visual image is not a replica of the object but an interiorized imitation of it.[11] Mrs. Woolf's use of the scanning process, an abstraction or simplification known to certain psychologists as "structural repression,"[12] occurs, for example, in her rendering of near-sleeping or hypnagogic states when "things simplify themselves"[13] or in her reduction of ordinary perceived visual objects, such as trees, furniture, or faces, to blurs or single lines.[14]

[10] Langer, *Philosophical Sketches*, pp. 71-73.

[11] Jean Piaget, *Play, Dreams and Imitation in Childhood*, trans. C. Gattegno and F. M. Hodgson (New York, n.d.), pp. 3-5.

[12] Langer, *Philosophical Sketches*, p. 78. In a footnote Dr. Langer refers the reader to Anton Ehrenzweig, *The Psychoanalysis of Artistic Vision and Hearing* (London, 1953), p. 15, for his discussion of structural repression.

[13] *Lighthouse*, p. 313; or see *Jacob's Room*, p. 12, in which the chest of drawers is a "sharp edge," the looking glass a "silver streak."

[14] See, for example, the description of Christopher feeding the chickens in *Night and Day*, p. 196; the Guy Fawkes's fire in *Jacob's Room*, pp. 72-73; the pot as a "reddish streak" in *The Waves*, p. 134; or faces as "bladder shapes" in *The Waves*, p. 147.

Perceptual vision is influenced in a similar manner by the mind itself with its own abstractive process[15] of combining unrelated percepts into the unity which we consider the object—a process that corresponds to what we loosely term "imagination."[16] Memory and thought likewise influence perceptual vision, since we tend to project our preconceptions about, and memories of, an object. Aware of these dual influences, Proust wrote that seeing someone we know is "an intellectual process" in which the actual face is merely a "transparent envelope" for the ideas which the perceiver forms about that person."[17] Perhaps learning from Proust, perhaps from her own powers of self-observation, Virginia Woolf demonstrates through the indirections of the reflecting modes how much the thinking process influences the way her characters view people and things.

How the character thinks. The influences on thought may be roughly termed the same as those on feeling; thought is merely the verbalization or abstraction of that feeling, as Dr. Langer noted. However, the modes or patterns of thought vary according to how they are directed by the conscious or the unconscious, and the mood or emotion of the individual character is more easily discernible to the reader if the particular flow and pattern of his thought is reproduced. In her novels, Virginia Woolf attempts to show the patterned sequences of at least three distinct modes by which the mind appears to operate:

[15] Langer, *Philosophical Sketches*, pp. 73-78. See also her *Philosophy in a New Key*, 3rd edn. (Cambridge, Mass., 1957), p. 72.

[16] ". . . the mind can never even perceive an object, *as* an object, till the imagination has been at work combining the *disjecta membra* of unrelated percepts into that experienced unity which the word 'object' denotes." Owen Barfield, *Poetic Diction: A Study in Meaning*, 2nd edn. (London, 1952), p. 27.

[17] Marcel Proust, *Remembrance of Things Past*, I, trans. C. K. Scott Moncrieff (New York, 1934), "Overture," p. 15. This passage may perhaps be the source for Mrs. Woolf's famous phrase, "the semi-transparent envelope."

that of logical or "everyday thinking," with its generaliza-
tions and wanderings; "artistic thinking," with its leaps
from " 'flash' to 'flash' " through steps which are perceptible
on a level other than conscious;[18] and dream or phantasy
thinking. Through her skillful rendition of these thought
patterns we can observe certain modes of subjectivity at
work, especially those primitive modes of image, metaphor,
and symbol and such means by which they work as abstraction, condensation, compression, and metamorphosis. Also
observable are the mechanisms which "trigger" memory and
idea association. The ways in which Mrs. Woolf shows
these aspects of thought activity suggest that a study of
their use in her novels might be of interest to psychologists.
Some of her techniques may well have been learned from
the psychologists themselves. As will be seen, she seemed
to follow the observations of William James who charted
certain directions of the flow of thought.[19] Proust, tutored
by Bergson, may have suggested to her the discontinuity
and "free association" of near-sleeping states. And certainly Freud apprised her, as did Frazer in *The Golden
Bough*, of the function of symbol and myth. Yet however
much these psychologists may have influenced her (perhaps they merely confirmed her own intuitions and perceptions), she made these techniques her own by extending
and refining them. In addition, she attempted to render, in
a less scientific and more poetic way, the quality and
rhythm of the thought itself. We are often aware of the
quality of our own thought: how at times it seems free,

---

[18] Sir Frederic Bartlett, *Thinking: An Experimental and Social
Study* (New York, 1958), pp. 164-86, 194-96. Bartlett quotes
Clive Bell's comment on the thought process of Virginia Woolf
as being different from that of any one else. See Bell's *Old
Friends: Personal Recollections* (New York, 1957), p. 95.

[19] She may also have been influenced by Dorothy Richardson's
patterns of reverie. See Mrs. Woolf's reviews of *The Tunnel*
(1919) and *Revolving Lights* (1923) in *C.W.*, pp. 121 and 124.
See also my Chapter IX, v.

light, racing, and at other times is sluggish or torpid. Mrs. Woolf communicates these qualities in vivid kinetic images whose sense of motion suggests the very flow and flux of the mental process with its accompanying charge of emotion. For example, Lily Briscoe's many thoughts dance, separately but simultaneously, like gnats in an "elastic net";[20] Orlando's emotion and feelings climb a "spiral stairway" to the brain;[21] later, Orlando feels her mind is "a fluid that flowed round things and enclosed them";[22] similarly Lily, from watching the sea, feels her mind rising and falling with it.[23]

How the character experiences time. Time for Virginia Woolf was not measured by the clock but experienced emotionally—hence her phrase "moment of being." By the clock, the span of the moment of being might be merely five minutes or five seconds. Experienced emotionally/mentally, it is seen to be composed, as is her moment of a summer's night, of a multiplicity of states of consciousness, a succession of awarenesses which take place not in five minutes—which posits a past, present, and future—but in the all-inclusive *now.* Although Mrs. Woolf did not consciously follow Bergson,[24] her moment of being, with its diversity in unity, resembles his con-

[20] *Lighthouse*, p. 43.   [21] *Orlando*, p. 17.
[22] *Orlando*, p. 283.   [23] *Lighthouse*, p. 231.
[24] According to a letter written by Leonard Woolf to James Hafley (*The Glass Roof*), Virginia Woolf had not read Bergson. Bergson, however, was very much "in the air" at that time. Proust, whom she did read as early as 1922, absorbed his concept of time from Bergson. Karin Stephen, a sister-in-law of Mrs. Woolf's, wrote a book on Bergson's thought called *Misuse of the Mind* (1922) but it is even doubtful that she read this. See Jean Guiguet, *Virginia Woolf and Her Works*, p. 33. An argument for the influence of Edmund Husserl's phenomenology, especially his concept of the moment, could just as readily be posed. Both philosophers reflect changing attitudes toward the concept of time.

cept of duration (*la durée*) in which time is qualitative, nonspatial, real, vertical, and always present.

Thus real (or psychological) time for the character may pass quickly or slowly, in response to emotional states such as excitement or boredom. It can contract or expand, contracting to attention on a single present fact or state, or expanding to include simultaneous memories from one or more periods of past time. For Bergson, the moment contained the whole of the past within it: a continuous "prolonging of the past into the actual" present.[25] Thus time enclosed within its walls aspects of thought, emotion, perception, memory, and even the personality itself, whose states of consciousness were mysteriously bound up with the moment.

The way the character experiences time, therefore, is another method of imparting to the reader the particular quality of that character's state of consciousness. We might term this, for lack of a definition, *rate of experience* or rate of being. Being is always moving, never static. Indeed, as Bergson explains, time or duration is actually the psychical state of becoming, poised on the brink between past and future and exhibiting qualities of motion, growth, and change[26] comparable to the biological processes in which every tissue and fluid of the body are in a state of constant transformation. In that sense, man does not experience time as such but rather sensation, motion, change. Experiencing the wealth of the myriad impressions of one moment of consciousness, he is in transition to a new moment which the duration he has just passed through will enrich.

[25] Henri Bergson, *Creative Evolution*, trans. Arthur Mitchell (New York, 1944), p. 7.

[26] Henri Bergson, *Matter and Memory*, trans. Nancy Margaret Paul and W. Scott Palmer (New York and London, 1911), pp. 177-78. See also *Creative Evolution*, pp. 3-10.

How the character experiences *clock* time—as opposed to real or psychological time—is rendered by Virginia Woolf as a sensory stimulus which may divert the stream of thought, summon memory, or change an emotional mood, as do the chimes of Big Ben and St. Margaret's throughout the novel *Mrs. Dalloway*. Thus, clock time (the "leaden circles" which "dissolved in the air" in *Mrs. Dalloway*) is metamorphosed into feeling and enters consciousness as one more aspect of duration. Time associated with the cyclical actions of the physical world and time as history (which compresses racial attitudes and instinctual patterns) function in a similar manner.

THE MULTIPLICITY of stimuli and responses within the moment of being suggests that the moment itself is not a single state of consciousness but rather an organization of many simultaneous states which interpenetrate and extend vertically from a surface layer we cognize to the deep levels of which we are scarcely aware. The moment, then, is a microcosm of being, for it includes the entire world of consciousness and organic response, and the experience to be found within that miniature world is even more complex than the simple categories of seeing, feeling, thinking, and experiencing time would suggest. The climax of Virginia Woolf's essay "The Moment" offers a final example of the many ways by which she places the reader within the character's mind. The particular state of consciousness shown here appears to transcend both feeling and thinking and push beyond into what might be termed a mystical or psychical state. If Mrs. Woolf's moment of being begins with a shower of atoms, it ends with a dissolving of them: what remains is a single awareness of space or the "not-me." In Virginia Woolf's essay, the "plausible glistening moment," whose walls reflect the surrounding material world, changes to one of "terror." She, as the narrator, wishes "to rush out unnoticed, alone; to be consumed; to be swept away . . . to be part of the eyeless dark." The world of objects and thought gives way to empty space, the self to the non-self. As the myriad atoms of the moment have converged to a substantive center, so they must dissipate. The walls of the moment break; new atoms will fall, and another cycle of the moment, with its pattern of tension and release, begins again.

This brief disintegration or fragmentation of the moment (which includes the temporary sense of loss of personality or self) may be termed a state of supraconsciousness. It is the "disembodied mood" which certain of Virginia Woolf's less stable characters, such as Rhoda, feel. Yet however related to the pathological it may be, its terrors are familiar; they are the fears felt in nightmares or anxiety dreams. Existing thus on the periphery of universal experience and rousing within the reader a flicker of subliminal response, these fears or terrors form yet another aspect of the complex of emotional reality which Mrs. Woolf attempts to convey.

CHAPTER FOUR

Three Ways of Seeing the Subject

For the psychological novelist there are three main ways of "seeing the subject"—that is, handling what we have termed *point of view*. The most obvious way to place the reader within the consciousness of a single character is to suggest the pattern of the flow of logical or conceptual thought through that consciousness. The second way is to present its phantasies, thereby entering peripheral areas of consciousness which the normal and reasoning mind does not explore. The thought of the character is thus "intuited" or inferred through image and story pattern rather than directly expressed. The third, most indirect, and therefore most difficult, way of presenting point of view is through what people do *not* say, through the silence "between the acts" of spoken thought or symbolic action, or through an attempt to verbalize feeling in artificial soliloquies, as Virginia Woolf does in *The Waves*.[1]

Mrs. Woolf freely uses all three of these methods, sometimes mixing them, other times interspersing them, as in *The Years*, with the traditional viewpoint of the omniscient author. Rarely, save in *The Waves*, does she remain with a single method of point of view, and it is this constant shift from one method to another—using whichever will best serve her purpose at the moment—which allows her a certain control over her story and keeps it free of the sense of narrowness and confinement for which she criticizes James Joyce.[2]

[1] See Edel, *The Modern Psychological Novel*, p. 199.
[2] "Modern Fiction" (*C.R.I*), *Essays*, II, pp. 107-108.

42

Possibly because of its limitations, Mrs. Woolf does not use the set formula of the internal monologue[3] as does Joyce. She is more concerned with giving the *illusion* of the flow of thought than creating the impression of transcribing it verbatim. This illusion, created by the suggestion of certain qualities rather than actualities of thought, is so skillful that we are scarcely aware that entrance into the character's mind is accomplished by such time-worn phrases as "she thought," "she felt," or "it seemed to him." What the reader is aware of is the *discontinuity* of the thought, its lack of organization, its sudden breaks and shiftings, which create a certain bewilderment as does the data of consciousness which thrusts itself upon us each moment and which we automatically sift and sort out for ourselves. Mrs. Woolf also makes the reader aware of the *simultaneity* of thought and perception, of the multiplicity of impressions within the moment so that the character's thoughts, or awarenesses, seem to be occurring on many levels at the same time—"multiple moments within the moment."[4] When Lily Briscoe feels her many thoughts dancing up and down like gnats in a net, she is experiencing the simultaneities of thought. Mrs. Woolf's presentation of these thoughts prepares the reader for the final revelation of multiplicity-within-unity which Lily feels and which communicates an extraordinary sense of the vitality of thought and its actions:

> Standing now, apparently transfixed, by the pear tree, impressions poured in upon her of those two men, and *to follow her thought was like following a voice which speaks too quickly to be taken down by one's pencil,*

[3] "Internal monologue" usually refers to a progression of thought associations and memories as they occur in the mind. The term is sometimes used loosely to include any method which places the reader "at the 'centre' of the character's thoughts." See Edel, *The Modern Psychological Novel*, pp. 56-64.

[4] *Ibid.*, p. 200.

and the voice was her own voice saying without prompting undeniable, everlasting, contradictory things, so that even the fissures and humps on the bark of the pear tree were irrevocably fixed there for eternity. You have greatness, she continued, but Mr. Ramsay has none of it. He is petty, selfish, vain, egotistical; he is spoilt; he is a tyrant; he wears Mrs. Ramsay to death; but he has what you (she addressed Mr. Bankes) have not; a fiery unworldliness; he knows nothing about trifles; he loves dogs and his children. He has eight. You have none. Did he not come down in two coats the other night and let Mrs. Ramsay trim his hair into a pudding basin? *All of this danced up and down, like a company of gnats, each separate, but all marvelously controlled in an invisible elastic net*—danced up and down in Lily's mind, in and about the branches of the pear tree, where still hung in effigy the scrubbed kitchen table, symbol of her profound respect for Mr. Ramsay's mind, until her thought which had spun quicker and quicker exploded of its own intensity; she felt released; a shot went off close at hand, and there came, flying from its fragments, frightened, effusive, tumultuous, a flock of starlings.[5]

Much of *To the Lighthouse*, as well as *Mrs. Dalloway*, attempts to define the movement, quality, and component parts of thought. In this particular sequence, not only is the multiplicity of Lily's thoughts given, but also the different levels on which they occur: pure logical abstraction in the case of the scrubbed kitchen table and its relation to the pear tree;[6] logical and emotional value judg-

[5] *Lighthouse*, pp. 42-44. Italics mine. Note the fragmentation of thought in the implied metaphor at the end of the paragraph, which ends the cycle of the moment, as described in the last chapter.

[6] The table represents for Lily Mr. Ramsay's philosophical work. "Subject and object and the nature of reality," with which

ments; past memories triggered through association. Lily's vision likewise shows how a central image (in this case the tree with a table caught in its branches) acts as an organizing agent or principle[7] which orders the mental landscape and aids in the observation and coalescence of many disparate elements.

Mrs. Woolf has noted in this paragraph, in the first italicized phrase, the impossibility of actually recording in words what occurs simultaneously—or in an incomprehensively swift succession of states—in the mind, and she has worked out several methods for suggesting simultaneity. One of these is the use of visual image as illustrated above by the gnats dancing in the net. Compression through symbol is another. A third is the use of parenthetical phrases to record a thought and an action transpiring at the same time. "Could I do it in a parenthesis? So that one had the sense of reading the two things at the same time?" she asks herself in her diary.[8]

Both Laurence Sterne and Lewis Carroll[9] had taught Virginia Woolf the advantages of the parenthetical remark, not to give additional information or an author's aside, but to place the inner and outer worlds as close as possible on the page and so achieve a three-dimensional quality. Sometimes the parentheses are used for something

---

his books deal, is abstracted in her mind into this image of a scrubbed board table, "grained and knotted, whose virtue seems to have been laid bare by years of muscular integrity" (p. 41). She sees it—stuck, "four legs in air," in a pear tree—as a symbol for the absurd relationship between man's sterile philosophy and nature's organic growth.

[7] See Chapter V, ii.

[8] *Diary*, September 5, 1926, while she was writing *Lighthouse*. She had used this method, however, as early as *Jacob's Room*.

[9] An example of Carroll's use of parenthesis for simultaneous thought and action: "First it [the Dodo] marked out a race-course, in a sort of circle ('the exact shape doesn't matter,' it said) and then all the party were placed along the course, here and there." *Alice's Adventures in Wonderland and Through the Looking Glass* (New York, 1946), p. 40.

45

as simple as recording the simultaneous thought and feeling,[10] speech and thought,[11] or thought and action[12] of a single person. At other times Mrs. Woolf juxtaposes the inner and outer worlds of two beings and sets up a contrast between them by presenting the feelings and thoughts of one character with the words and actions of another.[13] The parenthetical remark is not always enclosed in actual parentheses, however. Sometimes it is set off with dashes or inserted as a long interior modifying phrase. Indeed, all these "moments of being" contain the impression of parenthesis within parenthesis, simultaneous levels of feeling and action which make them stir like the city she describes in "Kew Gardens": "a vast nest of

[10] "But she could remember going cold with excitement and doing her hair in a kind of ecstasy (now the old feeling began to come back to her, as she took out her hairpins, laid them on the dressing-table, began to do her hair), with the rooks flaunting up and down in the pink evening light." *Dalloway*, p. 39. This passage combines, in addition, present action with past memory and action.

[11] See the passage of alternating thought and speech in *Jacob's Room*, p. 71.

[12] In *Lighthouse*, Mr. Bankes's long telephone conversation with and thought about Mrs. Ramsay is enclosed in parentheses. Within this parenthetical paragraph, Mr. Bankes muses on her beauty while he watches house builders next door: "So that if it was her beauty merely that one thought of, one must remember the quivering thing, the living thing (they were carrying bricks up a little plank as he watched them), and work it into the picture" (pp. 50-51). Here, as Mr. Bankes is listening to Mrs. Ramsay, and thinking about her, he is also busy watching a scene going on outside the window. This is a perfect juxtaposition of the inner and outer world of a single character. As usual the worlds are emotionally connected, for Mrs. Ramsay's creativity as a wife and mother—a builder of a home in the true sense—is symbolized by the house-builders Mr. Bankes is watching as he talks to her.

[13] "For Hugh always made her feel, as she bustled on, raising his hat rather extravagantly and assuring her that she might be a girl of eighteen, and of course he was coming to her party to-night, Evelyn absolutely insisted, only a little late he might be after the party at the Palace to which he had to take one of Jim's boys,— she always felt a little skimpy beside Hugh; schoolgirlish; but attached to him." *Dalloway*, p. 8.

Chinese boxes . . . turning ceaselessly one within another."[14]

The use of discontinuity is the other significant way in which Mrs. Woolf makes the reader aware of the flow of thought, a movement forward in time rather than a movement outward in space like simultaneity. William James in his chapter on the stream of consciousness likened this movement to the life of a bird with its "alternation of flights and perchings,"[15] and Virginia Woolf's description of Septimus Smith watching his wife Rezia in *Mrs. Dalloway* borrows James's image:

> . . . and as she sat there, waiting, looking down, he could feel her mind, like a bird, falling from branch to branch, and always alighting, quite rightly; he could follow her mind . . . and, if he should say anything, at once she smiled, like a bird alighting with all its claws firm upon the bough.   (pp. 161-62)

This flight-perching pattern of thought is carried throughout *Mrs. Dalloway* (her first full-length attempt to center a novel entirely within various characters' consciousnesses), aided by the bird image which is affixed to all three main personae.[16] In the opening pages Clarissa's mind darts from one thing to another. Sometimes we are given the sensory stimulus which impels the direction of the flight of her thought (the squeak of a hinge, the sound of Big Ben); at other times her mind makes the transition without links. We are conscious only of the thought's movement and the *"contrasts in the quality"*[17] resulting from the branchings or breaks.

---

[14] *A Haunted House*, p. 39.

[15] William James, *Psychology*, p. 160.

[16] Clarissa is said to have "a touch of the bird about her" and is likened to a jay by Scrope Purvis. Rezia thinks of Septimus as "a young hawk."

[17] William James, *Psychology*, p. 159.

These contrasts, which are emotional in quality, are illustrated perhaps even more vividly in *To the Lighthouse*, the novel which followed *Mrs. Dalloway*. The passage I am about to quote also utilizes the images of flight and perching, but it is far more complex, not only in its visual imagery, but in the emotional nuances conveyed by the constantly shifting pattern. The scene occurs near the end of the last section of "The Window." It is late at night; Mrs. Ramsay is knitting and thinking of a poem "Luriana, Lurilee," and she allows her mind to drift in relaxed semi-phantasy patterns which the poem itself, with its central images of flux and flow ("full of trees and changing leaves"),[18] seems to suggest. The rhythms of the poem's words assume pictorial form, first as waves, then as moving lights, finally as birds which seem to be "leaving their perches up there to fly across and across." Later, while she is reading, she becomes the words of the poem (and therefore the birds which are their image), climbing upward through lines of poetry as through petaled branches, swinging from one to another.

> And dismissing all this, as one passes in diving now a weed, now a straw, now a bubble, she felt again, sinking deeper, as she had felt in the hall when the others were talking, There is something I want—something I have come to get, and she fell deeper and deeper without knowing quite what it was, with her eyes closed. And she waited a little, knitting, wondering, and slowly those words they had said at dinner, "the China rose is all abloom and buzzing with the honey bee," began washing from side to side of her mind rhythmically, and as they washed, words, like little

[18] This line-fragment suggests the multiplicity of mental states and their constant change. Mrs. Woolf uses the image of the tree as dream-thought in *The Waves* (p. 40) and words as leaves in *Jacob's Room* (p. 92).

shaded lights, one red, one blue, one yellow, lit up in the dark of her mind, and seemed leaving their perches up there to fly across and across, or to cry out and to be echoed; so she turned and felt on the table beside her for a book.

And all the lives we ever lived
And all the lives to be,
Are full of trees and changing leaves,

she murmured, sticking her needles into the stocking. And she opened the book and began reading here and there at random, and as she did so she felt that she was climbing backwards, upwards, shoving her way up under petals that curved over her, so that she only knew this is white, or this is red. She did not know at first what the words meant at all.

Steer, hither steer your winged pines,
all beaten Mariners

she read and turned the page, swinging herself, zig-zagging this way and that, from one line to another as from one branch to another, from one red and white flower to another, until a little sound roused her—her husband slapping his thighs.   (pp. 183-84)

I have quoted this long section in order to convey the full sense of the movement of Mrs. Ramsay's mind. Virginia Woolf achieves this through a complex synthesis of outer rhythm and word sound, symbolic imagery, synesthesia, metamorphosis, and an *inner* rhythm expressed through the pattern itself and the imagery of falling ("diving . . . sinking"), then rising in an upward zigzag movement, *even as a bird would fly*. As in the sequence of Lily's thoughts quoted earlier, this long recording of a semiphantasy state emphasizes one of the most important factors in Mrs. Woolf's conveying of mental experience: the motion of the mind. Mrs. Woolf differs most perhaps from Joyce in this, for Joyce's "epiphanies"—moments of insight or vision—reflect perfect stillness (a working out of his aesthetic theories)[19] whereas hers are merely the climax of the moving moment and in themselves seem to constitute perceptions of eternal motion, as the quoted thought sequences of Lily and Mrs. Ramsay illustrate.

So far in this discussion, we have been concerned mainly with patterns of thought and their movement or direction. Now, in seeing how Mrs. Woolf shows the "breaks" in thought, which accentuate its sense of discontinuity, we are dealing with a still more subtle aspect of mental experience. The processes by which the mind accomplishes the transition from thought to thought—what William James refers to as the "transitive" as compared to the "substantive" part of thought[20]—are at the best obscure. The links are sometimes visible, such as word or idea association, or a sensory stimulus like sound or taste, which rouses a memory through what has been termed a "trigger mechanism." But other times the links are hidden, buried in the unconscious which, as Freud suggests, has a peculiar logic of its own and which, as seen in dreams, is able to dispense with the connectives so necessary to our grammatically oriented thought.[21]

[19] This is true, at least, in Joyce's *A Portrait of the Artist as a Young Man* (New York, 1928), in which the viewpoint is traditionally a romantic one (see pp. 205-15). Virginia Woolf's position, on the other hand, reflects the spirit of modern anti-romantic art, from Cubism onward, in which motion and speed are dominant. Music, starting with Stravinsky, and the French theatre of the absurd likewise rely on motion and speed.

[20] William James, *Psychology*, p. 160.

[21] Freud states: "All the linguistic instruments by which we express the subtler relations of thought—the conjunctions and prepositions, the changes in declension and conjugation—are dropped, because there are no means of representing them; just as in a primitive language without any grammar, only the raw material of thought is expressed and abstract terms are taken back to the concrete ones that are at their basis." *New Introductory Lectures on Psychoanalysis and Other Works*, Vol. XXII in *The Standard*

David Daiches, in describing Virginia Woolf's rendition of internal monologue, noted that "there was some deep and unconscious logic connecting these apparently random thoughts and images that crowd the drifting mind."[22] Where Mrs. Woolf makes such a leap from thought to thought, the underlying connection is an emotional one. Indeed, most of the links, seen or unseen, have a hidden relation with what the character *feels* about a certain person or thing. For instance, Clarissa always associates Peter Walsh with his criticism of her friends and her snobbishness. Her emotional reaction to his criticism, her hurt vanity, helps to supply the connecting threads.

What Mrs. Woolf recognized, then, was that the emotions which link thoughts are often deeply buried, that the process of awakening this kind of memory is not as recognizable as when it derives from a sensory stimulus. There lies beneath the conscious mind an intricate crisscrossing of impulse, like the electric wires which Mrs. Woolf metaphorically alludes to beneath cathedrals and city streets.[23] How complex this wiring can be is illustrated, again in *Mrs. Dalloway*, by Virginia Woolf's use of the sound of a bell (St. Margaret's) to bring a sudden memory of Clarissa to Peter Walsh's mind. The connection at first seems merely an arbitrary one: the quality of the sound of the bell is gracious and feminine, "the voice of the hostess," which Clarissa will be at her party that night. But there are underlying and conflicting emotions raised by the sound of the bell which Mrs. Woolf exposes enigmatically first in a memory, then a vision. The memory, one which Peter thinks of with deep emotion, is of

---

Edition of the Complete Psychological Works of Sigmund Freud, ed. and trans. James Strachey, Anna Freud, et al. (London, 1964), p. 20.

[22] David Daiches, *Virginia Woolf* (Norfolk, Conn., 1942), p. 71.
[23] *Voyage*, pp. 72-73; *Years*, pp. 107-108.

Clarissa "coming downstairs on the stroke of the hour in white," and he puzzles as to how this memory arose:

> . . . as if this bell had come into the room years ago, where they sat at some moment of great intimacy, and had gone from one to the other and had left, like a bee with honey, laden with the moment. But what room? What moment? And why had he been so profoundly happy when the clock was striking? Then, as the sound of St. Margaret's languished, he thought, she has been ill, and the sound expressed languor and suffering. It was her heart, he remembered; and the sudden loudness of the final stroke tolled for death that surprised in the midst of life, Clarissa falling where she stood, in her drawing-room. (p. 56)

On the surface, the linking is established by the bell; but less conscious connections are hinted in memories of different times—like the memory of the figure in white coming down the stairs—which converge in the death-thought of the beloved.

Virginia Woolf's means of transition from mind to mind are frequently the same as from thought to thought, and so give the reader the impression that he remains, somehow, *within the same mind or a facet of it*. By this method she achieves a continuity of subjectivity not possible with the usual change from one point of view to another. For example, the transference from the mind of Peter Walsh to Rezia on page 72 of *Mrs. Dalloway* is accomplished through a linking of emotional states. "It was awful," Peter Walsh remembers of his suffering with Clarissa. A moment later: "It's wicked; why should I suffer?" Rezia asks herself. Similarly, the emotional reactions of different characters to the Prime Minister's car and the airplane link the first section of the novel together and give the impression of a mass mind individualized now in Mrs. Coates, now in Mr. Bowley.[24]

In *The Waves*, emotions link the parts of each of the nine sections of the novel. Section V, for example, shows the emotional reactions of each of the characters to Percival's death, and the reader becomes aware of parallel or convergent memories and feelings. Thus Neville's sorrow over Percival's death ("I sob, I sob") connects with the emotion Bernard feels as "sorrow" in the next paragraph and forms a subtle emotional contrast and comparison. Neville's emotion is immature (a child "sobs" and a child repeats, as Neville does, "I sob, I sob") and centered on men, while Bernard's is a mature feeling of love for his just-born child and affectionate grief for his friend. This is only one way in which emotions form the links in the novel. All six characters (who can be seen as six aspects of one mind or multiple personality) are linked together through a network of leitmotifs or key words which vary slightly with each person. The reader, who has the common knowledge of the six minds (not merely that of the character whose soliloquy he happens to be reading at the moment) can therefore make linkings and associations beyond those offered by the single soliloquy. As the novel progresses, the emotional content of the key words or leitmotifs is enhanced and deepened because

[24] It is helpful here to see the emotions themselves as links rather than the car and airplane. The emotions are the reactions toward authority (the car) and the need for communication (the airplane writing "toffee")—the two underlying themes of the novel. "They are always talking about making the connection, but they never do," Septimus hears someone saying in the earliest manuscript version of this section of *Mrs. Dalloway* (*Notebook I*). Connection, or communication, is of course possible only on an emotional level. Mrs. Woolf, whose need for communication via fiction was imperative, may have felt that the novel which employs connectives on a purely technical level (such as *Ulysses* which uses a viceregal cavalcade to tie together a certain chapter) is missing out on the basic connections between people.

multiple associations cluster around them. Like the "little phrase" in Vinteuil's sonata which E. M. Forster feels becomes "a living being" threading its way through the Proustian reader's memory again and again,[25] the emotional life of each of the motifs in *The Waves* becomes rich in meaning.

৯ ৯

SO MUCH THEN for the direct way of placing the reader within the character's flow of thought. A second way of handling point of view is by showing the dreams and phantasies which the character's mind constructs when asleep and awake. The pattern of the flow of logical thought acquaints the reader with that character's everyday life, habits, and attitudes. Night dreams and day dreams, on the other hand, symbolize hidden areas which everyday speech and thinking cannot plumb —areas of which the character himself may be ignorant. Condensing and abstracting emotion in sharp pictorial images and patterns,[26] they can convey to the reader a subliminal or submerged realm of experience and feeling.

That Virginia Woolf was aware of the way dreams and phantasies reveal inner experience is clear from her essays on Lewis Carroll and De Quincey, in which she comments on their use of dream techniques.[27] She seems, moreover, to have been able to observe her own process of phantasy

[25] Forster, *Aspects of the Novel*, pp. 236-39.

[26] Freud noted that night dreams tend to employ more distortion and symbolization than day dreams. In general, dream material is subjected to compression and condensation which may bring together numerous elements in the latent dream thoughts. *New Introductory Lectures* (XXII), pp. 18-21.

[27] The brief essay "Lewis Carroll" (*M.*), *Essays*, I, comments specifically on metamorphosis, contraction and expansion of space and time, and lack of transition within "the world of sleep . . . the world of dreams" (p. 255).

—watching her "under-mind" working at incredible speed while her "upper-mind" drowsed[28]—and from this draw a sense of certain laws of operation within various levels of the imagining and dreaming mind. She was especially sensitive to the less obvious levels of phantasy—reverie, invention, even the simple process of "thinking about people" which, as Lily Briscoe observed in *To the Lighthouse*, consisted mainly in making up things about them, "not a word" of which was "true" (p. 267). Indeed, as Peter Walsh observed in *Mrs. Dalloway*, after he had invented an imaginary escapade with a girl, "one makes up the better part of life" (p. 61).

The way phantasy compresses experience and abstracts repressed emotion into symbol is illustrated, as we have seen, by Peter Walsh's imagining Clarissa falling in her dining room. Motives are suggested or implied, and different readers will attach different meanings to them. In a similar manner, Lily Briscoe's building up "a whole structure of imagination" on a single sentence which the Rayleys have spoken serves as a reflection of her state of feeling. Lily is fully aware of the invalidity of her speculation about the marriage of the Rayleys (who became engaged before Mrs. Ramsay's dinner) but only partially of its motivation. The imagined scenes of Paul Rayley's anger and infidelity may reveal her suspicion of men, for as she thinks of Paul Rayley and the idea of marriage, "a reddish light seemed to burn in her mind, covering Paul Rayley, issuing from him." This may be the memory of a beach fire, lit to help recover Minta's brooch. Or it may be a symbol by which her mind has abstracted her fears of love and its possible destructive power: "one had only to say 'in love' and instantly, as happened now, up rose Paul's fire again" (pp. 270-71).

Lily's structure of imagination exhibits the way differ-

[28] "The Leaning Tower" (*M.*), *Essays*, II, p. 166.

ent levels of the human mind interpenetrate and interact. An excellent example of this interpenetration on the dream level is seen in *Mrs. Dalloway* when Rezia has been given a sedative by Dr. Holmes after Septimus' suicide. Stimuli from the real world—the clock striking, Mrs. Filmer waving her apron—are incorporated into her dream. In the same novel but in a different way, the grey nurse who is knitting in Regent's Park beside the sleeping Peter Walsh enters his dream-phantasy metamorphosed into a series of protective yet vaguely threatening female figures.

The fairy tale, which the Regent's Park dream of Peter Walsh suggests, with its traveller-knight and giant awaiting at the end of the ride, is a specific phantasy pattern which Virginia Woolf uses, sometimes given as a thought-sequence, other times woven into incident, like the children's game played in the imaginary country of Elvedon in the opening chapter of *The Waves*. Isa's reverie in *Between the Acts*, in which she and her imaginary lover become two swans, has the fairy tale's denouement of wish fulfillment. In the psychologically astute short story, "Lappin and Lapinova," the young married couple play out their phantasy roles of two royal rabbits who inhabit a private wilderness—a sophisticated development of a brief scene in the earlier *Night and Day* in which Katharine leaves reality and goes wandering in a wilderness of her own with her lover/hero (pp. 144-45). The sense of freedom and escape—as well as the mysterious role which phantasy plays in reality adjustment—is conveyed by these sequences.

The various levels of phantasy which Virginia Woolf represents—from casual thinking about things to night dreams to phantasies of the disturbed mind such as those of Septimus Smith in *Mrs. Dalloway* and Rhoda in *The Waves*; or even the hallucinations of Rachel while ill with typhoid in *The Voyage Out*—employ what we have termed patterns or laws of operation which belong to phantasy and not to conscious logical thought. Some give gratification to the thinker, as Peter Walsh, for example, finds "a little glow of pleasure, a sort of lust, too" when he spins a phantasy of doctors and dead bodies.[29] Others bring pleasure to the reader as well, when he is able to identify with them.[30] When Mr. Ramsay on the way to the lighthouse stages "a little drama" by casting himself in the role of the widowed martyr,[31] the reader may respond, for he has probably created an analogous phantasy at some time or other. Likewise, the reader can understand Cam's double-level thinking when she imagines a shipwreck at the same time that she is observing the actual trip to the lighthouse:

> It seemed as if they were doing two things at once; they were eating their lunch here in the sun and they were also making for safety in a great storm after a shipwreck. Would the water last? Would the provisions last? she asked herself, telling herself a story but knowing at the same time what was the truth.[32]

These phantasy patterns which we, as readers, may know from our own experience appear like a flash from a remembered dream, or a scene from *Alice in Wonderland*. Much of *Mrs. Dalloway*, for example (which borrows many dream devices from Lewis Carroll) gives this hallucinatory sense. One after another of the characters "falls,"

[29] *Dalloway*, p. 166. Also see *Lighthouse*, p. 111, where Mrs. Ramsay muses on how "all sorts of horrors" seemed not to depress her husband but rather to cheer him.

[30] Simon Lesser's *Fiction and the Unconscious* (Boston, 1957) deals with this role of the reader, especially Chapter X, "Participation and the Pathways to Satisfaction."

[31] *Lighthouse*, pp. 256-57.

[32] *Ibid.*, p. 314. Before falling asleep, one can be aware of the process of phantasy going on in one part of the mind while the other part is consciously engaged in reality. Even the dreaming mind is aware of this dichotomy, knowing (especially in cases of extreme danger in a dream sequence) that "it is only a dream." See Freud's *New Introductory Lectures* (XXII), p. 17.

as does Alice, through a passageway.[33] Life seems to one "an unknown garden, full of turns and corners."[34] The obstructions which confront each character have the quality of those in dreams, appearing irrationally, rather than causatively as in life. The scenes of the novel "fade" and shift like scenes in dreams.[35] Finally, various characters suddenly swell to threatening proportions: the elderly nurse, Doris Kilman, Dr. Holmes, Dr. Bradshaw, Lady Bruton whose face becomes a clock dial with hands that keep slicing away at Clarissa's life. In no other novel has Virginia Woolf penetrated more deeply into subjective states and attempted in so many ways to reproduce the sense of the flow and pattern of the mind.

THE THIRD OF the ways of handling point of view is through what people do *not* say, but what their behavior and attitudes say for them.[36] This Virginia Woolf accomplishes by rendering unverbalized feeling in artificially "spoken" thoughts, such as the imagistic soliloquies of *The Waves*, and by such behaviorist means as drawing, doodling, or symbolic play.

The first two ways of handling point of view suggested in this chapter utilized the manner in which the mind works on conscious and partly conscious levels, i.e.,

[33] In the August 2, 1923, entry of the maroon leather *Dalloway* notebook, Mrs. Woolf speaks of a "scene of falling through into discoveries—like a trap door opening."

[34] *Dalloway*, p. 167.

[35] In her essay on De Quincey in *Granite and Rainbow* (*Essays*, I, pp. 170-71) she describes the scenes in his *Autobiographic Sketches* as having "something of the soundlessness and the lustre of dreams. They swim up to the surface, they sink down again into the depths. They have, into the bargain, the strange power of growing in our minds."

[36] Northrop Frye, *Anatomy of Criticism*, p. 234. Frye specifically cites *The Waves* as an example of this technique.

through thought and phantasy patterns which the conscious mind rationally recognizes and/or remembers from its own waking or sleeping experience. This third way depends heavily on what might be loosely termed the irrational element of the mind, the deepest levels of unconsciousness which surface only by chance. They may appear as symbolic thought—quick reactions to momentary experience which are rendered in image, verbalized for the reader, as in *The Waves*—or as a gesture, an action, a picture or diagram, verbal play, or a game which acts out or abstracts certain emotions too deep for conscious recognition.

It is useful to see *symbol* in Virginia Woolf's work as a key to the character's private experience rather than a writer's way of abstracting or accenting a situation. This is especially necessary in a consideration of *The Waves*, in which the buried or semiconscious feelings and responses of the characters are constantly projected through related series of images within the formal framework of a soliloquy. In this strange "submarine cave"[37] conscious thought in the logical sense has no place. What are continuously forming and reforming are the emotions of the characters toward the situation of the moment. Louis describes this movement of thought as Virginia Woolf herself presents it:

> "Now the current flows. Now we rush faster than before. Now passions that lay in wait down there in the dark weeds which grow at the bottom rise and pound us with their waves. Pain and jealousy, envy and desire, and something deeper than they are, stronger than love and more subterranean." (p. 102)

These waves of emotion, individualized into various passions directed toward different things, are pictorialized

[37] Winifred Holtby, *Virginia Woolf*, p. 189.

for the reader in numerous sets of images whose symbolism conveys their particular atmosphere: jungle and beast imagery, for example, or abstract geometric symbols (most of them variations of the *mandala*)[38] such as circles, globes, loops, and chains. Like the *mandala*, most of the images are rooted in myth or history, whether they be of a tiger leaping, women carrying red pitchers by the Nile, or a man casting a fling of seed. The actual situation to which the characters react is sketched in the sparest of detail; it is the images, with their many levels of meaning —some of which the reader senses only subliminally— which convey a complexity of emotion felt rather than intellectually comprehended.

Virginia Woolf's use of geometric images to represent states of feeling is not confined to *The Waves*. As early as *Night and Day* she experimented with behavioral means of expressing emotion by having her two main characters, Katharine Hilbery and Ralph Denham, work out in diagrams and doodles an abstraction or representation of their feelings. Whereas in *The Waves* diagrams appear merely as images on the screen of a character's mind, in *Night and Day* we see Katharine draw a circle and "scrub" it black, or halve and quarter circles and squares (again the *mandala* symbol).[39] Ralph, who wishes he could put his emotions into poetry, works out his feelings about Katharine on paper, with "blots" and "flames."[40] In subsequent novels behavioral patterns tend to grow more complex. Septimus Smith in *Mrs. Dalloway* conveys his feelings by drawing

[38] The *mandala* is a circle or square design which Jung sees as the symbol of "wholeness" or unity of personality. It occurs not only in Buddhistic religious paintings but also in the historic Greco-Roman world. C. G. Jung and C. Kerényi, *Essays on a Science of Mythology*, trans. R.F.C. Hull, rev. edn. (Princeton: Princeton University Press, 1969), pp. 12ff.

[39] *Night and Day*, pp. 324 and 323.

[40] *Ibid.*, p. 516.

stick figures, many of them obscene.[41] Isa Oliver in *Between the Acts* does what Ralph Denham wished he could do and offers throughout the novel a running commentary in rhyme on the relationship which she senses between herself and her son, her husband, and the gentleman farmer. The verse Isa composes, alliterative and full of refrain, is scarcely poetry; it seems to be a half-conscious attempt to accommodate herself to reality by placing her feelings in relationship to the world about her. What is communicated through her rhymes is the "ache . . . the crest of emotion" which Isa herself describes in an early version of the novel as producing the creative act of writing:

> The ache had gone; the crest of emotion had sunk; the desire for poetry was over; her anger was out; her mind was like a sea anemone when the feelers are curled up. . . .[42]

Symbolic play or action likewise externalizes hidden emotions. Rachel playing mermaid in *The Voyage Out* acts out her ambivalence toward her engagement to Terence Hewet.[43] In *The Years*, Rose Pargiter as a small child claps spurs to an imaginary horse on a secret mission in order to give herself courage to cross the deserted square to Lamley's store.[44] And in *Between the Acts* Isa plucks a leaf of Old Man's Beard to suggest perhaps her symbolic acceptance of love's bitterness.[45] All of Virginia Woolf's

[41] *Dalloway*, pp. 100 and 162. See also *Room*, pp. 46-49, in which Virginia Woolf describes drawing an "angry" and "ugly" picture of a lecturer who spoke of the inferiority of women. "Yet it is in our idleness, in our dreams, that the submerged truth sometimes comes to the top. A very elementary exercise in psychology, not to be dignified by the name of psycho-analysis, showed me, on looking at my notebook, that the sketch of the angry professor had been made in anger."

[42] *Pointz Hall Notebook III*, p. 35 (May 1938). This novel was to become *Between the Acts*. Note how the sea-anemone image conveys the half-formless world of the unconscious from which both emotions and poetry spring.

[43] *Voyage*, p. 365. Also see Chapter VIII, iv.

[44] *Years*, pp. 27-28.   [45] *Acts*, p. 243.

novels abound in instances of symbolic action, but nowhere is it as concentrated as in her final novel. There the best illustration can be seen in the child's game of kicking stones by which Giles Oliver acts out his feelings toward Isa, his wife; Mrs. Manresa, a flirtatious "child of nature"; and William Dodge, a semi-homosexual who is Mrs. Manresa's companion for the day. Walking toward the barn between the acts of the pageant, Giles saw that the "path was strewn with stones."

> He kicked—a flinty yellow stone, a sharp stone, edged as if cut by a savage for an arrow. A barbaric stone; a pre-historic. Stone-kicking was a child's game. He remembered the rules. By the rules of the game, one stone, the same stone, must be kicked to the goal. Say a gate, or a tree. He played it alone. The gate was a goal; to be reached in ten. The first kick was Manresa (lust). The second, Dodge (perversion). The third himself (coward). . . .

> He reached it in ten. There, couched in the grass, curled in an olive green ring, was a snake. Dead? No, choked with a toad in its mouth. The snake was unable to swallow; the toad was unable to die. A spasm made the ribs contract; blood oozed. It was birth the wrong way round—a monstrous inversion. So, raising his foot, he stamped on them. The mass crushed and slithered. The white canvas on his tennis shoes was bloodstained and sticky. But it was action. Action relieved him. He strode to the Barn, with blood on his shoes.

(pp. 118-19)

The situation diagrammed in this symbolic game is a complex one. Giles's hatred of Dodge is not the simple disgust of a man for an effeminate member of his sex; he sees that his wife Isa is drawn to Dodge, and a certain jealousy exists because of Dodge's relation to Mrs. Manresa. William Dodge is a "half-man"; " 'a flickering, mind-divided little snake in the grass . . . as Giles saw,' " Dodge says to himself (p. 90). Giles has already summed him up as a "toady; a lickspittle; not a down-right plain man of his senses; but a teaser and twitcher; a fingerer of sensations . . . not a man to have straightforward love for a woman" (p. 75). Giles's anger and jealousy are compounded by the lust he feels for Mrs. Manresa and by his sense of cowardice in not asserting himself either as Isa's husband or as Mrs. Manresa's lover. The stepping on the snake, as well as the rising tension and sudden release, dramatizes the strength of the conflicting emotions within Giles.

IT WAS ASKED in the last chapter how much Virginia Woolf owes to psychoanalytic theory, how much to her own self-observation and intuitive understanding. By 1911, Freud was certainly in the Bloomsbury air. Leonard Woolf, in his autobiography, mentions Freud as a revolutionary influence in 1911, although he himself did not read *The Interpretation of Dreams* until 1914, the year after its publication, when he reviewed *The Psychopathology of Everyday Life*.[46] Ernst Kris cites a monograph by a Dr. Hoops on the influence of Freud on English writers,[47] most of whom, when consulted,

disclaimed any familiarity with psychoanalytic writings, and the careful author concluded that they were therefore not "influenced" by Freud. A case in point is

[46] *Beginning Again*, pp. 37 and 167.
[47] The "monograph" is by Reinald Hoops, "Der Einfluss der Psychoanalyse auf die Englische Literatur," *Anglistische Forschungen*, ed. Dr. J. Hoops (Heidelberg, 1934).

Virginia Woolf, who stated she had become familiar with psychoanalysis only through ordinary conversation. Dr. Hoops overlooked the fact that Leonard and Virginia Woolf were Freud's publishers in England. But neither this, nor the fact that Virginia Woolf's brother was one of England's most distinguished psychoanalysists, need be quoted to understand that the "ordinary way of conversation" to which Virginia Woolf referred had some considerable influence on the formation of one of the great literary minds of Freud's century.[48]

Yet specific influence, save in the general area of symbolism, is difficult to trace. Kris lists J. Varendonck's *The Psychology of Daydreams* (1921) as an important influence on the writers of that time, but the book does not appear to have any bearing on the reveries of *Mrs. Dalloway* or the thought-patterns in *To the Lighthouse*. All we can acknowledge is the general orientation of a period in which the very ideas afloat in the air lodged in Mrs. Woolf's mind to develop in their own ways. Theories of the unconscious, of repressions, of the importance of childhood years; the more obvious sexual symbolism—all these were in the air. It is interesting, however, to note that the greatest concentration of the psychological appears in *Mrs. Dalloway*, which was begun in 1922, the year when the Woolfs' Hogarth Press began publishing *The International Psychoanalytical Library*. "The psychology should be done very realistically," Mrs. Woolf notes in the maroon leather *Dalloway* notebook in May of 1923, and as will be shown later, her rendition of Septimus Smith's pathological states in that novel is most exact.[49] After finishing *To the Lighthouse*, which followed *Mrs. Dallo-*

[48] Ernst Kris, *Psychoanalytic Explorations in Art* (New York, 1952), p. 268.
[49] See Chapter VI, ii.

way, Virginia Woolf wrote to Charles Percy Sanger, "I confess I sometimes want to cut the whole psychology business altogether."[50] Yet it continues to appear in her fiction, as *The Waves* demonstrates. Little as she may have been influenced by Freud, she was committed to her art of observing how her own mind and body mechanism worked. One of these areas of observation, related not to Freud but to G. E. Moore, is discussed in the following three chapters. They deal with perception—the ways in which the object is seen and how those ways penetrate and reflect the character's interior world.

[50] Dorothy Brewster, *Virginia Woolf* (New York, 1962), pp. 163-64.

CHAPTER FIVE

Three Ways of Seeing the Object

ONCE THE READER is committed to a given point of view—that is, established within the consciousness of the character—the world he finds himself in is a solipsistic one. Objectivity has all but vanished; even the subjective intrusion of the author has disappeared. The reality of the world of persons and objects that the character perceives—and hence that reality which the reader is made to feel—is governed by the physical and mental/emotional make-up of the character.

Virginia Woolf referred to this triangular interrelationship as "subject and object and the nature of reality." This phrase, occurring in *To the Lighthouse*,[1] is meant to draw the reader's attention to the novel's different views of reality which result from the various ways in which the characters see themselves, the world, and their relation to it. Three specific ways of seeing the object can be examined in *To the Lighthouse*: through the eye of the artist (Lily Briscoe), through the eye of a child (James, Nancy, and Cam), and through the feminine, creative eye of Mrs. Ramsay, whose vision might be said to be that of a poet. For her role in the novel is that of the creator of a world (a fictive world, but one which, like the poet's, is perhaps ultimately true) in which her husband, children, and even their guests move. There are, of course, other ways of "seeing the object," but these three modes of subjective vision seem to correspond to the

[1] Andrew Ramsay uses the phrase in describing what his father's books are about to Lily Briscoe (p. 40).

different ways in which Virginia Woolf herself saw the world. Although these modes tend to overlap somewhat, they are distinct enough to examine separately, for they show Mrs. Woolf's ability to communicate fine differences in the perceptive processes of various character types.

Before discussing these three modes, it is helpful to define the "object" as Virginia Woolf appears to have seen it. The "common-sense" view of the object is as a concrete, tangible thing. Virginia Woolf however, possibly under the influence of Hume and G. E. Moore,[2] seemed to consider the object in a subjective manner, as shaped by an individual's thoughts, memories, and sensations. In other words, *it is the emotional experience of the object, rather than the object itself, which is known.* Thus the object may be altered or colored by the character's mind and emotions; it becomes a mirror-image, an extension of the self.

The reverse or negative side of the mirror-object— "things . . . by themselves," as G. E. Moore phrased it in *Principia Ethica*—is the side we cannot know. Their existence appears to take place outside the semi-transparent envelope of human consciousness; the character can experience them only by dissociation as does Septimus, for example, in *Mrs. Dalloway*, or the man in the short story "Solid Objects" who loses his sense of human identity. They are glimpsed in the central section of *To the Lighthouse*: the flowers that stand there "eyeless, and thus terrible" (p. 209), or the "little airs" that nose and rub around the house (pp. 196-97). Unrelated to the human, they serve to sharpen the reader's sense of what *is* human and subjective. With this aspect of the object, there is no normal identification, no way of achieving the

[2] See Chapter II, ii. That Mrs. Woolf read Hume is substantiated by her diary. Maynard Keynes himself wrote on Hume, as did G. E. Moore (a chapter on Hume appears in his *Philosophical Studies*).

close relation between subject and object so necessary to express the poetic self.

For the role of the poet-hero, as Ralph Freedman expresses it in *The Lyrical Novel*, where he examines Mrs. Woolf's fiction as belonging to this genre, is to "absorb" the objective world and achieve a union with it.[3] Mrs. Woolf's characters, however, if we look more closely, appear to bring the objective world into subjective consciousness in order to dominate it. When, for example, Mrs. Ramsay in *To the Lighthouse* sees the bowl of fruit on the dinner table as a world over which one could move —"one could take one's staff and climb up hills . . . and go down into valleys"[4]—she is not absorbing that world of objects but rather bringing it under control. Through her intellectualized concept of the bowl of fruit as a microcosm, Mrs. Ramsay has won dominion over it. A similar instance occurs in her transforming the boar's skull into a bird's nest and flowering valley in her fairy tale for Cam. When, on the other hand, the world of objects is not under control, when furniture loses shape and form to Rhoda (*Waves*) or a dog turns into a man and landscapes change for Septimus,[5] there is no union between subject and object and hence a loss of balance or identity.

The world of objects, which Mrs. Woolf herself (as writer) assumed control of through verbal imagery, is mainly a visual world. It is because of this that *seeing the object* becomes the most important factor in a study of her modes of subjectivity. E. M. Forster noted that she "liked receiving sensations—sights, sounds, tastes—pass-

[3] *The Lyrical Novel: Studies in Hermann Hesse, André Gide, and Virginia Woolf* (Princeton, 1963), pp. 19, 20, 31.

[4] *Lighthouse*, p. 151. Mrs. Ramsay, noting "that Augustus too feasted his eyes on the same plate of fruit," observed that this "was his way of looking, different from hers."

[5] See Chapter VI, ii.

ing them through her mind, where they encountered theories and memories."[6] Actually, save in *Flush*, there are very few tastes or smells in her novels. The world is mainly *seen*, with an emphasis on form and color. Of the tactile sense there is almost nothing. A strange absence of it haunts the opening sections of *The Waves* which deal with childhood and youth; here the few images of touch are rendered visually, such as the "bright arrows of sensation" which Bernard feels in his bath. Generally, the characters in this novel fear touch: Neville hates "dampish" things, Louis and Rhoda fear sharpness. Jinny's sensuousness is conveyed mainly through images of color, light, and motion. Indeed, it could be said that Virginia Woolf, far from being an "elderly sensualist," as she was called by one critic,[7] was anti-sensual, transforming sensory contact with the object into an intellectualized image or concept of it rendered in abstract or visual terms. Finally, it might be stated that it is this confining of her world to that of sight which makes possible the existence of the object as a mirror-image of the self. Were the tactile sense fused with the visual, the object as mirror would be impossible, for touch validates the existence of a knowable world beyond that of the self.[8]

IN CHAPTER III we suggested some of the complexities involved in the act of perception, how the mind, the emotions, and the organic function of the eye itself all determine what we see and consider as the object. In discussing the first way Virginia Woolf sees the

[6] E. M. Forster, *Virginia Woolf* (New York, 1942), pp. 6 and 7.
[7] *Diary*, October 29, 1922.
[8] Wyndham Lewis, *Time and Western Man* (London, 1927), p. 432.

object, *through the eyes of the poet*, in which the image of the object organizes the entire thought or scene, we are dealing with just such complexities, for not only are such mental processes as "association" at work, but also the organic visual processes of "scanning," structural repression, and patterning. Linked with them are emotional values of the image itself.

Mrs. Ramsay's scanning of the centerpiece on her dinner table, letting her mind gather in associations (it is a "trophy" of "Neptune's banquet," a bunch of Bacchus grapes), then finally unifying and expanding the bowl of fruit into a little microcosm which she can exploit for its pleasure (the pleasure achieved in climbing and winning dominion over a little world), is a useful illustration of the poet's way of seeing the object. When, a few minutes later, Mrs. Ramsay looks at the Boeuf en Daube which she has created and sees in its savory confusion the sense of a festival celebrating in seriousness and mockery the birth and death of love, the same ordering of confusion has occurred; the disparate elements of the dinner and her own emotions are unified.

In both these cases, the principle of creativity is at work—the poet's ability to invent a fictive world or universe which he can dominate, enlarge, and order at his will. The long section (11) on Mrs. Ramsay's musings about the lighthouse beams are even more illustrative.[9] When she imagines herself as the "core of darkness" wedged in between the strokes of the lighthouse beams she is able, through the metaphor she creates, to master reality, shed the "attachments" of self for the moment, and be free to go anywhere. The same principle is used when

[9] This section comes, significantly, after Section 10 in which Mrs. Ramsay has told Grimm's fairy tale of the fisherman's wife. In this story the magic power of the flounder creates a fictive world for the wife and alters the aspect of land and sea in the fisherman's eyes.

she identifies with the long steady third stroke of the lighthouse beam; the power of this strongest stroke gives her an intense ecstasy. As the wedge of darkness and that of light are brought under control, she is able to see clearly her relationship to religion, her children, her marriage, and herself.

This idea that a *visual image*—usually one with an identifiable shape, such as a circle, wedge, dot, or dome—*can take disparate elements of thought and organize them into a harmonious whole* is a second principle which Mrs. Woolf used not only in *To the Lighthouse* but, to a certain extent, in all of her novels. We can term this the organizing power of the object. The simplest "object lesson" of this principle is contained in Mrs. Woolf's short story "The Mark on the Wall" in which a small dot becomes the center for a meaningful sequence of associations. The dot starts out as an unidentifiable mark on the wall; later it turns out to be a snail. As the narrator's mind plays around it ("how readily our thoughts swarm upon a new object, lifting it a little way, as ants carry a blade of straw so feverishly, and then leave it"), we believe that we have merely an impressionistic rendering of chance associations. By the time the story is ended, however, we realize that the reflections conjured up by the mark have arranged themselves not accidentally into a meditation on life, time, and history culminating in an apocalyptic vision. Nor does Virginia Woolf let her method go unapprehended by the reader. Novelists of the future will use this reflective method, she prophesies halfway through the story: "Those are the depths they will explore, those the phantoms they will pursue."[10]

The objects Virginia Woolf uses as organizing and exploring agents for the depths of consciousness are always interesting visually: the wedges of light and darkness, the

[10] *Haunted House*, pp. 40, 43.

dome or hive which concretizes Lily Briscoe's feelings about Mrs. Ramsay,[11] the lump of glass or the star-shaped china bit in the story "Solid Objects," the circular oily patch of water with a straw in the middle of it at which Mrs. Ambrose gazes fixedly in the opening of *The Voyage Out* and which gives off its own iridescences of thought and symbol. More complex visually are the trees which dominate so many scenes: Lily Briscoe's pear tree, the tree which "composes" the afternoon-tea scene in *The Voyage Out* (p. 316), the Regent's Park trees in *Mrs. Dalloway* which help Peter Walsh to arrange his ambiguous feelings about women (p. 64). The oak tree at the opening of *Orlando* allows Orlando to order both his emotions and the visual landscape:

> He sighed profoundly, and flung himself . . . on the earth at the foot of the oak tree. He loved, beneath all this summer transiency, to feel the earth's spine beneath him; for such he took the hard root of the oak tree to be; or, for image followed image, it was the back of a great horse that he was riding; or the deck of a tumbling ship —it was anything indeed, so long as it was hard, for he felt the need of something which he could attach his floating heart to. . . . To the oak tree he tied it and as he lay there, gradually the flutter in and about him stilled itself; the little leaves hung, the deer stopped; the pale summer clouds stayed; his limbs grew heavy on the ground; and he lay so still that by degrees the deer stepped nearer and the rocks wheeled round him and the swallows dipped and circled and the dragon-flies shot past, as if all the fertility and amorous activity of a summer's evening were woven web-like about his body.   (pp. 20-21)

[11] *Lighthouse*, p. 83.

In this passage the oak tree acts both as an organizer of Orlando's world and as an object which he can subdue and govern as Mrs. Ramsay does the bowl of fruit. E. M. Forster has compared Virginia Woolf's method of surrounding the object to that of Sterne; both "start with a little object, take a flutter from it, and settle on it again."[12] It is true that the oak allows Orlando to make associative images, but those images are metaphors by which Orlando's mind *dominates* the object, riding it like a horse or great ship, asserting through it a power over his surroundings. Like the poet who absorbs and transforms the identity of his external world, Orlando has achieved a union with the object which brings him satisfaction. The final knitting together of subject and object is imaged as a web, and one is reminded of Henry James's description of the consciousness of experience as a "huge spider-web of the finest silken threads." What has woven the symmetry of the moment, giving it texture and pattern, is this creative aspect of the subject-object relationship.

In summing up the poet's view of the object,[13] we might say that it is a principle which controls, arranges, even creates through certain emotional or mental needs of the subject perceiving it; that it uses free association as part of its process; that it gathers fact, fancy, memory, and feeling as a snowball rapidly accumulates size and shape as it rushes down a slope. Like the plain earthenware pot in *Robinson Crusoe*, it can dominate, subdue, and "rope(d) the whole

---

[12] Forster, *Aspects of the Novel*, p. 36.

[13] Virginia Woolf does not limit herself to the use of inanimate objects as organizers; a human figure can likewise dominate and rearrange a visual scene, bringing unrelated objects together, as does Jinny when she enters the dining room in *The Waves* (p. 86) for the farewell dinner for Percival: " 'She seems to centre everything; round her tables, lines of doors, windows, ceilings, ray themselves, like rays round the star in the middle of a smashed window-pane. She brings things to a point, to order.' "

73

universe into harmony."[14] Much of what we loosely term imagination is this mysterious ability of the object (as percept) to become the focus of a pattern and meaning.

🌿 🌿 🌿

WHEN LILY BRISCOE decides to move the tree to the middle of the canvas in order that the masses might hang together in her painting,[15] she is graphically working out the lesson of object-control learned from the paragraph about Orlando and the oak tree. Here the poet's and painter's eyes come together, for both seek to select, organize, and arrange. The painter's eye, however, goes one step further than that of the poet. He not only gives a rendering of the scene as the eye *and* mind actually perceive it; he also is concerned with the object itself, its color and its form. "Beneath the colour there was the shape," Lily Briscoe observes (p. 34). It is this aspect which is constantly before the reader's eyes in Virginia Woolf's novels: scenes and objects are simplified into a few lines; shapes are abstracted into flat forms such as trapezoids or ovals; color is squeezed out raw in blots of yellow, green, blue, red; an invisible frame is placed around the object so that it stands out whole, separate from, yet in spatial relationship to, the things around it.

As Bernard Blackstone has noted, Virginia Woolf learned a great deal about how to "see" natural form from her painter friends, especially her sister Vanessa Bell, Clive Bell, and Roger Fry. Clive Bell himself remarked that his sister-in-law had a "pure . . . almost painter-like,

[14] (*C.R.II*), *Essays*, I, pp. 74-75. Part of the original version of this essay appears in *Lighthouse Notebook I* in the middle of the first version of Section 4 of "The Window," with its focus, through Lily's eyes, on shape and form.
[15] *Lighthouse*, pp. 132-33.

vision."[16] What "pure vision" constituted for Virginia Woolf was the sense of the relation of the object to its surroundings (pattern and perspective), the relation of the shape to the emotion, and the concept of color not as surface-color, which seems united with the object, but as pure sensory stimulus which, like shape, releases energy within the viewer.[17]

Virginia Woolf's insistence on perspective—the spatial relationship of the object to its surroundings—is what separates her most clearly from the Post-Impressionists, who were interested mainly in the interrelationships of surface pattern and color. Placing the object in relationship to other objects in the foreground, middle distance, and far distance, gives them a depth of perspective corresponding to that of objects seen through normal binocular vision, and thus places the reader that much more firmly behind the eyes of the characters. When Lily Briscoe and William Bankes in *To the Lighthouse* stroll in the garden, with tennis lawn and pampas grass beyond them, they come "to that break in the thick hedge, guarded by red-hot pokers like brasiers of clear burning coal, between which the blue waters of the bay looked bluer than ever." The reader, through Lily's eyes, is given the view in perspective: the near flowers, the gap in the hedge, and the blue bay (infinity) beyond. The space in the hedge "frames" the distance and allows for the remarkable interaction between the near (red) and far (blue) colors which occurs in the viewer's eyes.[18]

[16] Clive Bell, *Old Friends*, p. 113.

[17] In her essay "Pictures," a painting of flowers ("red-hot pokers") is an "orgy of blood and nourishment" for the viewer. "We nestle into its colour, feed and fill ourselves with yellow and red and gold till we drop off, nourished and content." *M*. (not reprinted in *Collected Essays*), p. 143.

[18] *Lighthouse*, p. 35. Note, too, the contrast and interaction between the images of water and fire, which create an emotional tension. The use of perspective occurs throughout Virginia Woolf's novels.

In this passage, the colors are rendered as a landscape artist sees them, separated from the form of the object; their brightness corresponds "with the intensity of the light on the retina" rather than the brightness of the colors themselves which appear to be part of the flowers and water.[19] This type of subjective color perception—seeing colors as "disembodied"—allowed Mrs. Woolf to duplicate the sense of color in a more psychologically accurate manner. It also facilitated her abstracting shapes from the object and presenting them as *units of color* whose color vibrations and interactions (which the mind/eye relates) are more important than the forms themselves. The bed of red-hot pokers, for example, is abstracted into an oval or rectangle (brasier of coals), but it is the color that dominates the shape. The same holds true for the space of blue in the gap in the hedge.

A longer quotation, from *Jacob's Room*, concentrates on color shifts, though its sequences are timed exactly by the clock:

> By six o'clock a breeze blew in off an icefield; and by seven the water was more purple than blue; and by half-past seven there was a patch of rough gold-beater's skin round the Scilly Isles, and Durrant's face, as he sat steering, was of the colour of a red lacquer box polished for generations. By nine all the fire and confusion has

[19] Dr. James J. Gibson, in *The Perception of the Visual World* (Cambridge, Mass., 1950), posits two types of color perception: that of surface-color, which he calls the everyday type of perception, and that of "disembodied" color, which only a trained eye learns to see. The landscape painter, Dr. Gibson says, has learned that the "disembodied color of an object is the color which must be reproduced on his canvas." The "natural kind" of seeing takes an objective attitude—it is "naive and is directed toward the real object." The "introspective kind" adopts the subjective attitude and is "critical, analytic, or photographic, and is directed toward the stimulus" (pp. 166-68). Although the two kinds of seeing may be mixed, Mrs. Woolf's color perception is constantly directed toward the stimulus.

gone out of the sky, leaving wedges of apple-green and plates of pale yellow; and by ten the lanterns on the boat were making twisted colours upon the waves, elongated or squab, as the waves stretched or humped themselves. The beam from the lighthouse strode rapidly across the water. Infinite millions of miles away powdered stars twinkled; but the waves slapped the boat, and crashed, with regular and appalling solemnity, against the rocks.

(pp. 50-51)

In this passage, Timmy Durrant's face is abstracted to a red rectangle, sky reflections to wedges, lantern-light to long or fat shapes that constantly move and change. Because of the simplification of form, the succession of scenes is rendered with utmost clarity, and a sense of depth perception is achieved by the swift running-together of the sequences. Thus, through Jacob's eyes, we see in the foreground the face of Timmy Durrant, the boat lanterns behind him, and the reflections of the waves beyond; in the middle distance, the rocks of the Scilly Isles and the lighthouse; in the far distance, the stars. Although the forms aid in the eye's swift arrangement and comprehension of the scene, it is the colors which, with their interactions and associations,[20] stimulate the mind and retina. The colors are rendered with more vividness than they would display in natural light, and thus assume their proper function of sense stimuli.

The relationship between masses of color and form— what connects them emotionally as well as visually—is still another aspect of the artist's vision which concerned Virginia Woolf and which she expressed through Lily

[20] The "red lacquer box polished for generations" can stimulate, for example, associations connected with red (fire, sunburn, blood, etc., raising energy values linked with violence and pain) as well as Oriental images and ideas connected with inscrutability, history, red dragons, firecrackers, etc. This is merely the beginning of the long train of associative thought which might occur to the reader.

Briscoe's problem of "how to connect this mass on the right hand with that on the left" of a canvas she is painting (p. 86). Lily's search in *To the Lighthouse* is for a way to connect the darkness of the triangular purple shadow, representing Mrs. Ramsay and James in the window, with the mass of light outside. This is finally achieved at the very end of the book through a series of slanting lines "running up and across" the canvas which connect, symbolically, the emotional world of Mrs. Ramsay within the house and the outside world of her husband.[21] Thus the eye, artfully led by the writer along a particular path, serves as the link between conscious perception and the world of feeling which Mrs. Woolf wishes to present.[22]

🦎 🦎 🦎 🦎

THE THIRD WAY in which Virginia Woolf sees the object is through the eyes of the child. As the painter's vision is related to that of the poet, so the vision of the

[21] This symbolic relationship or connection between the two worlds dominates the book, and Lily Briscoe's painting may be seen as an "abstract" of the relationship. The first part, "The Window," takes place in the house which Mrs. Ramsay emotionally fills. The final part, "The Lighthouse," dominated by Mr. Ramsay, is outdoors. These two opposing "masses" of light and shadow are connected by "Time Passes," the central section of the novel in which there is an interaction between the outdoor and indoor worlds: nature threatens to overtake and destroy the house, which is then saved by human intervention or life-force. The slanting lines which finally connect the two masses, or worlds, in Lily's canvas are the enduring emotion between wife and husband which Lily at first did not perceive, seeing them as two separate and antagonistic worlds.

[22] The same sense of emotion pictorialized is seen in the paragraph on feeding the chickens in *Night and Day* (p. 196). Mary Datchet's hand casting grain moves into the "centre of a circle," connecting the "wavering discs" of light that are the chickens and her brother Christopher, and establishing an emotional connection which Ralph, on the outside, feels.

child resembles that of the painter, for the child is concerned above all with the visual process, with seeing, and with form. Indeed, the child's life seems to be dominated by the "appearance" of things.[23] Through young Jacob in *Jacob's Room*, Cam, Nancy, and James in *To the Lighthouse*, the children in *The Waves*, and Isa's son George in *Between the Acts*, the reader's vision is accommodated to the vivid clarity of childhood,[24] its ability to infuse the perceived object with emotion, its delight with the isolated object which is experienced wholly and separately.

The preliminary version of Virginia Woolf's essay on *Robinson Crusoe*—drafted while she was writing *To the Lighthouse*, in which much is seen from the child's point of view—notes that "every stick & stone on the island has its own weight & shape," and that "what is true [is] miraculously freshened renewed & sharpened, so that we are children, enjoying life liberally."[25]

This concern with "every stick and stone," seeing each individually rather than as a class—a liberation from the complexity and relatedness of the adult world—helps to achieve a sense of the sharpness of things seen for the first time. The object is isolated—the moment of perception is all. Thus James cuts out a refrigerator from a catalogue, concentrates on it, and fringes it "with heavenly bliss" which reflects his mood at the moment. Jacob's attention is diverted now to a rock, a crab, a sheep's skull, each of which looms singly in his world. Rachel, in *The Voyage Out*, who reverts at times to childhood, feels the

[23] Jean Piaget, *The Construction of Reality in the Child*, trans. Margaret Cook (New York, 1954), p. 381.

[24] Of her niece Ann, Virginia Woolf wrote in her diary, September 7, 1924: "The walls of her mind all hung round with such bright vivid things, and she doesn't see what we see."

[25] This fragment from *Lighthouse Notebook 1* does not appear in the final, much revised version of the essay in *C.R.II.* Cf. Neville's remark in *The Waves* (p. 7): " 'Stones are cold to my feet . . . I feel each one, round or pointed, separately.' "

companionability of flowers and pebbles as if they were individuals, and sees a tree not just as "an ordinary tree," but as one "so strange that it might have been the only tree in the world. Dark was the trunk in the middle, and the branches sprang here and there, leaving jagged intervals of light between them as distinctly as if it had but that second risen from the ground" (pp. 204-205).

Virginia Woolf's method is seen more explicitly perhaps in the opening of *The Waves* where each young child, presumably of nursery age, observes a single object and reports on it in a brief speech. The sun, a spider-web, a shadow, birds' eyes, and a caterpillar are commented on by the six children reciting in turn. This concentration on the isolated object is not accidental; it forms part of the original working plan of *The Waves* in which the novel is visualized as a poetic-encyclopedic reconstruction of the creation and development of man and his mind, moving from his earliest awareness of objects—"the beginning with pure sensations," Mrs. Woolf noted in an early outline of part one[26]—to a perception of the world, death, and time. The earliest manuscript shows the opening section entitled "The Mind," with emphasis on the change in the process of visual perception from the very young to the older child. As the child begins to separate himself from the external world and confront it rationally, perceptual vision changes:

Appearances were no longer enough. The snail, the butterfly, the green seat off which one could scrape green dust, no longer burned larger & larger till they filled the mind's eye & were seen. . . . Messages were no longer burnt upon the innocent ear by a branch stiff against the sky; by a shaken leaf. Things no longer happened outside their context.[27]

[26] *Small Waves Notebook.*
[27] *Waves Notebook I*, p. 115 (1929).

This tendency of the child to see things larger than they are in reality appears to be part of seeing the object whole and isolated. With single-focus concentration Jacob sees his rock as something tremendous and primitive.[28] Nancy can make conscious use of this focus, enlarging things at will and turning a small pool into the sea and "minnows into sharks and whales."[29] George, grubbing in the grass on a walk with his nurse, sees a flower:

> George grubbed. The flower blazed between the angles of the roots. Membrane after membrane was torn. It blazed a soft yellow, a lambent light under a film of velvet; it filled the caverns behind the eyes with light. All that inner darkness became a hall, leaf smelling, earth smelling of yellow light. And the tree was beyond the flower; the grass, the flower and the tree were entire. Down on his knees grubbing he held the flower complete. Then there was a roar and a hot breath and a stream of coarse grey hair rushed between him and the flower. Up he leapt, toppling in his fright, and saw coming towards him a terrible peaked eyeless monster moving on legs, brandishing arms.
>
> "Good morning, sir," a hollow voice boomed at him from a beak of paper.
>
> The old man had sprung upon him from his hiding-place behind a tree.[30]

In this single, concentrated passage are several of the elements which, in Mrs. Woolf's work, seem to distinguish the child's vision from that of the adult.[31] George's view is limited to the world of the root, flower, and tree. He is aware of a primitive spatial relationship in that he per-

---

[28] *Jacob's Room*, pp. 7 and 8.   [29] *Lighthouse*, p. 119.
[30] *Between the Acts*, pp. 16-17.
[31] The normal non-artistic adult, that is. Certain aspects of so-called artistic vision bear a resemblance to modes of vision of primitives and children, as well as those experienced in pathological states. An example would be the all-absorbing focus on the single object.

ceives the tree as being beyond the flower, but the rest of the garden is unseen. He concentrates on the flower's color, which he experiences metaphorically as light and which so engrosses his emotions that flower, tree, and grass—the sight, smell, and feel of his surroundings—seem part of himself and of his mind. He sees the objects whole; the flower is "complete," the tree "entire" (though he cannot possibly see it all from his stooping position). When his grandfather puts a newspaper hood over his face to frighten the boy, he becomes the single object to fill George's world. Later, when his grandfather disciplined the dog, "George looked at the dog only."

Another glimpse of the child's relation to the objects surrounding him appears in a brief description of George's world in an early manuscript version of the novel. It is a world of nurses and prams, bears and quilts, "that complete cosmogony which was now surrounding as with a hedge of snowdrops her son George."[32] This "cosmogony" is composed only of the things with which George is immediately concerned. What is near at hand is the child's whole reality, and he is free to create fancies, embroider the objects, ascribing personality to them or changing their make-up to create out of them, as Nancy does with her seaside pool in *To the Lighthouse*, a little universe of his own. However limited the child's view may appear in one respect, it is a perception of the objective world which, to some extent, Virginia Woolf retains throughout her entire work, for there is a common ground on which the vision of the poet, painter, and child can be said to meet. All suggest heightened modes of perception; all convey a freshness which a "common sense" view of the object scarcely could. Another mode which offers a fresh view is the "angle of vision," the physical or psychological position from which objects are seen, and this is the concern of the following chapter.

[32] *Pointz Hall Typescript*, p. 23 (April-May, 1938).

CHAPTER SIX

The Angle of Vision

SHOWING THE object through the eyes of the poet, the painter, and the child might be termed giving perspective to point of view, for commitment to the consciousness of a particular character inflicts its own limitations and relationships on object and scene. In this sense, perspective is governed mainly by mental and visual elements, as suggested in the last chapter. But there is a further way in which Virginia Woolf achieves perspective, and that is through the *angle of vision*, the physical or psychological position or angle from which an object is viewed. Not only is the reader placed behind the prescription lens of the character, he also sees what the character sees from the position of his body or from his state of mind at the time.

In the beginning of *A Portrait of the Artist as a Young Man*, Joyce shows a football game from Stephen's vantage point:

> He was caught in the whirl of a scrimmage and, fearful of the flashing eyes and muddy boots, bent down to look through the legs. The fellows were struggling and groaning and their legs were rubbing and kicking and stamping. Then Jack Lawton's yellow boots dodged out the ball and all the other boots and legs ran after.
>
> (p. 4)

Virginia Woolf in *Jacob's Room*, some eight years later, following perhaps Joyce, perhaps her own sense of perspective, describes the view from Jacob's eyes as he lies in a boat moored by the river bank:

83

The meadow was on a level with Jacob's eyes as he lay back; gilt with buttercups, but the grass did not run like the thin green water of the graveyard grass about to overflow the tombstones, but stood juicy and thick. Looking up, backwards, he saw the legs of children deep in the grass, and the legs of cows. Munch, munch, he heard; then a short step through the grass; then again munch, munch, munch, as they tore the grass short at the roots. . . .

"Oh-h-h-h," groaned Jacob, as the boat rocked, and the trees rocked, and the white dresses and the white flannel trousers drew out long and wavering up the bank. (p. 35)

The oblique angle of vision has increased the reader's feeling that he, too, like Jacob, is lying in the boat; he sees the world from the level of the roots of the grass that the cows are munching, not from the position of the traditional narrator who hovers, suspended like an illuminating light, above the scene. Moreover, a secondary angle of vision has been added: the appearance of the scene changes because of the motion of the boat; the trees rock and the shapes of the dresses and trousers, already altered by the position at which they are viewed, become elongated. In *The Waves* a similar effect is achieved when Bernard and Jinny, hidden in the currant brush, watch the skirts of Miss Hudson and Miss Curry move past, then Susan's white socks and Louis' shoes (p. 16). *The Years* contains several scenes in which passing legs and feet are seen through a basement window, an angle which not only lends sharpness to the view but also conveys Mrs. Woolf's sense of the submerged life—that which is hidden or repressed —which people lead.[1]

[1] *Years*, esp. pp. 311 and 415. The scene on p. 311 occurs in an air-raid shelter. The view of the lower-half of the bodies is

Indeed, Virginia Woolf rarely employs a specific angle of vision for its effect of novelty alone. In her early short story "Kew Gardens," published in 1919, the snail's-eye view of the gardens and people walking by the flower beds— who appear merely as feet or vague butterfly-like forms— contributes to the story's theme of life as a phenomenon of exquisite but meaningless pattern and color. The use of the snail, her symbol of the "victim," deepens the emotional effect of beauty-and-horror which the theme suggests. In the "biography" *Flush*, the angle of vision is used to far more complicated ends. Here especially it must be remembered that the connection between subject and object, the viewer and the viewed, is invariably one of emotion, and that a particular angle conveys a particular atmosphere with its cluster of emotional meanings. Jacob's prone position communicates the languor of the afternoon and of youth itself; Bernard and Jinny in the hedge suggest the hiding games of children with their secret joys. In *Flush*, might not the view from the rug at the foot of Elizabeth Barrett's bed, where the famous cocker spaniel lay, be symbolic of the many possessive human relationships in that story, just as the underground world in which Flush is held captive suggests Miss Barrett's own captivity in the house on Wimpole Street? This novel directly preceded *The Years*, in which, as we have just noted, certain cellar scenes symbolize the submerged or imprisoned life.

Virginia Woolf was also aware that the emotional value of an angle of vision is increased in direct proportion to the narrowness of the visual field. When the focus is beamed on a specific object, a sense of emotional compression results, as when Orlando, kneeling, offers a bowl of rose water to the Queen:

---

suggestive of mutilation as well as the primitive withdrawal from fear into a cave.

> Such was his shyness that he saw no more of her than her ringed hand in water; but it was enough. It was a memorable hand; a thin hand with long fingers always curling as if round orb or sceptre; a nervous, crabbed, sickly hand; a commanding hand too; a hand that had only to raise itself for a head to fall; a hand, he guessed, attached to an old body that smelt like a cupboard in which furs are kept in camphor. . . . All this he felt as the great rings flashed in the water.   (p. 23)

Because of Orlando's position, his visual field is limited to the area of the bowl, and his focus quite naturally goes to her hand. Translating the rhetorical principle of synecdoche into perception, Virginia Woolf has conveyed the whole by the part, and like a symbol with its penumbra of associations, the hand calls up to Orlando all manner of emotional response. Following this passage, Mrs. Woolf repeats her method and describes Orlando from the Queen's angle of vision as she looks down on him, seeing only a head.

Virginia Woolf's direct and exclusive focus on the object has been compared to the cinematic close-up.[2] And such it is, in its most superficial sense. But the term *close-up* fails to convey both the freshness of the angle and the object's isolation from its background which makes of it a microcosm, a little world in which the emotions of the moment—and sometimes of the entire novel—move. When in *Jacob's Room* the sun suddenly blazed and "gilded the great blackberries trembling out from the hedge" (p. 9), or when in *Orlando* she emerged from a dark tunnel of time and saw everything "as if she had a microscope stuck

[2] See Robert Humphrey, *Stream of Consciousness in the Modern Novel* (Berkeley, 1954), p. 49; Dorothy Brewster, *Virginia Woolf*, p. 101; Maxime Chastaing, *La Philosophie de Virginia Woolf* (Paris, 1951), pp. 33-44. Winifred Holtby, *Virginia Woolf*, p. 111, notes Mrs. Woolf's discovery of the "powers of expansion and contraction" in cinematic techniques.

to her eye"—"the intricacy of the twigs," every blade of grass distinct, "the markings of veins and petals," even the blue sheen on flies' bodies[3]—the space of the world is contracted to a hard and shining point which is illumined for us with an almost preternatural light. Yet this focus escapes the theatrical; it is our own vision at its concentrated best. Virginia Woolf's narrowing of the visual field to a single beam of focal vision—dispensing for the moment with peripheral awareness, which nevertheless mentally surrounds the object with its " *'psychic overtone'* or *'fringe'* "[4] as shown by Orlando's focus on Queen Elizabeth's hand—is consistent with her entire treatment of the visual process.

VIRGINIA WOOLF'S use of the physical angle of vision is paralleled by her use of the psychological state of mind in which a particular object is viewed. If the physical dimensions of an object appear distorted for being seen from an unusual position, mental and physical illness and emotions such as love[5] can likewise alter the appearance of the object. Since Mrs. Woolf's subjective modes are related to the over-all meanings of her novels, it can be

[3] *Orlando*, pp. 287-88. It must be remembered that Orlando, kneeling as a boy to the Queen, has changed into a woman.

[4] See Chapter I, iii. A parallel exists between "peripheral vision" and mental awareness on the edge of consciousness, just as there exists, as noted, an analogy between other visual and mental processes. See Arthur Koestler's *The Act of Creation* (New York, 1964), pp. 158-59.

[5] The resemblance between the effects of love and physical illness is noted in Mrs. Woolf's essay "On Being Ill" in which she states that "illness often takes on the disguise of love, and plays the same odd tricks" (*M.*), *Essays*, IV, p. 194. These are shown in *Jacob's Room* when Fanny Elmer feels love as illness (p. 117) and in *Voyage* when the perceptual distortion of Rachel's world through love foreshadows that produced by her illness (pp. 346-47).

expected that the psychological angle of vision, like that of the physical, is interwoven with the novel's emotional and thematic values.

The most obvious example of visual distortion caused by abnormal perception is that of Septimus Smith in *Mrs. Dalloway*. Septimus, as Bernard Blackstone wrote, sees the world through the eyes of a poet whose vision of things has been carried to the extreme;[6] for he not only thinks in metaphor, he *experiences* it, projecting his inner vision onto outward reality. He literally sees Rezia as a flowering tree, or the sound of music as "smooth columns." Instead of feeling emotionally one with nature, he imagines red flowers growing through him, communicates with leaves, and hears birds speak Greek.[7] As the reader becomes accustomed to the angle of Septimus' vision, he realizes that it is one of a dissociated world:[8] objects and events are dislocated; normal spatial relationships change, with corresponding shifts in meaning; scenes are fragmented and reassembled in bizarre ways.[9] This is the schizophrenic's

[6] *Virginia Woolf: A Commentary* (New York, 1949), pp. 79 and 96.

[7] *Dalloway*, pp. 163, 76, 26, 28. "Cosmic delusions—of being one with the world—part of the trees—of being able to know what the birds are talking about . . . are frequent schizophrenic disturbances of the sense of reality." Leopold Bellak, M.D., ed., *Schizophrenia: A Review of the Syndrome* (New York, 1958), p. 12. Leonard Woolf, in *Beginning Again*, mentions how Virginia Woolf heard birds speak Greek during her periods of insanity (p. 77). Since the maroon *Dalloway* notebook suggests that Septimus is patterned after herself (November 19, 1922), we can assume that much of what Septimus "sees" and "feels" was taken from her own experience.

[8] The syndrome of Septimus' illness corresponds closely to that of the schizophrenic, probably of the manic-depressive type. The difficulty that schizophrenics have in meaningful communication, their reactions to emotionally-toned words, their lack of consistent reaction to a given stimulus, their response on the symbolic rather than the realistic level, and the tendency to fragment, are carefully detailed in the thoughts and actions of Septimus. See Bellak, *Schizophrenia*, pp. 7-55.

[9] A motor horn is dislocated from its audial background to be-

landscape, in which internal and external reality are confused and private meanings (externalizing inward anxieties) are projected onto the perceptual world.[10] Septimus
shows us how close Clarissa herself is to the brink: Clarissa
identifies with him, his anxieties are hers, and the distortions they assume make the total meaning more clear to us.
Virginia Woolf is very careful to detail Septimus' psychological history—his self-education, first love and friendship, job, war years, and marriage. And we are reminded
how, in her essay "The Leaning Tower," she stresses the
influences (heredity, education, socio-political elements of
the times) that determine a writer's particular angle of
vision.[11] In showing the world through Septimus' disor-
dered vision, Virginia Woolf helps the reader to discover
the rich resources of human perception.

Rhoda in *The Waves* exhibits a similar use of abnormal
perception for thematic and artistic values. Although a
member of a closely-knit group of six friends, she is isolated, shrinks from contact with others, and spends most of
her time day-dreaming. This isolation and autistic behavior
result in a distortion of reality. Time loses its sequence;
she can neither make moments merge nor find the unity
that the self-within-time can bring.[12] Solid objects do not
remain constant, but at times appear to become so fluid that

come chimes on a grass stalk; the disparate elements of a child
crying, the sight of sparrows against tree branches, and the sound
of a horn are synthesized to symbolize an abstract truth. *Dalloway*,
pp. 77, 26.
    [10] Dr. Holmes notes that Septimus "was attaching meanings
to words of a symbolical kind. A serious symptom. . . ." *Dalloway*,
p. 106.
    [11] (*M.*), *Essays*, II, pp. 167-72.
    [12] *Waves*, p. 46. See also p. 15, where Rhoda is afraid of " 'being
blown for ever outside the loop of time' " which encloses the others.
"Primary process thinking" includes a lack of comprehension of
time and space relationships (Bellak, *Schizophrenia*, p. 389).

she fears falling into them,[13] or seem to move with rapidity.[14] The colors on their surface lift and part like veils.[15] It is as if she glimpsed the world through the waters of her unconscious dreaming mind whose ripples contract and expand the shape of the objects. There is more than a suggestion of Alice's wonderland of the unconscious.[16]

🏃🏃🏃

VIRGINIA WOOLF'S placing of the reader behind the eyes of Septimus Smith might be termed the first serious attempt in the English novel to give the illusion of abnormal perception. Dostoevsky had explored the mental worlds of the psychotic and schizophrenic in a number of short stories and novels, most notably in *Crime and Punishment*, and Raskolnikov's inability to feel, his withdrawal, paranoid feelings, hallucinations, and sense of unreality and isolation find their way into his English counterpart, Septimus Smith. Dostoevsky, however, emphasized the dramatic rather than the visual. We know how Raskolnikov feels, but we rarely see the effect of his emotions on the visual world around him, save in his hallucinations or dreams. Virginia Woolf, on the other hand, concentrates on the visual manifestations of Septimus' mental state, and

[13] She seems to fear falling into a cupboard and into the nursery looking-glass (p. 20).

[14] " 'Look at the table-cloth, flying white along the table' " (p. 8). " 'When Miss Lambert passes, she makes the daisy change; and everything runs like streaks of fire when she carves the beef' " (p. 32).

[15] " 'Our eyes . . . seem to push through curtains of colour . . . which yield like veils and close behind them, and one thing melts into another' " (p. 96).

[16] Not only her fear of sinking and falling suggests this, but her constant looking at things " 'on the other side of the world' " (pp. 76 and 90), the place to which Alice literally fell and which is the side furthest from the conscious self. Rhoda's schematic place in the novel (see Appendix) is that of the imagination, which Mrs. Woolf feels to be mainly in the unconscious.

we feel his emotions through the terrifying or beautiful images in which his thoughts present themselves and through the manner in which the images form and dissolve like the visions in De Quincey's opium dreams.

It is to De Quincey that Virginia Woolf may owe much of her perceptual method, especially the sense of the contraction and expansion of time, space, and matter, and the projection of internal emotions, notably certain fears, on the external visual field. Joan Bennett notes the similarity between De Quincey's bizarre description of ocean waves "paved with innumerable faces"[17] and a passage from one of the chapter prologues in *The Waves*, but bases the comparison mainly on rhythm.[18] However, a section in the original opening of *The Waves*,[19] as well as a passage on page 20 of the published version, is close to De Quincey's in concept. In the latter passage Rhoda feels herself " 'tumbled . . . stretched, among . . . these long waves, these endless paths, with people pursuing, pursuing' " (p. 20). Rhoda's vision of reality is based on the same feeling of persecution as De Quincey's vision of "faces imploring, wrathful, despairing." Moreover, the images of the waves themselves, with their endlessly surging motion—the very metaphor of pursuit—have already been prepared for in the novel and continue their theme throughout. In Virginia Woolf's essay on De Quincey, she perceived that in his writing "the emotion is never stated; it is suggested and

[17] "Now it was that upon rocking waters of the ocean the human face began to reveal itself; the sea appeared paved with innumerable faces, upturned to the heavens; faces imploring, wrathful, despairing; faces that surged upwards by thousands, by myriads, by generations: infinite was my agitation; my mind tossed, as it seemed, upon the billowy ocean, and weltered upon the weltering waves." De Quincey, *Confessions*, pp. 116-17.

[18] Joan Bennett, *Virginia Woolf: Her Art as a Novelist*, 2nd edn. (Cambridge, England, 1964), p. 106.

[19] The original opening pictures the waves as "many mothers . . . endlessly sinking, falling, & lying prostrate, & each holding up, as the wave pass[ed] its crest, a child." *Waves Notebook I*, pp. 17, 19 (September ? 1929).

brought slowly by repeated images before us until it stays, in all its complexity, complete."[20]

We can see how this particular method is accomplished in *The Waves*, developed to its utmost until the reader himself senses the "faces" of the many emotions whose fluid images haunt him long after the book has been laid down. Although it is a method which appears to have been invented solely for *The Waves*, an examination of her first novel, *The Voyage Out*, shows that even then she was aware of the effect of emotional and bodily states on the appearance of the external world as well as the use of certain key images whose very repetitions bring forth the emotions she wished to convey—emotions whose full impact is not felt until the end of the book. The water images in their many variations, from surface to under-sea symbols; the corridors, tunnels, vaults, and cul-de-sacs; the various images of death (clustering around the guillotine), chance, and fate—all converge in the final delirium scene. Most dreamlike, perhaps, is Rachel and Terence's walk down the corridor of a jungle forest which was like "walking at the bottom of the sea." The "cruel churning" of the water of the Amazon is in the distance; Rachel wonders, " 'Is it true, or is it a dream?' " The sea, jungle, water, corridor, and death images shift from one set to another. Time expands and contracts. Like "people walking in their sleep" they discover the love which has shifted and distorted the walls of their mental world (pp. 330-37). When the final illness comes—one probably developed on the trip —the delirium atmosphere has already been created (indeed, it has been there from the first moment when the ferryboat with the Ambroses crossed the river Thames/ Styx to reach the ship where Rachel is), and the "appearance" of the jungle world becomes the "reality" of her illness.

[20] "De Quincey's Autobiography" (*C.R.II*), *Essays*, IV, p. 2.

Because of this novel's conventional trappings—a plot, an intervening narrator, the traditional third person point of view—most critics fail to see Virginia Woolf's final achievement, one which even to her did not seem like much in retrospect.[21] Yet as earlier and subsequent chapters of this study show, there is not a single mode of subjectivity used in her later novels which is not present in *Voyage*. The most consistent use of these modes does not occur until Chapter XIX, where the dream-action patterns, which dominate the final third of the book, begin. But they are scattered here and there in the first part of the novel, as in the scene of Rachel's experience of dissociation. Here she is aware simultaneously of time and eternity and experiences a sense of dissolution of personality. The figure of her aunt Helen entering the room appears as merely "a tall human being" with "the toneless voice of a ghost." Meaningful reality has vanished, and figure and action are seen as "utter absurdity" (pp. 144-45).

Lytton Strachey sensed something of the subjective atmosphere of *The Voyage Out* when he wrote to Virginia that there was something "very unvictorian" and "Tolstoyan" in the account of Rachel's illness.[22] He was evidently referring to the fusing of inward and outward reality which Tolstoy accomplished at the end of *Anna Karenina*, when she is close to suicide, by mixing sensory data with memory and emotion.[23] Yet not even Virginia Woolf's reading of Tolstoy could have schooled her for the rendering of the distortion of Rachel's perceptual world. As has been suggested, Mrs. Woolf's own illnesses probably furnished her with ample experience; what is notable, however, is the accuracy of her observations and the methods by which she

[21] *Diary*, February 4, 1920.
[22] *Virginia Woolf and Lytton Strachey: Letters*, February 25, 1916.
[23] See Leon Edel's illuminating chapter on Tolstoy's "dialectic of the mind" in *The Modern Psychological Novel*, pp. 147-53.

presents them—modes which De Quincey or Tolstoy could not have disclosed to her. Nor could Proust, Dorothy Richardson, or Joyce have been of any help. She was not to read Proust until 1922,[24] Dorothy Richardson until 1915 or later.[25] At the time she began *The Voyage Out*, in late 1906–early 1907, Joyce's *A Portrait of the Artist* was a mere unpublished sketch. The observation of subjectivity was her own; she could experience emotionally and, at the same time, stand back and examine the very processes of those emotions.

It is perhaps the cool, exact way in which she presents her subjective material in *The Voyage Out* which makes it appear traditional to those critics who tend to find in a Joycean obscurity and confusion the sign of true mental reality. It is perhaps also the omniscient narration. The following scene from Rachel's illness is not presented as stream of consciousness, but the psychological and physical angle of vision is there—Rachel's world with its shifts and changes, its lack of object constancy, its emotional distortions:

> On this day indeed Rachel was conscious of what went on round her. She had come to the surface of the dark, sticky pool, and a wave seemed to bear her up and down with it; she had ceased to have any will of her own; she lay on the top of the wave conscious of some pain, but chiefly of weakness. The wave was replaced by the side of a mountain. Her body became a drift of melting snow,

[24] *Diary*, October 4, 1922, and April 8, 1925.

[25] 1915 is the date of the publication of *Pointed Roofs*. The first documentary evidence that Virginia Woolf read Dorothy Richardson is the former's review of *The Tunnel* in 1919. However, as Horace Gregory points out, "Miss Richardson's publisher, Gerald Duckworth, was Virginia Woolf's half-brother." There is a possibility that she may have read the manuscript of *Pointed Roofs* when it was first submitted to Duckworth in 1913. *Dorothy Richardson: An Adventure in Self-Discovery* (New York, 1967), prologue, p. ix.

above which her knees rose in huge peaked mountains of bare bone. It was true that she saw Helen and saw her room, but everything had become very pale and semi-transparent. Sometimes she could see through the wall in front of her. Sometimes when Helen went away she seemed to go so far that Rachel's eyes could hardly follow her. The room also had an odd power of expanding, and though she pushed her voice out as far as possible until sometimes it became a bird and flew away, she thought it doubtful whether it ever reached the person she was talking to. There were immense intervals or chasms, for things still had the power to appear visibly before her, between one moment and the next; it sometimes took an hour for Helen to raise her arm, pausing long between each jerky movement, and pour out medicine. Helen's form stooping to raise her in bed appeared of gigantic size, and came down upon her like the ceiling falling. (p. 423)

This quotation is from the final version of 1913, but its basic ingredients were present in the earliest of the three surviving manuscripts,[26] which means that Virginia Woolf was aware of her inner world at the beginning, merely expanding and enlarging it in subsequent versions. The most notable addition to Chapter XXV, made in the 1912 hand-written version, was the mythic figure of Sabrina from Milton's "Comus"; she is used to personify the

[26] I have determined the sequence of the manuscripts through the evolution of certain textual corrections and changes. The earliest version, typed, is only approximately half the length of the two later ones, manuscript and typewritten, dated 1912. The "Ur-Voyage" from which the first typescript was made could have been written anytime from 1907 to 1911. Leonard Woolf, in *Beginning Again*, states that *The Voyage Out* was "rewritten (I think) five times from beginning to end" (p. 81). The final chapters were written "for the tenth, or, it may have been, the twentieth time" (p. 87). Aileen Pippett states that the novel "took her seven years to finish," in *The Moth and the Star* (Boston, 1955), p. 65.

existing metaphor of the sticky pool of Rachel's illness. With Sabrina and her "cool, translucent wave," Virginia Woolf was able not only to show the effect of illness on the meaning and connotation of words (as Rachel listens to Terence reading the poem)[27] but also to present the exact quality of the distortion of Rachel's mental world through the image of water, whose rippling movement constantly changes the appearance of all objects within and beyond it and which forms a constant reminder of the irrational and unconscious into which Rachel descends.

THE "RIPPLING" quality of both Rachel's and Rhoda's perceptual worlds suggests the final category of the angle of vision: that of the *screens* or *filters* through which a scene or object is viewed to give the illusion of an emotional state, much as a photographer's screens and filters are employed to give emotional texture to a picture. Virginia Woolf uses both color and water as screens, and the use of color—as in Bernard's description of the effects of first love as " 'a purple slide . . . slipped over the day' "[28] —graphically points out how our vision of things is "coloured" or altered by our emotions.

Water, with its constantly changing surface pattern, likewise makes an excellent screen. When Helen Ambrose at the opening of *The Voyage Out* looks at a "circular

[27] Rachel notes that the words of Milton's "Comus" which Terence is reading to her mean different things than they usually do and suggest "unpleasant sights" independent of their meaning (p. 399). Cf. the section in Mrs. Woolf's essay "On Being Ill" devoted to words in illness and the "mystic quality" they possess at this time—(*M.*), *Essays*, IV, pp. 199-200. Much of the material in this essay seems an exposition of the "drama of the body" recorded during Rachel's illness. This essay first appeared in January, 1926, and was later revised.

[28] *Waves*, p. 177.

iridescent patch slowly floating past" in the river "with a straw in the middle of it," she sees the straw and patch swim "again and again behind the tremulous medium of a great welling tear."[29] Tears also alter Mrs. Flanders' perception of the bay at the opening of *Jacob's Room*, and we are given the literal effect of the water-screen (which is an improvement over the earlier technique):

> . . . her eyes fixed, and tears slowly filled them. The entire bay quivered; the lighthouse wobbled; and she had the illusion that the mast of Mr. Connor's little yacht was bending like a wax candle in the sun. She winked quickly. Accidents were awful things. She winked again. The mast was straight; the waves were regular; the lighthouse was upright. . . . (p. 5)

In this paragraph, angle of vision joins with refraction. The mood of Betty Flanders—one of grief and anxiety—is reflected by or refracted from the bay, the lighthouse, and the yacht which quiver because of the prism of Mrs. Flanders' tears. What we see are not the objects but Mrs. Flanders' emotions (her anxiety is emphasized by her thinking that "accidents were awful things"). The principle may be seen as identical to that of light itself which touches the object and refracts from its surface.

A similar combination of refraction and angle of vision occurs when Mrs. Woolf places the object against a background which interacts with the object in the mind of the viewer. Again the effect is similar to that of the photographer's use of background to bring out an emotional angle. Thus in *Jacob's Room*, when Jacob sees

[29] Here, the "filter" adds meaning, for the iridescent patch of water with its straw is a generalized symbol of a "patch" of iridescent life (Rachel's) which will be tossed this way and that, like the straw, by Fate. Mrs. Ambrose at the novel's end will glimpse Rachel literally through her tears.

Clara Durrant high on a ladder picking grapes, the effect of his angle of vision is enhanced by the effect of the background on Clara:

> "There!" she said, cutting through the stalk. She looked semi-transparent, pale, wonderfully beautiful up there among the vine leaves and the yellow and purple bunches, the lights swimming over her in coloured islands. Geraniums and begonias stood in pots along planks; tomatoes climbed the walls.   (p. 61)

Here color also makes a screen, dappling Clara with reflections from the grapes and the flowers. In a more complicated manner, the rather "worried and garrulous" face of St. John Hirst in *The Voyage Out* is seen by Helen Ambrose against a background of "smooth and inarticulate" magnolia flowers, and a pattern composed of St. John's face against the magnolia bush weaves itself into their talk (p. 247).

It might be said that these latter modulations of angle of vision come under the general heading of reflection, since they mirror the emotion of the viewer. Yet they are separated from the main modes of reflection by their very obliquity; their function is to emphasize or give a fresh meaning to an object or a relationship. Because their purpose is that of distortion, they can set up in the reader's mind a tension between the distorted or "angled" view and the normal one so that the object is isolated from its surroundings and appears in a new light. By this means the ordinary is made odd.

The modes with which the forthcoming chapter deals are more direct; they reflect the viewer without any "bend" in the refracting beam. They constitute, perhaps, the most important of Mrs. Woolf's subjective modes since they are the primary way in which she renders the illusion of her characters' mental worlds.

CHAPTER SEVEN

The Mirror Modes

ॐ

THE LAST TWO chapters presented various ways in which the subject sees the object, how it uses that object for its particular needs, mental and emotional, and how states of mind and physical positions can influence or alter the perception of that object. Now our concern shifts from the subject to the object itself and the many modes by which Virginia Woolf makes of it a reflecting surface—not only for the specific emotions of the character who perceives it, but also for the more general emotional atmosphere of the scene. People, objects, landscapes—all the world which forms the boundaries of that semi-transparent envelope of consciousness—become a series of mirrors reflecting the many aspects of the character himself. The character, however, is not aware of this mirroring process. It is the reader who has the double vision; who, seeing how the character sees his world, catches from it the reflecting gleams.

The most vivid illustration of Mrs. Woolf's use of surface or background as a reflector of the self occurs at the climax of *Between the Acts*. The audience has been watching a pageant of historical England, each scene of which may be said to represent a certain attitude or emotion discernible in the thoughts or actions of those who watch it. In the final scene, "Present Time," the stage is filled with mirrors; in a parabolic gesture, the mirrors are turned to the audience—they see nothing but themselves. As the audience winces ("the mirror bearers squatted; malicious; observant; expectant; expository," p. 217), the reader becomes aware that the ideals and idiocies, the stumblings toward truth, the romantic intrigues, and the deceptions and self-deceptions depicted in the pageant resemble those of the novel's characters. In a sense, reflector and reflected merge.

This may be seen as Virginia Woolf's final statement regarding the process of reflection, for it was the last novel she would write. But it illustrates another attitude toward a principle with which she was concerned from the beginning: the validity of the emotional experience of the object as reflected by what the subject sees. Her novels are filled with mirror surfaces: the closed blinds of the Prime Minister's car in *Mrs. Dalloway* which reflect the watchers' emotions toward authority; the glass which reproduces a perfect flower in *The Waves*; the mirror in *Orlando* which Queen Elizabeth shatters with her sword, annihilating the image of Orlando kissing a girl and thus confirming the reality not of the act but of its reflection— i.e., its image in the Queen's mind.[1] What the sum of mirror images suggests is that the way in which people perceive the object may yield the most truthful expression of themselves.

There are three "direct" modes by which the external mirrors the internal to create this subjective reality. In each of these modes, the character colors the object with his own emotions or attitudes, or endows it with a different meaning which mirrors a complex feeling or state of mind. The first of the direct modes, which shows the object as a mirror of basic character attitudes or a permanent psychological state, has been glimpsed in the way Rhoda sees objects in *The Waves*, a vision reflecting the arrested

---

[1] P. 27. Cf. the suggestion that the reflection itself may be the reality in Mrs. Woolf's short story "The Lady in the Looking-Glass" (*Haunted House*, p. 87). What Mrs. Woolf seems to imply is that, since the mind-eye is a camera lens in which the image is reflected, the picture in the mind (the way we know the object) is the reality, rather than the object itself.

state of her psychological development and the loneliness and terror which engulf her. This mode of reflection may be said to operate to a lesser extent with all of Virginia Woolf's characters. The opening of *The Waves*, for example, suggests how even through the young child's view of objects the reader can be made aware of incipient emotional tendencies:

> "I see a ring," said Bernard, "hanging above me. It quivers and hangs in a loop of light."
>
> "I see a slab of pale yellow," said Susan, "spreading away until it meets a purple stripe."
>
> "I hear a sound," said Rhoda, "cheep, chirp; cheep, chirp; going up and down."
>
> "I see a globe," said Neville, "hanging down in a drop against the enormous flanks of some hill."
>
> "I see a crimson tassel," said Jinny, "twisted with gold threads."
>
> "I hear something stamping," said Louis. "A great beast's foot is chained. It stamps, and stamps, and stamps." (p. 6)

What the children see or hear, in these opening lines,[2] is indistinct; a ring, a globe, a tassel; a bird's call; a beast stamping. The reader is not certain whether it is metaphoric fancy or what the child actually thinks he observes. What is clear, however (when the book has been read and the data assorted by the reader), is that these early experiences of objects reflect viewpoints and emotions which the character will display in adult life. They are

---

[2] Cf. the scene in Chapter XVI, "Doubloon," of Melville's *Moby-Dick* in which Pip, as Ahab and the three mates soliloquize on what they see in the gold coin, conjugates the verb "to look" with its six persons: " 'I look, you look, he looks, we look, you look, they look.' " Mrs. Woolf's six-sided conjugation has a slight variation; four persons say "I see," two "I hear." The visual object is similar to the coin nailed to the masthead—a gold, glittering thing, perhaps the sun.

the very beginnings of an impulse, what we might term a psychological movement toward a particular position or attitude. Thus Jinny sees " 'a crimson tassel twisted with gold threads' "—the rising sun with its rays of gold, or perhaps simply a tassel; she is drawn to it by her instinctive response to color. Her reaction to physical sensation (" 'I burn, I shiver . . . out of this sun, into this shadow' " —p. 8) seems already developed and anticipates her later love of the social and sensuous life.[3] Bernard sees the handle of a cupboard above him as a ring which " 'quivers and hangs in a loop of light.' " The ring will, later in the novel, symbolize his need for communication through writing and friendship; his sense of proportion is already reflected by his exact observation of the object which he describes in spatial relation to himself.[4]

The second of the direct modes shows the object as a reflector of a momentary state of mind or a complex feeling. In *To the Lighthouse*, Paul Rayley, filled with the excitement of his engagement, sees the lights of the town below him as the "things that were going to happen to him—his marriage, his children, his house" (p. 122). A complexity of feeling radiates from the lights which he has

[3] On the next page, Jinny kisses Louis; later in the chapter (p. 17), images of a snake and "an apple tree" innocently come into her thoughts. This is typical of Mrs. Woolf's close interweaving of image and motif to suggest emotional attitudes.

[4] The particular ways in which the other children will "see" things are already reflected in this passage. Neville tends to see things enlarged in relation to reality: the sun is a "globe" hanging against " 'the enormous flanks of some hill.' " Susan looks at the earth and sees light and shadow rendered as solid, palpable things —a "slab" of yellow. (Ralph Freedman, in *The Lyrical Novel* [p. 248], suggests that this is a "stylized image of grainland and rural sky of dawn," prefiguring the farm life she will lead.) Rhoda does not "see" reality; but she finds an up-and-down pattern in the bird's song. Louis, who will later be involved emotionally in the historical past, likewise "hears" rather than sees; the sound of the waves is a stamping beast, later an elephant, a symbol of memory.

converted into symbols of his future life. In *Night and Day*, stronger but more confused emotions are suggested by Ralph Denham's looking through a shop window to see the people outside as "a dissolving and combining pattern of black particles" (p. 242). He has just realized that Mary Datchet is in love with him. The dehumanization of people to black dots reflects his single focus on himself; nothing exists save his state of mind which this discovery has severely agitated. Mrs. Woolf then offers "the involuntary procession of feelings and thoughts which formed and dissolved in rapid succession in his own mind": one moment Ralph wants to marry Mary Datchet; the next moment, to disappear. But a more vivid sense of Ralph's conflicting emotions has been cast back from the "black particles" themselves.

Night and Day, which is partially a study of the conscious and unconscious forces which influence man and his emotions, seems to make greater use than Mrs. Woolf's other novels of images which the character imbues with a particular meaning. Rodney sees "a fiery glen" of coals in the grate as representing his emotion for Cassandra (p. 304); Katharine imagines dead leaves to be symbolic of her and Rodney's immaturity and the "dry" quality of their love (p. 256).[5] A similar effect is achieved in two parallel scenes, also in *Night and Day*, which show the technique of double reflection, the third of the direct modes. Here, background and object reflect each other and in turn serve to mirror the subject seeing them. The first sequence occurs in Kew Gardens when Ralph Denham watches Katharine Hilbery in the orchid house:

[5] Later in the novel, Ralph Denham while talking to Katharine will uncover "with the point of his stick a group of green spikes half smothered by the dead leaves" (p. 349). This reflects not only the emergence of new love but also its contrast with the old.

Nevertheless, when he saw Katharine among the orchids, her beauty strangely emphasized by the fantastic plants, which seemed to peer and gape at her from striped hoods and fleshy throats, his ardour for botany waned, and a more complex feeling replaced it. . . . The orchids seemed to suggest absorbing reflections.

(p. 351)

Here, the flowers reflect both Katharine and Ralph's feeling for her. The orchids, suggesting "absorbing reflections," take on certain features of Katharine in Ralph's eyes as Katharine herself takes on the coloration of the flowers. This mutual mirroring hints at subtle, perhaps even dangerous, aspects of femininity, and we are somehow reminded of the scene in Hawthorne's "Rappaccini's Daughter" when Giovanni realizes the sisterhood of Beatrice and the deadly flowers. Two chapters later, at the Zoo, Ralph once more sees Katharine against an exotic background, one of "pale grottos and sleek hides," of pythons and lizards, of "deep green waters" and "slim green snakes stabbing the glass wall again and again with their flickering cleft tongues" (pp. 390-91). If, in the orchid house, Ralph's reaction has been a "complex feeling," here the reader is left to guess Ralph's emotions for himself. Immediately afterward, Mrs. Woolf changes mood and emotion and further confirms her method. Standing by the monkey cage, Katharine sees William Rodney mirrored in "a wretched misanthropical ape, huddled in a scrap of old shawl." Katharine's humorous observation reflects her annoyance with and scorn of William—feelings of which she is perhaps not yet consciously aware, thinking only that he "had pulled her down into some horrible swamp of her nature where the primeval struggle between man and woman" still raged (pp. 392-93).

VIRGINIA WOOLF's brother Adrian Stephen once described her method of telling a story in a way that furnishes us with a parable of the mirror modes. She would take hold of an anecdote, he wrote, as though it were a painted top, "tossing it in the air, setting it spinning, and then describing, not the top, but the radiations it gave off as it whirled around."[6] In this manner, the top itself disappeared; in its place appeared motion, the whirl of color, the emotional vibrations which it evoked. It is this sense of the subject's experience of the object which characterizes Virginia Woolf's use of the object as reflector. The principle also operates in the indirect mirror modes in which color, landscape, and parallel scene may be said to send forth emotional vibrations which increase the intensity of the particular situation or the character's feelings.

We have termed these modes "indirect" because the character himself is not necessarily involved in the visual synthesis. It is the reader for whom the color, landscape, or scene reflects a particular emotion; what "vibrations" or reflections he feels he then associates with the character. Of the three indirect modes, that of color is the most easily understood, for we tend to respond to colors in specific ways, calling them "cool" or "warm" as they affect us emotionally, or being more sensitive to colors at different times. In *The Waves*, for example, a green jar shows the eye's changing response to color as the child grows older.[7] Or the red and gold which Jinny loves—

[6] Pippett, *Moth and Star*, p. 63.
[7] For example, the young eye reacts violently to the green jar (p. 79); the older eye rejects the color for the form (p. 107). See also pp. 21, 118, and 130.

she wants " 'a fiery dress, a yellow dress, a fulvous dress' "
—serve to mirror the intense, electric quality of the girl.[8]
A cooler color range, and therefore a different emotional
response, is suggested by the "purple light" of Miss Lambert's ring, " 'a vinous . . . an amorous light,' " which
reflects Rhoda's feelings about her teacher and possibly her
mental imbalance.[9]

A graphic lesson in the way landscape, as well as color,
reflects emotion is given by the Grimm's fairy tale which
Mrs. Ramsay tells James in *To the Lighthouse* and which
bears a curious relationship to the novel. The story is
"The Fisherman's Wife," and the fears of the fisherman
and anger of the flounder are reflected by the ocean
which changes color and grows more stormy with each of
the greedy wife's requests. Mrs. Woolf includes two sections of the tale: first, the sea " 'was quite dark gray, and
the water heaved up from below' " (p. 90); later, " 'the
sea came in with black waves as high as church towers' "
(p. 97). The fairy-tale landscape which mirrors its own
characters' emotions reflects in turn the diverse angers of
the morning—James's fury at his father, Mrs. Ramsay's
anger at Charles Tansley for agreeing with her husband
that it would rain, Mr. Ramsay's own inexplicable rage.
Ten years later, when James is sailing to the lighthouse,
memories of those angers are revived.

A progression of emotion similar to that which the
fairy tale reflected in its changing seascapes is used by

[8] P. 15. Cf. the crimson and gold tassel of Jinny's first speech.
Jinny also invests "gold" and "black" with meaning. Her negative
and positive " 'body signals,' " as she calls them, are imaged as
the " 'rough black "No," the golden "Come" ' "—emotional vibrations of revulsion and attraction (pp. 74 and 126).

[9] P. 24. In Bellak's *Schizophrenia* it is noted that subjects with
this syndrome "use or like colors of the blue-red series (purple and
mauve) more than do non-schizophrenics" (p. 749). The violets
which Rhoda flings into the river as an offering to Percival lie in
this same color-range.

Mrs. Woolf in the descriptions of landscape and weather which preface the chapters of *The Waves* and *The Years*. Here too the appearance changes according to the mental atmosphere, whether that of the collective minds of the characters in *The Waves* or the obscure emotions of a generation in *The Years*. In the latter novel especially, the outer weather of the London landscapes reflects the "inner weather" of the Pargiters—the endless rain in the opening section which echoes the atmosphere of the mother's death; the smoke and burning of the autumn of 1891 which emphasizes the necessity of the family to "consume their own smoke," as Abel Pargiter says; the frozen darkness of the cold winter's night in 1917 that mirrors the frozen emotions of the night in the air-raid shelter. As the images of light on sea or landscape suggest the increasing awareness in the growing minds of the characters in *The Waves*, so the rain, smoke, frost, fall of rotten leaves, and wind of a sterile spring throw back the uneasy vibrations of the cycles of hope and despair which make up *The Years*.

Virginia Woolf's earliest use of landscape reflection occurs at the opening of Chapter XXV in *The Voyage Out* where the heat vibrations of the Santa Marina afternoon prefigure the fever and distortions of Rachel's coming delirium (p. 398). In *Jacob's Room*, Mrs. Woolf expands landscape description to reflect facets of Jacob's personality; London and its environs and the Greek landscape become a series of mirrors in which we glimpse aspects of Jacob and the civilizations which have formed him.[10] In *The Waves*, the most sophisticated use of this

[10] The multiple Greek images and object-symbols all seem to form a vast mosaic of tiny mirrors which reflect the abstract idea of Greek civilization. This idea then becomes a mirror for the parallel civilization of pre-war England and finally for Jacob himself, whose head is like the Hermes of Praxiteles in Sandra Wentworth's eyes. These images include the neo-classic eighteenth-

mode is not in the poem-essays but in the depiction of certain outer landscapes which reflect the characters: Rhoda's shifting world of solid objects; the cool Flemish interiors of Susan's farmhouse from which elements of her personality emerge like the symbolic details of a painting by Van Eyck; the Dante-esque scene of the London Underground in which Jinny, like one of Dante's sinners in the fiery desert of the sodomites, asserts the lust which gives a mechanized motion to her world.[11]

In Virginia Woolf's essay on George Meredith she comments on how "the landscape always makes part of the emotion" and is "brought forward to symbolize what the human beings are feeling or looking." The following scene from a Meredith novel she calls a "description of a state of mind": " 'The sky was bronze, a vast furnace dome. The folds of light and shadow everywhere were satin rich. That afternoon the bee hummed of thunder and refreshed the ear.' " Another description, that of a winter morning, she sees as "a woman's face."[12] Virginia Woolf's use of landscape reflection, especially in *Jacob's Room*, may be said to follow this method; here feeling and personality are not so much concretely imaged as suggested almost inaudibly through an abstract arrangement of landscape forms. As her work tightens and progresses, she moves from the reflective to the symbolic, compressing the image into one of more definite outline which is nearly identical to the subject's feeling about it.

The use of parallel scene, the third of the indirect modes of reflection, is similar to that of landscape in that

---

century interiors (p. 69), Jacob garlanded in grapes (p. 74), Florinda compared to Greek women (p. 77), the Scilly Isles episode with its Greek-island flavor (pp. 45-47).

[11] Bernard's final assessment of Jinny in the last chapter as " 'a crinkled poppy, febrile, thirsty with the desire to drink dry dust. . . . So little flames zigzag over the cracks in the dry earth' " (p. 179) confirms this view.

[12] (*C.R.II*), *Essays*, I, pp. 228-29.

it poses an emotional duplicate of the original scene. The characters and situation may differ, but the basic emotion is the same, so that the original receives reinforcement through its somewhat distorted mirror twin. Virginia Woolf experiments with this technique especially in *Jacob's Room* and *Mrs. Dalloway*, then discards it in her later novels for a more complicated arrangement of mirrored memory panels to be discussed in Chapter X. The method she pursues in the early books is best illustrated by the brief scene, in Section VIII of *Jacob's Room*, that follows Jacob's disillusionment with the demi-prostitute Florinda as he sees her going up Greek Street on the arm of another man. It opens with Rose Shaw (a friend of Jacob's) crying that life is wicked and detestable and proving it by a story of two people who love each other yet cannot communicate. He is killed in the war, she visits hospitals; what should have been love is turned into death. Following this brief scene, which condenses certain elements of the novel (for example, the young man is buried in Flanders Field, an omen of Jacob Flanders' death), is a harshly-drawn city landscape in Soho; then a flash of Jacob reading the *Globe*, which is full of tragedies; then a snow storm on a lonely country road. This series of four scenes closes the section. By itself, each is meaningless; together they synthesize the original emotion of betrayal and the resultant death of the heart. In a similar manner, the Regent's Park scenes in *Mrs. Dalloway* mirror or parallel each other in their basic emotional situations: non-communication and the inability to love.

THE FINAL mirror mode—which can be classed as still another "direct" method of reflection—is that of

the self by other people. "Nobody sees any one as he is
. . . they see all sorts of things—they see themselves,"
the narrator in *Jacob's Room* remarks (pp. 28-29). In a
letter to Vita Sackville-West, Virginia Woolf asked: "Do
we then know nobody? Only our own versions of them,
which as likely as not, are emanations from ourselves?"[13]

These "emanations," Mrs. Woolf suggests, are various.
They may be reflections of our own feelings, which make
us ascribe negative characteristics to another person, as
Lily Briscoe admittedly does when she uses Charles Tansley as her "whipping-boy."[14] Or they may be elements of
our own nature, real or imagined, which we glimpse in
the other person, as Rhoda and Louis in *The Waves* are
drawn to each other by their similarities. *To the Lighthouse*, especially the dinner scene, makes frequent use of
characters as mirrors of one another. In *The Waves*, in
which scenes and even images and symbols continually reflect their duplicate, this mirror mode is carried to the
extreme. As with Rhoda and Louis, each character has at
least one aspect of himself mirrored in another; Bernard's
normal urge for family and children is reflected by Susan,
Neville's sensuality by Jinny's, and so forth. In a different
manner, Percival serves as a giant reflector for the feelings of his six friends. Like the mirror itself, Percival is
never seen; all we know is the light glancing from his
surface[15]—the emotions of the characters toward him. At
the close of the farewell dinner, Jinny says: " 'Let us hold
it for one moment . . . this globe whose walls are made
of Percival,' " thus confirming his position as the reflecting outer boundary of their world. In the final chapter,

[13] Pippett, *Moth and Star*, p. 255.
[14] "Half one's notions of other people were, after all, grotesque.
They served private purposes of one's own. He did for her instead
of a whipping-boy. She found herself flagellating his lean flanks
when she was out of temper" (*Lighthouse*, p. 303).
[15] Percival's very essence is that of "light"; see Chapter VIII, iv.

when Bernard sums up the experience of his life and that of his friends, the reflections multiply indefinitely, like those in the hall of mirrors at Versailles, and we seem to gaze down a long corridor in which the various personalities form a series of continuous cross-reflections, successive images-in-depth whose totality we can now experience for ourselves.

Virginia Woolf's treatment of personality as the sum of emotion felt by one person for another (as Percival is created from his friends' feelings in *The Waves*) is parallel to that of Proust in *Remembrance of Things Past*, especially to the way Swann considers Odette and the narrator thinks of Albertine. Of the latter, the narrator says that she was merely "the generating centre of an immense structure which rose above the plane of my heart."[16] In other words, she was the stimulus which inspired the response, and the result was not necessarily connected with the real Albertine. Virginia Woolf's portraits of people through the consciousness of another character have this same separate structure. We perceive the people as detached from the personality they actually represent, and the "structure" takes on the outlines not so much of that person as of the consciousness perceiving it.

In this way the characters in a novel like *Mrs. Dalloway* develop through their views and appraisals of other people. We feel Clarissa intimately (far more than any conventional heroine) because Mrs. Woolf places us at the very center of her emotions which ray out to the people she encounters and remembers and refract with energy. All around Clarissa stand characters who, like mirrors placed at various angles, send back different aspects of herself—reflections which may at first appear monstrous but which become clear as the novel progresses. For example, the "brutal monster" which Clarissa releases in the form

[16] Proust, II, p. 689.

111

of Miss Kilman—an ogre about to "seduce" her daughter[17] —is shaped not so much of the unfortunate and pathetic Miss Kilman but of the irrational hatred which the possessive and inherently snobbish Clarissa feels. As the novel progresses, various elements of Clarissa, which she unwittingly shapes from her own emotions, appear. As she thinks of Peter, of Sally Seton, of Ellie Henderson whom she does not want at her party, of Millicent Bruton who elicits her jealousy, of her husband Richard, of her own daughter, and of herself, her violent aversion to Miss Kilman falls into its place in the cauldron of conflicting feelings deep within Clarissa—so deep, in fact, that in the original plan of the novel Clarissa herself was to have committed suicide at the end of the party.[18] Like Mrs. Giles Oliver in *Between the Acts*, gazing into the "three-folded mirror, so that she could see three separate versions" of her face (p. 19), Clarissa seems to hold people up to her gaze only to show the reader her multi-emotional self.

[17] *Mrs. Dalloway*, pp. 14-15, 138-39, 192 ("Elizabeth's seducer").
[18] Introduction to the Modern Library edition, p. vi.

CHAPTER EIGHT

A Multiplicity of Self

Mrs. Giles Oliver, gazing at her triple reflection in the mirror, suggests the attempt of the psychological novelist for " 'a multi-dimensional effect in character, a sort of prism-sightedness.' "[1] The method of reflection, however, constitutes only one panel of the triple mirror by which Virginia Woolf makes the reader aware of the multi-dimensional quality of self. Two other modes view the depth and complexity of personality in different ways. The first of these two modes is the *quantitative* method used by Proust: the splitting of the self into time/memory selves or separate states of consciousness which take place in time and are imaged as separate identities. The second mode is *qualitative* and achieves its effect by dividing the character's emotional aspects into different selves or doubles so that their exact nature can be seen.

Before describing how Virginia Woolf uses these modes, it might be useful to examine in a more general way what she seems to mean by the self or personality. It can be said that all of her novels, from *The Voyage Out* to *Between the Acts*, seek to explain and redefine the self in terms of her increased awareness and understanding of it. Certainly the view becomes more complicated with each work. Bernard in *The Waves* recognizes that he is " 'not

[1] Lawrence Durrell, *Justine* (New York, 1957), p. 27. Darley, the narrator, remembers Justine "sitting before the multiple mirrors at the dressmaker's, being fitted for a sharkskin costume, and saying: 'Look! five different pictures of the same subject. Now if I wrote I would try for a multi-dimensional effect in character, a sort of prism-sightedness. Why should not people show more than one profile at a time?' "

one and simple, but complex and many' " (p. 55), and
the novel goes to exquisite lengths to explain how. Yet
the view of personality achieved earlier in *Mrs. Dalloway*
seems clear enough to cover her entire work: that of the
self as a bundle of divided and disparate parts which the
outside world views (mistakenly) as a single person:

> She pursed her lips when she looked in the glass. It
> was to give her face point. That was her self—pointed;
> dartlike; definite. That was her self when some effort,
> some call on her to be her self, drew the parts together,
> she alone knew how different, how incompatible and
> composed so for the world only into one centre, one
> diamond, one woman who sat in her drawing-room. . . .
>
> Strange, she thought, pausing on the landing, and
> assembling that diamond shape, that single person. . . .
>
> (pp. 42-43)

The question, then, becomes one not of the diversity
of personality but of what that diversity consists. The
basic nature of the multiple selves is emotional. But "feeling" or emotion covers the entire conscious and unconscious
range of response in the human organism; and so the
selves constantly appear in new guises. Sometimes they
are the particular attitudes toward the situation of the moment which embrace the entire being—philosophical, im-
pulsive, eager, abrupt, or observant, as Mrs. Woolf terms
five of the selves which she analyzes, one after another,
in her essay-colloquy "Evening Over Sussex."[2] At other
times they seem to constitute specific emotional responses
to sensory stimuli or, in a more complex way, to people
or conditions. In still another manner they represent abstract qualities which in turn are syntheses of a complex
of emotional reactions: the feminine or the masculine self,

[2] (*D.M.*), *Essays*, II, pp. 290-92.

for example, or the intuitive or analytical self. Or they may be symbolic of one aspect of the physical or mental being, such as the conscious or ego, the id,[3] the "I-self" who watches, or the body, independent of the mind.[4]

Whatever quality the subjective and momentary self assumes, it is defined by, or at least related to, the objects which it encounters. The state of consciousness is never a vacuum, and each state's particular quality or identity as a "self" is comprised of emotion toward a particular object whether that object exists outwardly in space or inwardly as memory. This connection between self (the subject) and object can be said to constitute the momentary "reality" of the self. The quality of that reality consists of the quality of the "connection" at that particular moment. When Virginia Woolf speaks of the self as attaching itself by threads to particular objects (Mrs. Ramsay to the lighthouse beam, Louis to the world,[5] Orlando to the oak tree), she is establishing that "connection" and defining the quality of that moment's self.

Showing these separate selves of the moment—each of which has its own identity yet is part of the whole—forms the first mode to examine here: that of the time/memory selves. With this mode Mrs. Woolf shows herself aware, as R. L. Chambers explains, of the theory of the discontinuity of personality, in which the self "consists not of a homogeneous entity capable of gathering experience to itself, but rather of discrete moments of experience."[6] Proust's narrator, searching through time for his memories

[3] The "id" is symbolized by Albert, the idiot in *Between the Acts*, whose identity as "something hidden, the unconscious . . . sex" (p. 233) is discussed by the audience.

[4] The body is the final self to appear in "Evening Over Sussex" and speaks its concern with warmth, cold, food, and sleep.

[5] " 'My roots are threaded, like fibres in a flower-pot, round and round about the world' " (*Waves*, p. 14).

[6] R. L. Chambers, *The Novels of Virginia Woolf* (Edinburgh, 1947), p. 77.

115

of Albertine, wrote that "our ego is composed of the superimposition of our successive states," each state supplying a "fresh memory," a "different Albertine."[7] It is in this manner that Virginia Woolf's Orlando, nearing the end of the "biography," calls upon "her great variety of selves," of which the narrator remarks that she had "many thousand":

> Choosing then, only those selves we have found room for, Orlando may now have called on the boy who cut the nigger's head down; the boy who strung it up again; the boy who sat on the hill; the boy who saw the poet; the boy who handed the Queen the bowl of rose water; or she may have called upon the young man who fell in love with Sasha; or upon the Courtier; or upon the Ambassador; or upon the Soldier; or upon the Traveller; or she may have wanted the woman to come to her; the Gypsy; the Fine Lady; the Hermit; the girl in love with life; the Patroness of Letters; the woman who called Mar (meaning hot baths and evening fires) or Shelmerdine (meaning crocuses in autumn woods) or Bonthrop (meaning the death we die daily) or all three together—which meant more things than we have space to write out—all were different and she may have called upon any one of them.[8]

These swift successions of selves, however, do have a "Captain self," a "Key self, which amalgamates and controls them all," as Orlando observes, and which gives a unity to the diversity,[9] keeping the reader feeling that he

[7] Proust, *Remembrance of Things Past*, II, p. 764.

[8] *Orlando*, p. 278. Marmaduke Bonthrop Shelmerdine is Orlando's husband, and she calls him by various parts of his name according to her emotional state at the time, linked always to sensory or psychic perceptions.

[9] *Orlando*, p. 279. The search for this key self, and the expression of its captaincy (like Clarissa's attempt to consolidate her various selves into "one diamond") appears the goal of the in-

is at least within a single personality if not a single integrated self. This key self appears as a sense of identity,
able to call up the other selves, which are linked through
the threads of memory, sensory stimulus, or association. In
Orlando, the narrator terms these emotional connections
"attachments" and "sympathies" which have "little con-
stitutions and rights of their own . . . so that one will only
come if it is raining, another in a room with green curtains, another when Mrs. Jones is not there, another if you
can promise it a glass of wine" (p. 277). The sound or
look of rain, the color green, the impress of personality,
the taste of wine—these, with their clustering threads of
emotion, make up the connections which link the "scraps,
orts and fragments" of the personality to the parent whole.

THE SECOND mode by which Virginia Woolf
suggests the multiplicity of self is that of personifying its
separate aspects as individual characters. She accomplishes this through the use of divided or dual personalities
(such as Orlando, who appears in the novel first as a man,
then as a woman), complementing personalities, doubles,
and abstract figures embodying mental/emotional qualities
which, when considered together (as the six characters
in *The Waves*), form a unified though various whole.
These personalities are not to be confused with the time/
memory selves; rather, they form the instinctual or psychic
bases upon which the time/memory selves are built.
They may be called the directives which control the
moment. Out of their many patterns and combinations

---

dividual in each of her novels—what psychology would term
individuation. The "diamond" in Oriental philosophy is the symbol
of total personality integration.

the characters, or group of characters, in Virginia Woolf's novels are composed.

When Virginia Woolf was writing *Mrs. Dalloway*, in which she planned Septimus Smith as a double of Clarissa,[10] she was sketching out the essay "The Russian Point of View" with its emphasis on passion and "soul" (the latter word is perhaps rendered better in English as "psyche").[11] Dostoevsky's novels she saw as "seething whirlpools, gyrating sandstorms, waterspouts which hiss and boil and suck us in. They are composed purely and wholly of the stuff of the soul." And again: "He cannot restrain himself. Out it tumbles upon us, hot, scalding, mixed, marvellous, terrible, oppressive—the human soul."[12] The emphasis on the diversity of personality, its passions and its submerged elements, is implicit in these quotations, and one need only take one step further and remember how Dostoevsky dramatized aspects of personality by presenting them as different characters or as submerged elements which "split away" from the parent psyche, to realize at once the psychological relationship between Septimus and Clarissa.

It is in this sense of repressed aspects of personality that Septimus is the double of Clarissa. Both, in different ways, exhibit the failure to feel.[13] But what Clarissa is unable to externalize as either active affection or rejection is expressed by Septimus in a self-destructive violence of revolt against society, marriage, and procreation. His refusal to give Rezia a child or be a proper husband and his hostility toward society, expressed in his obscene drawings,

[10] *Dalloway*, introduction to Modern Library edition, p. vi.

[11] *Dalloway Notebook II* (1924). This appeared in 1925 in *The Common Reader* together with "Modern Fiction" which devotes considerable space to the Russian "mind" and "heart." In 1921-22, Mrs. Woolf was also collaborating with S. S. Koteliansky on a translation of Dostoevsky's *Stavrogin's Confession*.

[12] (*C.R.I*), *Essays*, I, pp. 242 and 244.

[13] Leon Edel, *The Modern Psychological Novel*, p. 132.

118

are distorted parallels of Clarissa's coldness and prudish-
ness. As her "double," Septimus may also be said to atone
for Clarissa's guilt arising from her power-drives (her love
of authority and society) by his rebellion against these
forces.[14] (A deeper motive for guilt may be Clarissa's intense friendship for Sally Seton which is similar to Septimus' ambivalent feelings for his dead friend Evans.)[15] It
is for these reasons that Clarissa feels a sense of purgation,
almost of joy, at hearing of the death of Septimus. "Death
was defiance," she thinks—and seems to believe that Septimus had, in his madness, defied the society and conventions which imprisoned her and turned her into a
snobbish hostess. " 'If it were now to die, 'twere now to be
most happy,' " the refrain comes to her.

> Somehow it was her disaster—her disgrace. It was her
> punishment to see sink and disappear here a man, there
> a woman, in this profound darkness, and she forced
> to stand here in her evening dress. She had schemed;
> she had pilfered. She was never wholly admirable. She
> had wanted success, Lady Bexborough and the rest of it.
>   (p. 203)

And two paragraphs later:

> She felt somehow very like him—the young man who
> had killed himself. She felt glad that he had done it;

[14] Septimus thinks of himself as "the scapegoat, the eternal
sufferer" (p. 29).

[15] It is a mistake to see the suggestion of homosexuality in the
cases of Septimus and Clarissa as overt; it is obviously latent.
And calling Sally Seton a "homosexual," as does Monique Nathan
(*Virginia Woolf*, p. 91), seems a distortion. Sally is indeed bold
and daring, smokes cigars, clips off the heads of flowers and
floats them in bowls (see Freud on castration symbolism in
dreams—*The Interpretation of Dreams* [V], p. 357), but in the
end produces five boys, raises flowers, and is called maternal. What
Virginia Woolf is probing in the characters of Septimus, Clarissa,
and Sally is the varying amounts of masculine and feminine in each
nature and the psychological conflicts which an imbalance may
present.

thrown it away. . . . He made her feel the beauty; made her feel the fun.[16]

Septimus Smith can be seen as Clarissa's double on two counts. He is the irrational, uncontrolled unconscious as opposed to her controlled rational conscious. In this sense, Septimus represents the "not-me," the so-called bad self personifying the drives and conflicts that rule him. In another sense, Septimus is the prophet, possessed of a divine madness as he raves against a wicked generation and foresees a future world in which there is "universal love" and "no crime."[17] In notes for a revision of the novel's opening chapter, Virginia Woolf wrote: "Sanity & insanity. Mrs. D. seeing the truth. S. S. seeing the insane truth."[18] Like the Greek figure of Cassandra, Septimus touches on another perhaps more traditional aspect of the unconscious mind.

🐦 🐦 🐦

IN *The Waves*, Virginia Woolf takes the self of a single being, ultimately represented by Bernard, and slices it into six sections which personify, on a varying number of levels, the conscious and unconscious selves and drives within the human personality.[19] Instead of

[16] *Dalloway*, Harbrace edn., pp. 283-84. The Uniform edition omits the last sentence, which emphasizes Clarissa's sense of catharsis.

[17] *Dalloway*, pp. 28, 75, 162.

[18] *Dalloway Notebook I* (October, 1922). An entry in the maroon leather *Dalloway* notebook speaks of a "scene of falling through into discoveries" which appears to refer to a reality which, Virginia Woolf notes, is "not at all apparent" to Septimus' doctor.

[19] Bernard, in the final section of *The Waves* (p. 205), asks himself, " ' "Who am I?" I have been talking of Bernard, Neville, Jinny, Susan, Rhoda and Louis. Am I all of them? Am I one and distinct? I do not know. . . . But now Percival is dead, and Rhoda

simply Septimus and Clarissa, we have three men and three women—Bernard, Neville, and Louis; Susan, Jinny, and Rhoda—who explain their identities through their reactions to a given situation or object. A seventh self, Percival, who is felt but never actually heard or seen, appears to be a mystical presence perhaps analogous to "soul," "spirit," or "life-force,"[20] for he is that influence which unifies and binds the six characters so that they are able to merge their separate identities. In a chart in the appendix, I have illustrated certain ways in which Mrs. Woolf has divided the self to illustrate various aspects of mind and body, of conscious and unconscious. Throughout the novel, the various members combine and recombine, exhibiting the numberless possibilities of interchange and fusion within the personality, even as the waves of the sea break and reform again.

The perfect balance of male and female (three men, three women) which makes up the total Bernard exhibits Virginia Woolf's concern with the androgynous nature, a concern which appears in her first novel and follows through to the last. Sometimes Mrs. Woolf shows the two natures in a single person, as in Terence Hewet, who in *The Voyage Out* is said to have "something of a woman in him," or Richard Dalloway in the same novel who is "man and woman as well."[21] Other times she shows complementing personalities which, taken together, form a Platonic whole, as Lily Briscoe in *To the Lighthouse*, exhibiting a nearly sexless, perhaps partially masculine personality, yearns for spiritual completion and fullness of

is dead; we are divided; we are not here. Yet I cannot find any obstacle separating us. There is no division between me and them.' "

[20] He plays another mystic role as Attis-Parsifal, discussed in the next section on the mythic double.

[21] *Voyage*, pp. 302 and 65.

self as she puts her head on Mrs. Ramsay's knee.[22] *Orlando* describes no less than three androgynous natures: that of Orlando who starts as a man and finishes as a woman; her husband Marmaduke Bonthrop Shelmerdine; and the Archduke (or Archduchess) Harry who, like Orlando, changes sex, but in the opposite direction. Indeed, so much has been written of Virginia Woolf's concept of androgyny, surely her most flamboyant theme, that it is unnecessary to repeat it here. Its relevance to this discussion is to show Mrs. Woolf's awareness of the conflicting masculine and feminine drives within the single person whose aspects she dramatizes as dual or separate personalities for the reader.

If *Orlando* is the apex of her concern with this theme, its beginning is to be found in her second novel *Night and Day*, whose very title suggests the polarities of personality and whose five characters constitute differing aspects of the masculine and feminine worlds—a set of variations which anticipates the intricate partitioning of self which she was to accomplish in *The Waves*. Night, with its mysteries, intuitions, and dreams, is related to woman; daylight, with its rationality and logic, to man. In this sense the two women Katharine Hilbery (interested in astronomy and mathematics) and Cassandra Otway (suggesting the intuitive and prophetic aspect of woman) belong to the night; Ralph Denham and William Rodney to daylight. But there are also twilight regions where day and night merge and the landscape contains aspects of both light

[22] *Lighthouse*, pp. 81-83. In Chapter VI of *A Room of One's Own*, Mrs. Woolf elaborates on Coleridge's theory "that a great mind is androgynous" and posits the idea that "a mind that is purely masculine cannot create, any more than a mind that is purely feminine" (p. 148). The "two sexes in the mind" must spiritually cooperate and "have intercourse" with each other. In *To the Lighthouse*, Lily Briscoe's artist nature lacks the feminine creative aspect which Mrs. Ramsay so abundantly possesses, and it is this which Lily seeks from her. At the novel's end, when Lily achieves her vision of Mrs. Ramsay, her nature is symbolically complete and she is able to finish her painting.

and darkness. Ralph Denham is seen as the "masculine" man, Rodney as the "old-womanish" type. In a parallel manner, Katharine and Cassandra, as the novel's narrator notes, "represented very well the manly and the womanly sides of the feminine nature."[23] Opposed to these four characters (who, after much mixing, find their proper mates) is Mary Datchet, whose very name seems to exhibit feminine and masculine characteristics[24] and who, complete in herself, does not need to marry but devotes herself to Women's Rights—a cause surely androgynous in spirit. Like the imagery of sun, moon, stars, and planets, the characters dramatize these sexual aspects of self which revolve around the central core of being.

VIRGINIA WOOLF's final method of showing multiple personality is by the use of the mythic double, the archetype or myth-twin of the self whose shadow stands just behind that of the character, projecting it into time and prehistory and endowing it with an emotional aura deriving mainly from a level below that of personal memory.[25] This technique was not, as might be imagined, a late development but one of her earliest attempts to give dimension to character. Rachel Vinrace

[23] P. 362. Katharine is also considered for the part of Rosalind in a performance of *Twelfth Night* (p. 323), again an indication of her "manly" side.

[24] I.e., Mary suggests the feminine (the Virgin); Datchet has a sharp, masculine sound, like hatchet.

[25] Jung terms archetypes as " 'the psychic residua of numberless experiences of the same type' encountered by our ancestors, and stamped into the memory of the race—that is, into the deep layers of the 'collective unconscious' below the level of personal memories. Hence, whenever some archetypal motif is sounded, the response is much stronger than warranted by its face value—the mind responds like a tuning fork to a pure tone." Koestler, *Act of Creation*, p. 353.

has a myth-twin, the nymph Sabrina, in Mrs. Woolf's first novel, *The Voyage Out.* Sabrina's purpose here is to personify certain psychological qualities of Rachel Vinrace which would otherwise be exceedingly difficult to present, and it is worth examining the nature of Sabrina in Milton's "Comus" to see her peculiar and illuminating relationship to Rachel.

When Rachel falls ill with a headache, a precursor of the typhoid which will destroy her, Terence is reading her the speech of the "attendant Spirit": "There is a gentle Nymph not far from hence." Sabrina is described as "a Virgin pure," descended from the Trojan founder of Britain, and because of her virginity possesses the power of unlocking spells or enchantments. She is "swift," explains the Spirit, in aiding a "Virgin, such as was herself." The Virgin in Milton's poem is the Lady enchained by the magician Comus, who represents the lusts of the flesh. After the Spirit sings a song, "Sabrina fair," to invoke the river goddess, the nymph releases the Lady from Comus' spell by touching her with "chaste palms moist and cold."[26]

It is not coincidence that the "saving" of Rachel consists of being released through her own death from her coming marriage to Terence Hewet—the fulfilling of the fleshly self from which she shrank earlier in the novel when Richard Dalloway kissed her (a kiss which brought terror and an ensuing nightmare of being trapped with a deformed man in a vault). Even when she found herself finally in love with Terence, she played mermaid to evade his embraces, a role which anticipated her later identification with Sabrina.[27] At the novel's end, Rachel and Sabrina

[26] "Comus," *John Milton: Complete Poems and Major Prose*, ed. Merritt Y. Hughes (New York, 1957), lines 824ff.
[27] *Voyage*, p. 365. Rachel moves through the room, "bending and thrusting aside the chairs and tables as if she were indeed striking through the waters." Finally, caught by Terence, "gasping

join as the sheets on her bed turn to water and she is submerged in the pool of her illness. Sabrina, the water spirit, a lovely death-wish, has come for her.[28]

The use of myth in connection with Rhoda in *The Waves* is likewise subtly linked with an unconscious fear. Rhoda, whose leitmotif is " 'the nymph of the fountain always wet,' " has an implied myth-twin in Arethusa, a nymph who fled the embraces of the river-god Alpheus by turning into a fountain. Rhoda's fear of the flesh is compounded by another mythical image, that of being pierced by a bird's beak,[29] which suggests the myth of Leda. Male fears of castration appear in the farewell dinner for Percival which assumes, through the eyes of two of the participants, the shape of the ancient fertility rite of Attis, who sacrificed his manhood to the mother-earth goddess Cybele.

Percival, the unseen grail-questing hero of *The Waves* who is about to leave for India, embodies Virginia Woolf's most complicated use of the mythic double. His manliness and purity, as well as his destination, suggest Perceval, the last of the Grail kings.[30] But just as the Christian legend

---

[28] and crying for mercy," she tells him, " 'I'm a mermaid! I can swim . . . so the game's up.' " The final idiom suggests their love-game being over at the book's end.

[28] In *The Golden Bough* (1 vol., abr. edn.; New York, 1951), Sir James Frazer recounts the myth that water spirits steal human souls by letting the body die (Chapter XVIII, p. 223).

[29] Rhoda's fear of birds is sounded, in the opening chapter, in her first sensory awareness of their cries. Louis sees her eyes as " 'the colour of snail's flesh,' " thus connecting her with the image of the snail as "victim," the snail being impaled by a bird's beak or broken upon a rock by a bird. The antagonistic male force—which appears as the "beak of brass" which young James in *To the Lighthouse* fears in his father (pp. 62-63)—is thus mythicized into the bird-image. Louis, during the dinner for Percival, thinks that " 'to be loved by Susan would be to be impaled by a bird's sharp beak' " (p. 86). Louis too is connected with the snail motif, and the image here appears to be one of castration.

[30] Percival "has the name, and certain qualities, of the last of the Grail Kings, Perceval; both have physical beauty but limited

merges with the far older one of Attis, as Jessie L. Weston explains in *From Ritual to Romance*,[31] so Percival includes not only Perceval (or Parsifal) but also the Phrygian counterpart of Adonis. Percival is in love with Susan, who appears to represent Cybele. His young manhood is to be sacrificed, for he will die in India. In the middle of the celebration, speaking as if in a trance, Rhoda and Louis experience the dinner as its mythic archetype. The use of the Attis fertility ritual, which Virginia Woolf renders in swift images (complete with the symbol of the violets which sprang from Attis' blood), suggests the creative and destructive aspects of the relationship between the sexes, which find their individual counterparts in the characters.[32] The mythic presence of Cybele dramatizes the demanding power and cruelty of the maternal role which Susan (who has rejected Percival to raise a farmer's sons) exemplifies. Rhoda and Louis, too, raptly adoring during the mythic experience, reveal a certain cruelty and coldness in their nature. Through the ritual enactment of the myth of the sacrifice of the beloved, the conflicting emotions and personalities of the different diners are brought forth.

As Perceval the Grail king and as Attis-Adonis, Percival's multi-mythic personality is still not complete. The

---

intelligence. Percival in the novel dies when he falls from a horse in India, and the Grail hero is supposed to have carried the Holy Cup from England to India, where it disappeared." F. L. Overcarsh, "The Lighthouse Face to Face," *Accent*, Winter 1950, 122.

[31] See especially Chapters IV and XII in Weston's *From Ritual to Romance* (New York, 1957) and Chapter XXXIV, "The Myth and Ritual of Attis," in Frazer's *The Golden Bough*. Another suggestion of this myth occurs in *Jacob's Room* in the image of the tree falling in the forest (pp. 21 and 30) which is linked with the sound of shots (p. 175), connecting tree-Jacob-death.

[32] The incredibly complex interweaving of Mrs. Woolf's symbols can be seen in the fact that Neville, who loves Percival, has somewhat adopted the role of Catullus, the Latin poet who wrote a famous poem on the myth of Attis.

Grail king is identified with the earlier knight of the Arthurian Court who accompanied Sir Galahad, and with the Parsifal of German legend. Together with the image of the Grail comes that of light. Percival is called "a God,"[33] and so another fusion of late-and-early myth is achieved: that of the sun-god and a Christian god whose primary aspect is light (I John 1:5). The dinner for Percival is a "last supper" with his friends, and the Grail image is suggested when, at his coming, " 'the chair, the cup, the table—nothing remains unlit. All quivers, all kindles, all burns clear' " (p. 100).

To Perceval, Attis, Sabrina, and Arethusa we must add Antigone in *The Years* and the archetypal wife and husband who appear briefly in *To the Lighthouse* and at the closing of *Between the Acts*. Taken together, they show how Virginia Woolf used universal myth to underline the particular character or situation, and relate her material to the archetypes of human experience.

FINALLY, it may be suggested that Mrs. Woolf's use of the various aspects of self—whether *quantitative* (time/memory), *qualitative* (emotional), or *mythic* (also emotional)—makes possible for the reader not only the illusion of participating in the constantly shifting perceptual and emotional stimuli of the character but also the sense of living inside a personality whose very essence is that of variation, motion, and internal change. In the opening pages of *Mrs. Dalloway*, for example, the reader not only inhabits Clarissa's mind and sees a London morning through her eyes, but is inhabited by a series of Clarissa-selves, quantitative *and* qualitative, which appear in the succession in which they would normally in life. They lift the reader on the "wave of divine vitality" which

[33] " 'The multitude cluster round him, regarding him as if he were—what indeed he is—a God' " (*Waves*, p. 97).

is that of Clarissa's personality. We are made to sense Clarissa solid and entire, and we sense her fluid component parts. In *The Waves*, we are immersed in even deeper and more hidden aspects of personality which, like the ghosts in Henry James's stories who "have their origin within us,"[34] we furtively recognize as parts of our self. Ritualistic in their movements, they glide in and out of us in a formal interchange, a ballet of behavioral patterns so instinctive that at first we scarcely recognize their meaning.[35] Each of the multipersonal selves speaks a similar language. It is the voice of subjectivity, and its tone, that of an almost impersonal fusion of personality, will be discussed in the next chapter.

[34] "Henry James's Ghost Stories" (*G.R.*), *Essays*, I, p. 291.
[35] I am indebted to Joan Bennett for this metaphor. She describes the over-all pattern of *The Waves* as that of "some classical ballet in which from time to time the dancers come forward singly or in pairs and at times all combine in a concerted movement" (p. 110).

CHAPTER NINE

The Voice of Subjectivity

ONCE VIRGINIA WOOLF had discovered a way of expressing the "multi-dimensional" effect of character, another problem still remained: that of finding a voice which would speak for these different selves, sometimes individually, at other times synthesized into a representative voice or tone.

If we set aside the traditional meanings of such terms as "point of view," we can perhaps more closely approach the question of *voice* which appears to have been one of Mrs. Woolf's major concerns and which constitutes still another of her subjective modes. It is not the spoken voice of the character or the conventional narrator; it is the inner voice whose exact nature resists definition yet attempts, through language and rhythm, to articulate feeling. It is the tone of the internal monologue, but it represents more than mere verbalized consciousness. It is verbalized *being*; giving voice to the total moment, transcending self and time, its vibrations strike the inner ear of the reader as a familiar voice. Since it is at once conscious and unconscious, personal and impersonal, individual and collective, it is the voice of everyman and, conversely, of no-man— "the voice that was no one's voice," as Mrs. Woolf wrote in *Between the Acts* (p. 211). To achieve this particular quality, Mrs. Woolf used every possible means: phrases such as "he thought," "it seemed to her," "one felt"; the question asked;[1] the cause and effect noted;[2] the impulse

---

[1] "Was he not being looked at and pointed at; was he not weighted there, rooted to the pavement, for a purpose? But for what purpose?" *Dalloway*, p. 18.

[2] The "for" indicates reason behind act or cause behind effect,

stated which gives rise to memory or sensory response.[3] It is not always certain from which direction the voice comes—it issues, at different times, from within, from above, or from the surrounding atmosphere. Indeed, we might say that, like T. S. Eliot's "three voices of poetry," three distinct voices are heard in Virginia Woolf's novels. But whatever the direction of their origin, they have the same tone and speak the same language. Together, we may call them the *voice of subjectivity*.

The first of these voices comes from within the character and at times resembles the usual voice of the internal monologue: it is that of the character talking to himself at a particular moment. The second voice, sometimes mistaken for that of the narrator, belongs to what has been better termed "a central intelligence"[4] which hovers above the character but has access to certain obscure areas of his personality. The third voice, like the second voice, discerns certain hidden truths of the individual. It is not, however, of the moment but reaches far back into memory and time. Sometimes two, or even the three, voices are blended; other times they are distinct.

With the exception of *The Waves*, Virginia Woolf does not keep to a single voice. She employs instead a rapid, sometimes dizzying sequence, darting in, around, and above her characters.[5] In the opening pages of *Mrs. Dallo-*

"the inexplicable half-logic of reverie." David Daiches, *Virginia Woolf*, p. 71.

[3] See how the sound of Big Ben gives direction to thought-streams of several characters in *Mrs. Dalloway*, pp. 129-30.

[4] In speaking of the "narrator" in *To the Lighthouse*, James Hafley calls it "a central intelligence that approaches and assumes the characters' consciousness." *Glass Roof*, p. 90.

[5] In *To the Lighthouse*, Lily Briscoe says of Mrs. Ramsay, "One wanted fifty pairs of eyes to see with. . . . Fifty pairs of eyes were not enough to get round that one woman with" (p. 303). If we transpose this metaphor from the visual to the aural field, we can discern Mrs. Woolf's handling of voice as similar to the stereo principle of musical broadcasting, in which two or more

way, for example, voice follows voice. We see how the morning "seemed" to Clarissa herself, how "one" feels at night hearing Big Ben (the implied "I" is exchanged for a more universal pronoun), how time and motion (the third voice, concretized in the "whirling young men, and laughing girls" in transparent muslin, "unwound" by the morning) form part of the world surrounding Clarissa. The result is a whole Clarissa, an emotional tonality not limited by confinement to her thoughts. The use of "I" (stated or implied by "she") would shrink Clarissa to the mere observing, inactive self. The reverie, on the other hand, is a reflection of Clarissa's total participation in life. Like the voice in *Orlando* (which is now Orlando's, now the "biographer's," now that of an elusive "spirit of the age"), it communicates a sense of tremendous vitality.

🜃 🜃

THE VOICE OF the character "talking to himself"—which resembles the first of T. S. Eliot's three voices[6]—finds outlet in Virginia Woolf's two earliest novels in traditional reveries rendered in third person but made subjective through image and pattern. *Jacob's Room* experiments in voice: Mrs. Flanders talks to herself, but the second and third subjective voices also speak.[7] As Vir-

---

speakers beam the sound from different directions so as to approximate actual listening conditions. Mrs. Woolf's inner, outer, and encompassing voices try to reproduce or express a tonal sense of reality.

[6] T. S. Eliot, "The Three Voices of Poetry" in *On Poetry and Poets* (New York, 1957), p. 96. This is "the voice of the poet talking to himself—or to nobody." The two other voices, however, appear to have little relationship to Mrs. Woolf's.

[7] As when Jacob and Florinda are together in Jacob's room and Mrs. Flanders' letter (personified into a watchful, knowing presence —that of the second voice) utters her anguish at what is transpiring in the room (pp. 90-91).

ginia Woolf progresses from novel to novel, the alternation and blending of voice become more complex. By the
time she had completed *Orlando*, she was ready for the
more complicated fusion of voice which she achieved in the
"I"-monologues of *The Waves*.

This "I"-voice, whether in first or third person, James
Hafley sees as related to the "indivisible 'I' " which Tolstoy
referred to in the conversations translated by Virginia
Woolf with S. S. Koteliansky: "True life exists where the
living being is conscious of itself as an indivisible 'I,' in
whom all impressions, feelings, etc., become one."[8] There
is a strong resemblance between this consciously feeling
and integrated being and Virginia Woolf's concept of the
multipersonal self as shown in *The Waves*, even to Tolstoy's belief that two consciousnesses exist, animal and
spiritual, which Bernard acknowledges. It took Mrs. Woolf
a long time, however, to find the exact voice she wanted
for the novel. As late as March, 1930, her diary complains
of her not having mastered "the speaking voice,"[9] which
she had referred to earlier as that of "a mind thinking."[10]
Still earlier she had thought of the novel (then called *The
Moths*) as "some continuous stream, not solely of human
thought."[11] It was not until three years after she had begun
The Waves that the soliloquies approached their present
form, and what she had called the "continuous stream"
divided into the non-human voice of time and nature, heard
in the prologues to each section, and the voice of human
thought.[12] Significantly, too, the tense had changed from

[8] *Talks with Tolstoi* (Hogarth Press, 1923), p. 92. See Hafley's
The Glass Roof, pp. 74-77.

[9] March 28, 1930. By this time she had completed at least one
full version of the novel plus a variation of beginnings.

[10] May 28, 1929. This was before any of the actual notebook
manuscripts, which start July 2, 1929, were begun.

[11] June 18, 1927. She had just finished *To the Lighthouse*.

[12] *Waves Notebook IV*, p. 83, June 1930, contains the children's
speech, but sandwiched in between descriptions of dawn on the

past to present. It was the moment of *now*, and what converged upon that "indivisible 'I' "-voice were all the different tones sounded from the various levels of being: memory and imagination, sensation and perception, and repressed elements not usually surfacing to consciousness.

Because these soliloquies give voice to the moment only, or to a random cluster of moments or durations, there is a fragmentary, unfinished quality to them which gives them a different tone from that of the stage soliloquy or internal monologue. Bernard, searching for words to express his feelings, longs for " 'a little language such as lovers use . . . as children speak . . . a howl; a cry.' "[13] The cries themselves (howls of anguish, such as those over Percival's death)[14] are heard throughout the novel as a spontaneous expression of emotion. The "little language," formal though its external appearance may be, imitates the primitive or child-mind's mode of thought which expresses itself directly in pictorial images that symbolize its emotion rather than in word sequences. For example, " 'The door opens and the tiger leaps. . . . I circled round the chairs to avoid the horror of the spring' " renders the feeling of Rhoda's fear of people far more vividly than the explanation—" 'I am afraid of you all' " (p. 93)—which follows. In this sense, we can describe the language of *The Waves* as that of

---

sea. The soliloquy had been experimented with as early as November 29, 1929, in *Notebook II*, but used only sporadically.

[13] *Waves*, p. 209. Here she may be showing the influence of Vico's theory that all original words were monosyllables reproducing either a natural sound or "immediate expressions of emotion, interjections of pain or pleasure, joy or grief, surprise or terror." Ernst Cassirer, *The Philosophy of Symbolic Forms*, trans. Ralph Manheim, 3 vols. (New Haven, 1953-57), I, p. 149. The "little language such as lovers use" may be illustrated in the "cypher language" that Orlando and her husband invent to describe "a whole spiritual state" (*Orlando*, p. 254).

[14] Voiced in the " 'I sob, I sob,' " of Neville. A similar tone is heard in *Jacob's Room* in which Archer's call "Ja-cob! Jacob!" for his brother has a tone which seems, with its "extraordinary sadness," to forecast Jacob's death.

articulated feeling. The entire novel is composed of these symbolic images of emotion which are translated very simply for the reader's benefit. With the cries, however, we have no such translation. They speak for themselves, allowing the reader to supply the meaning from his own emotional store. The following passage, "spoken" by Rhoda at a concert after Percival's death and probably referring to an opera aria, illustrates both the power of the image and the cry:

> "An axe has split a tree to the core; the core is warm; sound quivers within the bark. 'Ah!' cried a woman to her lover, leaning from her window in Venice. 'Ah, ah!' she cried, and again she cries 'Ah!' She has provided us with a cry. But only a cry. And what is a cry?"
>
> (p.116)

In Virginia Woolf's later novel, *The Years*, the sounds of half-sentences add their clamor:[15] " 'And you—' "; " 'I saw . . .' "; " 'The dawn!' "; " 'The roses. Yes . . .' "; " 'And now?' " All suggest but do not complete a meaning; they supply an exclamation point rather than a thought. Bernard states that beneath our surface life there is always "a rushing stream of broken dreams, nursery rhymes, street cries, half-finished sentences."[16] Although *The Years* does not have the consistent "indivisible 'I' "-voice of *The Waves*, it does stress this undercurrent of the unconscious, which contributes so much to the voice quality of the earlier novel.

A final problem remains in connection with the first voice of subjectivity: "But when the self speaks to the

---

[15] Throughout the novel, Mrs. Woolf stresses the "cry" by repeating it three times, such as " 'North! North! North!' " (c.f. " 'Louis! Louis! Louis!' " in the opening pages of *The Waves*, and the quotation above). Street cries from various hawkers likewise add their "verbal noise."

[16] *Waves*, p. 181. *The Years* specifically employs all these devices.

self," Virginia Woolf asks in "An Unwritten Novel," "who is speaking?" In other words, which of the multipersonal selves is talking, which listening? Ralph Freedman, treating Mrs. Woolf's novels from the standpoint of poetry, calls the voice the "lyrical 'I' " and answers Mrs. Woolf's question—which she herself never does precisely[17]—by saying that it is *"Je suis* made *Je est*."[18] Speaker and spoken-to have fused; the personality and its "double" talk in a single voice.

Like the "indivisible 'I' " of Tolstoy which blends bodily and spiritual self, the "lyrical 'I' " fuses two aspects of being, the personal feeling self and the impersonal observer. All through *The Waves* this dual aspect of *Je est—* " 'the double capacity to feel, to reason' "[19]—is exhibited. Bernard, though he grieves at Percival's death, weighs this emotion with his joy for his new-born son. Rhoda, terrorized by the physical world disintegrating about her, can nevertheless analyze her anguish. In *Between the Acts,* which approaches the "shape of pure poetry,"[20] Isa Oliver becomes the ultimate "lyrical 'I,' " transforming through a process half-conscious, half-unconscious, her observations and feelings into poetry, banal though it may be.

𝕩 𝕩 𝕩

BEFORE Virginia Woolf found the speaking voice of *The Waves,* she noted in her diary that "several problems cry out at once to be solved. Who thinks it? And

[17] Mrs. Woolf states that the voice is that of "the entombed soul, the spirit driven in, in, in to the central catacomb; the self that took the veil and left the world"—a definition exasperatingly vague. *Haunted House,* p. 24.

[18] Freedman, *The Lyrical Novel,* p. 33.

[19] Bernard in *The Waves,* p. 55.

[20] "Looming behind *The Pargiters* [*The Years*] I can just see the shape of pure poetry beckoning me." *Diary,* January 26, 1933.

am I outside the thinker?"[21] This narrating "I"—not the author but a person who has "no real being," as Virginia Woolf makes clear in *A Room of One's Own*[22]—never appears in the final version. But it does take form briefly in an early manuscript of the novel as "the lonely mind,"[23] a spiritual rather than physical presence, endowed with supra-narrating powers, which filters experience and emotion. And it appears, in various other guises, in nearly all of her novels.

This second voice of subjectivity differs from that of the usual narrator in a number of ways. It does not furnish, or even possess, a complete dossier on the character. It is there not to give facts but to ask questions, to suggest, or perhaps even to divulge a little of the character's mystery. In *Jacob's Room*, Virginia Woolf describes this narrator's curious position and role:

> But something is always impelling one to hum vibrating, like the hawk moth, at the mouth of the cavern of mystery, endowing Jacob Flanders with all sorts of qualities he had not at all . . . what remains is mostly a matter of guess work. Yet over him we hang vibrating.[24]

[21] September 25, 1929.

[22] *A Room*, p. 7. This narrative "I" is the one Mrs. Woolf uses to refer to herself in the speech, giving it the name of "Mary Beton, Mary Seton, Mary Carmichael or . . . any name you please" (p. 8). The rhyming names and same first name suggest, however, sibling selves.

[23] " 'I am not concerned with the single life but with lives together. I am trying to find in the folds of the past such fragments as Time, who has broken the perfect vessel, keeps safe.' There was nobody to hear these words; they were spoken, perhaps not even aloud, by somebody, where sex could not be distinguished, in this very early light; the lonely mind brooded over a table spread with odds & ends; a napkin & a flower pot & a book . . . in a small room, where windows were open." *Waves Notebook I*, p. 83 (1929).

[24] *Jacob's Room*, p. 72. Here, the image of the moth, which Virginia Woolf associates with her creative self throughout her diary, gives the impression of potential creativity, a humming "energy" which will evoke the character.

136

Here, the narrating presence seems to take the position of the reader, who injects his own subjectivity, inventing where the author has left silences and spaces for just this purpose. Elsewhere, it sheds the reader's persona and assumes a more abstract, immaterial form. Erich Auerbach, analyzing Section 5 of "The Window" in *To the Lighthouse* (which he calls "The Brown Stocking"), comments on the fact that in part of this scene we are in the "consciousness of some observer (to be sure he is not identified)" whose position "verges upon a realm beyond reality."[25] As this nameless observer comments on Mrs. Ramsay ("Never did anybody look so sad") and describes a tear that "perhaps" had fallen in the interior of her being, Erich Auerbach himself observes that the voice belongs not to a human speaker but to "spirits between heaven and earth, nameless spirits capable of penetrating the depths of the human soul, capable too of knowing something about it, but not of attaining clarity as to what is in process there, with the result that what they report has a doubtful ring."[26]

In an early version of *Between the Acts*, called *Pointz Hall*, Virginia Woolf has written a description of this nameless narrator which can be seen to confirm Erich Auerbach's perception of it. The scene is the empty dining room set for lunch, and Virginia Woolf appears to have wished to describe the room so that the reader himself could enter subjectively into all its corners, preparing himself for the eventual entrance of the characters, and so experience more thoroughly the total reality:

[25] Erich Auerbach, *Mimesis: The Representation of Reality in Western Literature*, trans. Willard Trask (Princeton, 1953), pp. 540, 532.

[26] *Ibid.*, p. 532. This is consistent with Mrs. Woolf's concept of character as an enigma, an iceberg whose bulk is mainly hidden from view. See my Chapter II, i and iv.

But who observed the diningroom? Who noted the silence, the emptiness? . . . This presence certainly requires a name, for without a name what can exist? . . . Certainly it is difficult, to find a name for that which is in a room, yet the room is empty; for that which perceives pictures knife and fork, also men and women; and describes them; and not only perceives but partakes of [the]m, and has access to the mind in its darkness. And further goes from mind to mind and surface to surface, and from body to body, creating what is not mind or body, not surface or depths, but a common element in which the perishable is preserved, and the separate become one. Does it not by this means create immortality. And yet we who have named other presences equally impalpable—and called them God for instance or again The Holy Ghost, have no name but novelist or poet, or sculptor or musician, for this greatest of all preservers and creators. . . .

This nameless spirit then, who is not "we" nor "I," nor the novelist either, For the novelist all agree must tell a story; and there are no stories for this spirit; this spirit is not concerned to follow lovers to the altar, nor to cut chapter from chapter; and then write as novelists do   The end with a flourish; since there is no end; this being, to reduce it to the shortest and simplest word, was present in the dining room at Pointz Hall for it observed how different the room was empty from what the room was when—as now happened—people were about to enter.[27]

The presence which Virginia Woolf here compares to the "Holy Ghost," the creative spirit, is the same as that which "broods," like the "lonely mind," quickening the

[27] *Pointz Hall Typescript*, pp. 57-58 (July 3, 1938).

chaos into life,[28] over the few articles in the room at the beginning of *The Waves*. Thus related to the *élan vital* of the moment and containing an intuitive perception of it, it is the most pervasive, if elusive, of the subjective voices, and as such allows the reader to penetrate into the mysteries of the cavern over which the hawk moth stood vibrating.

There are, of course, additional guises which this name-less and observing presence assumes in Virginia Woolf's work. There are the ubiquitous "one," "people," or "passers-by" who say or think a particular thing about a character. Their identity too is nameless, but like the "ghostly" presence just discussed, or the chorus in Greek tragedy, they embody emotional aspects of the reader (or audience) and so assume, in a collective way, another subjective link between character and reader. In *Mrs. Dalloway*, for ex-ample, Virginia Woolf specifically used the idea of the Greek chorus, if we are to take seriously certain notes she made while reading Aeschylus' *Choephori*. In the first part of the novel there was to be "an observer in the street at each critical point who acts the part of chorus—some nameless person."[29] Later the idea of "chorus" became more subjective and was formulated, as in Greek tragedy, to convey the emotions of the character to the reader (audi-ence). For the Regent's Park scene, while Peter Walsh sleeps, she planned "a chorus, half of calm & security . . . half of fear & apprehension," consisting of the nursemaid, sleeping baby, and a little girl.[30]

In the final version of the novel, only the "elderly grey nurse" and sleeping child remain of the chorus. But Vir-

[28] Cf. Milton's image of the Holy Ghost as "brooding on the vast Abyss" in *Paradise Lost*, Bk. I, line 21.

[29] *Maroon Leather Dalloway Notebook*, November 19, 1922. The notebook's entries appear at intervals and present a short running commentary on the writing of the book. The back part of the notebook has jottings on the *Choephori*.

[30] *Maroon Notebook*, July 22, 1923.

ginia Woolf, out of Peter Walsh's dreaming mind, has drawn another ghostly presence, that of a "solitary traveller," who presents a series of mythic visions which embody the feelings of fear and apprehension which the notebook entry advised.[31] Like the ubiquitous spirit which haunts the Pointz Hall dining room, or the "certain airs" which move about the Ramsay's house at night,[32] the "traveller" allows the reader to enter obscure areas of Peter Walsh's psyche which would otherwise remain unknown. The voice of the chorus, although removed to the unconscious world of dream and myth, is still able to engage the reader with its strong emotional tones.

THE THIRD VOICE of subjectivity exists in time rather than in space (as does the second voice) or in personality (as does the first).[33] It is the voice of history, myth, legend—the most interior and least conscious of the three voices. There are reflections of it early in Virginia Woolf's work; in the hilltop scene in *Jacob's Room*, in the central section of *To the Lighthouse*, and in the interludes which preface each section of *The Waves*. It is the "voice from underground" which bubbles up in the song of the old woman in Regent's Park in *Mrs. Dalloway*; it is also the rapt, tense telling of the Attis legend by Rhoda and Louis during the dinner for Percival.

The original opening passage of *The Waves*, taken from her notebooks, sets this tone:

> It was all very pale, & discordant too; the cock crowing
> & the blank music of the melodious birds; the moth . . .

[31] *Dalloway*, pp. 62-65.   [32] *Lighthouse*, pp. 196-97.
[33] This would suggest that the three voices of subjectivity speak for the three aspects of reality (to Virginia Woolf): time, space, and personality.

the white plate; the plant; the sea turning the shells over, and then over again, on the beach. They interrupted each other, as if the mind of a very old man or woman, had gone back to the dawn of memory; & without being able to finish any sentence; without being sure in what order things came; without attempting to make a coherent story.[34]

The voice described here is older than that of "the lonely mind" or of the presence which infused the dining room of Pointz Hall. It is the mythical figure which speaks for a race, a kind of Tiresias, or Cathleen O'Houlihan. The voice has gathered to itself sea-like echoes from all past ages which fuse, simultaneously, in a single faint roar, like that of the shell. The effect is a montage of history and memory—the sentences unfinished, the order of experience scrambled, the story the incoherent, apparently haphazard unfolding of life. Twice Mrs. Woolf emphasizes the intelligibility of its language: in the song the Cockney children sing at the end of *The Years*, a voice of time future; and in "this rusty pump, this battered old woman" whom Peter Walsh hears in Regent's Park in *Mrs. Dalloway*.

A sound interrupted him; a frail quivering sound, a voice bubbling up without direction, vigour, beginning or end, running weakly and shrilly and with an absence of all human meaning into

ee um fah um so
foo swee too eem oo—

the voice of no age or sex, the voice of an ancient spring spouting from the earth; which issued, just opposite Regent's Park Tube Station, from a tall quivering shape, like a funnel, like a rusty pump, like a wind-beaten tree

[34] *Waves Notebook I*, p. 3 (July 2, 1929).

141

for ever barren of leaves which lets the wind run up and down its branches singing

> ee um fah um so
> foo swee too eem oo,

and rocks and creaks and moans in the eternal breeze.

Through all ages—when the pavement was grass, when it was swamp, through the age of tusk and mammoth, through the age of silent sunrise—the battered woman—for she wore a skirt—with her right hand exposed, her left clutching at her side, stood singing of love—love which has lasted a million years. . . . (p. 90)

Is it a woman, or a spring? It hardly matters, for it is the voice of water, of time—an early Anna Livia Plurabelle.[35] She appears again, this time as an actual washerwoman (or char), in "Time Passes" in *To the Lighthouse*—Mrs. McNab, an old creature who moves as if through the waters of time[36] and who hums a song which, "robbed of meaning, was like the voice of witlessness, humour, persistency itself." Able to see into the past ("Some cleavage of the dark there must have been, some channel in the depths of obscurity"), she is time and memory commenting on the present. Indeed, she puts the present into order as does memory itself, refurbishing the Ramsays' house as, "wantoning on with her memories," she recalls Mrs. Ramsay in her grey cloak or Mr. Ramsay talking to himself on the lawn.

[35] As the washerwomen in "Anna Livia Plurabelle" turn into an elm and a stone, so the rusty pump metamorphoses into a tree and an old woman, suggesting the mutability and metamorphosing quality of time itself. *Mrs. Dalloway* was published May 4, 1925. The section of *Finnegans Wake* entitled "Anna Livia Plurabelle" first appeared in the *Navire d'Argent*, October 1, 1925.

[36] She "rolled like a ship at sea," "lurched about . . . like a tropical fish oaring its way through sun-lanced waters" (pp. 202, 206). On page 215 the decaying house is imaged as "the pool of Time that was fast closing over them" [Mrs. McNab and her helper].

The inner tone of *Orlando* and of *Between the Acts*—a tone more historical than mythic—is also that of time, but time of a particular moment, a vocal "spirit of the age." In *Orlando* it speaks indirectly in the passages mimicking the literary fashions of the day, more directly in the descriptions of each century. In *Between the Acts* it changes its voice in a similar manner as the historical scenes of the pageant change. "Was that voice ourselves?" the narrator questions as the pageant ends. "Scraps, orts and fragments, are we, also, that?"[37] Taken together, the voice was a vocal synthesis of the many aspects of self which make up historical personality. Individual as well as universal, it became the voice of the audience's own past. In her diary, while she was struggling for the exact tone to be heard in the novel, Virginia Woolf commented on the necessity of changing the narrating "I" to "we": " 'We' . . . the composed of many different things . . . we all life, all art, all waifs and strays—a rambling capricious but somehow unified whole—the present state of my mind?"[38]

The question mark at the end of the quotation indicates that even in her last novel she was searching for new modes with which to express the whole of consciousness, for an exact voice to speak for the multipersonal self. *Between the Acts* may blend different voices—Isa's own, as well as that of a central intelligence, fuses with the historical—but the novel as a whole conveys a single tone in which individuality is submerged in the voices of the unreachable past, in which all the "waifs and strays" (those emotions which hover at the periphery of being) are recognized. Here, more than in *Orlando*, the multi-leveled aspects of the moment (a moment which goes back to the time of the mastodons in the Outline of History which Lucy Swithin is reading) find their voice.

[37] *Acts*, p. 221.   [38] April 26, 1938.

THERE REMAINS another aspect of voice which we have only briefly mentioned: style. By this we mean the words themselves, Bernard's " 'warm soluble words' " capable of dissolving into the individual stream of consciousness of character and reader; the cadence and flow that Bernard refers to as " 'the speed, the hot, molten effect, the laval flow of sentence into sentence' "; the sequent rhythms of paragraph and chapter which, related to the rhythmic organic flow of life, " 'expand, contract; and then expand again.' "[39]

Seeking as she did a vocabulary and a rhythm which would express thought and feeling at once personal *and* universal, the voice-tone of Virginia Woolf's different characters of necessity remains the same. By contrast, Leopold Bloom in *Ulysses* uses only words that Bloom himself would use; his thoughts, vocabulary, tone, and voice rhythm are peculiarly his own. Yet we must be reminded that Joyce himself worked toward an expression of universal language in *Finnegans Wake* and that H. C. Earwicker's voice, called "the collective mind" by Leon Edel,[40] bears at least a resemblance to the "indivisible 'I' "-voice of the characters in *The Waves* as well as to that heard in *Between the Acts*. Individualized by their actions and thoughts, rather than by their speech, Mrs. Woolf's characters allow the reader to go "in and out of her people's minds like the blood in their veins,"[41] or to shift from character to character without losing the sense that he, the reader, is inside some universal consciousness of which

[39] *Waves*, pp. 50, 57, and 68. See my Chapter XII, i and ii.
[40] *The Modern Psychological Novel*, p. 136.
[41] Virginia Woolf writes this of Jane Austen in "Phases of Fiction" (*G.R.*), *Essays*, II, p. 79.

he has become a perceptive part. This stylization imposes certain limitations: it sheds the externals with which the reader is accustomed to drape the characters; it offers not the "social" voice used by most novelists but a deep, sometimes troubling, inner voice. It does, however, give the reader a closeness of identification with the character which is not possible otherwise. He knows the characters not as he knows his friends; he knows them as he knows himself or, more accurately, the various selves of his own composite personality.

The vocabulary in Virginia Woolf's novels, as Maxime Chastaing notes, constantly guides the reader to an awareness of emotional or sensory reality. Verbs of perception or of intellection are constantly used (thought, felt, looked, seemed, appeared, imagined); in *The Waves*, "les manifestations du mot 'voir' paraissent innombrables." Chastaing also notes that "les produits de fantaisie et de sensibilité sont envahis par la légion des vocables porteurs de passion ou d'émotion: aimer, haïr, craindre, compatir, envier, respecter."[42] In addition to these words, which signal the character's mood, Virginia Woolf uses the more direct verbal means of suggesting emotion, such as exclamations and half-phrases, noted earlier in this chapter; the poetic conventions of rhyme, repetition, and refrain which especially mark *The Years*; or onomatopoetic constructions like "the walloping Oxford bells, turning over and over like slow porpoises in a sea of oil."[43]

The base upon which vocabulary and rhythm are set is, of course, the sentence. Neville in *The Waves* remarks that it " 'would be a glorious life . . . to follow the curve of the sentence wherever it might lead.' "[44] This sentence-curve Virginia Woolf manipulates according to the need of

[42] *La Philosophie de Virginia Woolf*, pp. 14 and 15.
[43] *Years*, p. 50. Variations of this phrase, pp. 52 and 66.
[44] *Waves*, p. 63. Cf. *Diary*, March 11, 1935.

the novel or the character's particular emotion. It is loosest in her earlier novels (*Jacob's Room* or *To the Lighthouse*);[45] in her final novel it is compressed to a kind of verbal shorthand to convey intensity of feeling and a foreshortening of time. But everywhere it follows the individual curve of the character's thoughts.[46] The "ascending" or "descending" passages of *Mrs. Dalloway*, for example, carry the desperation or exaltation of Septimus' or Clarissa's feelings. In *The Waves*, the more organic rhythms of tidal ebb and flow or the rise and fall of emotion seem echoed in passages such as Bernard's visit to St. Paul's cathedral, which combines outward visual movement with a carefully arranged series of rising iambs and falling trochees and dactyls:

"I stray and look and wonder, and sometimes, rather furtively, try to rise on the shaft of somebody else's prayer into the dome, out, beyond, wherever they go. But then like the lost and wailing dove, I find myself failing, fluttering, descending and perching upon some curious gargoyle, some battered nose or absurd tombstone, with humour, with wonder, and so again watch the sight-seers with their Baedekers shuffling past, while the boy's voice soars in the dome and the organ now and then indulges in a moment of elephantine triumph."[47]

[45] In *Lighthouse Notebook I* (August 6, 1925) she states that her aim is "to find a unit for the sentence which shall be less emphatic & intense than that in Mrs. D: an everyday sentence for carrying on the narrative easily."

[46] Susanne K. Langer, in *Feeling and Form* (New York, 1953), cites the "relation between the length of rhythmic phrases and the length of chains of thought" (p. 258).

[47] P. 200. A similar passage, utilizing the Miltonian technique of rising and falling rhythms to emulate emotion, occurs in one of the chapter prologues of *The Waves*:

[the birds] sang emulously in the clear morning air, swerving high over the elm tree, singing together as they chased each other, escaping, pursuing, pecking each other as they turned high

Yet however Mrs. Woolf bends and curves her language to achieve the exact subjective tone she wants, it remains "a woman's sentence," as she calls that of Dorothy Richardson—a "psychological sentence of the feminine gender . . . of a more elastic fibre than the old, capable . . . of suspending the frailest particles, of enveloping the vaguest shapes." Miss Richardson invented it "consciously," Mrs. Woolf claims, to "descend to the depths and investigate the crannies of Miriam Henderson's consciousness."[48] Virginia Woolf's sentence, on the other hand, with its swoops and dartings, its quick contradictions, its occasional chattering tone, seems to have been reproduced unconsciously, catching the spontaneity and constantly changing quality of feminine thought.[49] It is perhaps this personal immediacy—as if the sentences were "thought out loud"[50]—that gives Virginia Woolf's language "that curious sexual quality" which she feels a woman's writing should possess.[51] It exists most strongly in the long curving sentences of Mrs. Ramsay's reveries, which suggest her maternal infolding of everything about her. *Orlando*, too, breathes out a certain musky feminine sentence; one

---

in the air. And then tiring of pursuit and flight, lovelily they came descending, delicately declining, dropped down and sat silent on the tree. . . . (p. 53).

Compare with the third stanza of Milton's "Nativity Hymn": "She crowned with Olive green, came softly sliding / Down through the turning sphere" or with the falling passage from *Paradise Lost*: "How art thou lost, how on a sudden lost,/Deface't, deflower'd, and now to Death devote?" (Bk. IX, lines 900-901).

[48] Review of *Revolving Lights*, *C.W.*, p. 124.

[49] In Mrs. Woolf's review of *The Tunnel*, she observes that "here we are thinking, word by word, as Miriam thinks" (*C.W.*, p. 121). This perhaps most clearly shows the distinction between the two writers—Dorothy Richardson explicitly reproducing a thought in words, Virginia Woolf conveying that thought through the flow and direction of the sentence, which renders more fully its emotional quality.

[50] In her diary, Mrs. Woolf records striding down the moors and composing entire scenes out loud. October 2, 1934.

[51] *A Room*, p. 140.

is not surprised to find, on page 126, that Orlando has become a woman. However imprecise the definition of a feminine sentence might be (compare, for example, Betty Flanders' thoughts with those of Isa Oliver), this "mode of femininity" has its part in shaping the voice-tone not only of the characters themselves but also of the novels they dominate. Susanne K. Langer, in *Feeling and Form*, calls the rhythm of language "a mysterious trait that probably bespeaks biological unities of thought and feeling which are entirely unexplored as yet" (p. 258). The resonances of the "woman's sentence" suggest just such underlying unities and mysteries, and posit the very real question of the relation of the woman writer to the larger symbolic form of the work itself.

CHAPTER TEN

Three Modes of Time

THE MOST DRAMATIC way of entering the character's consciousness is by the modes of time—those modes intimately connected with the moment of being and the way the character apprehends it emotionally. In Chapter III a brief attempt was made to define the psychological concept of time as an aspect of reality—how it is mental, rather than mechanical; how it is qualitative, measuring by emotions rather than by the clock; how it is always present, containing the past within it; and how it is non-spatial, dependent on the physical universe only for the sensory stimuli of the moment. These concepts, derived partly from Bergson, govern the modern psychological or "time" novels, as some critics call them, from Proust and Joyce to William Faulkner.

As Leon Edel has noted in his chapter on time in *The Modern Psychological Novel*, each of these writers had his own preoccupation with time, his own method of dealing with it. Joyce in *Ulysses* wanted to preserve "eighteen hours of experience" at the exact rate of speed at which time passed for the individual. Proust wished to " 'seize, isolate, immobilize for the duration of a lightning flash . . . a fragment of pure time in its pure state.' " Faulkner was absorbed by the omnipresence of the past in the "now." Virginia Woolf, fascinated by the living reality of the moment, voiced each of these concerns in her three modes of depicting time. More sensitive than the others, save Proust, to the intimate relationship between time and personality, she used these modes to confirm her sense of the effect of time's quality of transience, change, and transformation upon the individual. Indeed, time for Virginia Woolf seemed to be regulated by the mysterious inner workings of the human mechanism—time-clocks wound up by biophysical as well as mental impulse.[1]

The first mode, the *kinetic mode*, is concerned with this sense of time's movement, the emotional speed at which it passes. In *Orlando*, the narrator states that "an hour, once it lodges in the queer element of the human spirit, may be stretched to fifty or a hundred times its clock length" or "be accurately represented . . . by one second." Accelerating or decelerating time, Virginia Woolf has Orlando live twenty-five years between breakfast and dinner, a few moments in several weeks;[2] or she stops and "freezes" time as she does literally in the Great Frost scene. Carrying out acceleration and deceleration by the quantities of thoughts and emotions which swell the moment,[3] or by the speed at which the paragraph itself moves, she conveys the emotional response of the character to the situation. In the opening of the novel *Orlando*, when he is under the oak tree on the hilltop and hears the trumpet announcing the Queen, he stands transfixed. Time slows;

---

[1] Joseph Church, *Language and the Discovery of Reality: A Developmental Psychology of Cognition* (New York, 1961), pp. 42-43. More explicitly, Dr. Church writes that "our knowledge of time has its foundations in the biological rhythms of activity and repose, of feeding and digestion, and the external events with which these rhythms are coordinated. All animal organisms . . . have daily and seasonal cycles, which are to some degree under the control of external stimulation (such as the alternation of daylight and darkness, the rise and fall of the tides, the phases of the moon, and so forth), but which also become stabilized . . . as 'biological clocks' which regulate the organism's activities from within."

[2] *Orlando*, pp. 91-92.

[3] ". . . his whole past, which seemed to him of extreme length and variety, rushed into the falling second, swelled it a dozen times its natural size, coloured it a thousand tints, and filled it with all the odds and ends in the universe." *Orlando*, p. 92.

as in a trance he watches the lights of the estate and the movements of welcome (their motion intensifies his stillness). Then at once the mood changes; the long curving sentences shrink to short declarative ones:

> Orlando looked no more. He dashed downhill. He let himself in at a wicket gate. He tore up the winding staircase. He reached his room. He tossed his stockings to one side of the room, his jerkin to the other. He dipped his head. He scoured his hands. He pared his finger nails. With no more than six inches of looking-glass and a pair of old candles to help him, he had thrust on crimson breeches, lace collar, waistcoat of taffeta, and shoes with rosettes on them as big as double dahlias in less than ten minutes by the stable clock. He was ready. He was flushed. He was excited. But he was terribly late. (pp. 21-22)

The speed of the paragraph conveys haste, excitement. Orlando, breathless by its end, has lived far more than the ten minutes by the stable clock. The body, experiencing the rush downhill, the flight up the stairs, and the energetic preparations, feels the sequence of moments by its combined sense of stimulation and fatigue. The mind, reacting mechanically to the initial order given by the sight of the Queen, suspends thought. (We do not have Orlando's voiced feelings; his actions are enough.) The delight of this sequence for the reader lies in the awarenesses of the contrasting emotional states and their differing "rates of experience."

In a similar manner, when Orlando is wooed (as a woman) by the Archduke and looks in the glass at her loveliness, time decelerates to nearly a standstill; we are given a series of formal pictures which, though they have motion in them, suspend the moment as a fish is suspended in a bowl of water:

151

What woman would not have kindled to see what
Orlando saw then burning in the snow—for all about
the looking-glass were snowy lawns, and she was like
a fire, a burning bush, and the candle flames about her
head were silver leaves; or again, the glass was green
water, and she a mermaid, slung with pearls, a siren in
a cave, singing so that oarsmen leant from their boats
and fell down, down to embrace her. . . .

(pp. 168-69)

After this series of pictures drawn from levels of racial
memory and myth,[4] Orlando sighs. Time in the unconscious is no-time.[5] But suddenly it starts again. A thought,
" 'Life, a lover,' " fills her mind with possibilities. And
in an accelerated paragraph, whose pace moves "with
extraordinary rapidity," Orlando drives off to London
"within an hour."

Orlando is not the only novel in which Virginia Woolf
dramatizes emotional states through the kinetic mode. In
The Voyage Out, for example, she slows down the jungle
love-scene to a languorous dream state. Rachel and Terence
move like "people walking in their sleep"; a very long time
seems to pass, although it is only half an hour. Rachel
raises her arm slowly, yawns, is tired. They arrive " 'later
than we arranged.' "[6] Like time in dreams (in which
lateness can appear as part of an anxiety syndrome) it has
come nearly to a stasis: an emotional sense of suffocation
and anxiety which, in this novel, is equated with the state
of love. By contrast, the opening of *Mrs. Dalloway* with its

[4] Greek and Celtic myth here mingle with the neo-Christian
paradox of fire and ice presented in Robert Southwell's poem
"The Burning Babe."

[5] Freud says that "there is nothing in the id that corresponds to
the idea of time; there is no recognition of the passage of time
. . . no alteration in its mental processes is produced by the passage
of time." *New Introductory Lectures* (XXII), p. 74.

[6] *Voyage*, pp. 332-34.

creation-morning scene or the Underground sequence of Jinny (who represents motion) in *The Waves* accelerate time to a fever pitch to convey the energy and restless vitality of the two women.

When Virginia Woolf freezes time, as she does in *Orlando*'s Great Frost scene, she is extending that moment of consciousness whose evanescence William James compared to "a snowflake crystal caught in the warm hand."[7] This particular moment does not melt. The frost brings the country to a standstill: the Thames is frozen to twenty feet and turned into a pleasure park; bonfires blaze on the ice, skaters dally, courtiers rush to and fro. The color, energy, and movement dramatize the motion and *élan vital* of the moment itself, which becomes a microcosm of amazing brilliance. But more than this, it is the moment of Orlando's passion for Sasha, the Muscovite princess. The metaphor of the frost allows Mrs. Woolf to prolong the moment almost indefinitely so that we can experience its energy and examine its emotional values. Were it rendered in clock time instead of emotional duration, we would be unaware of its intensity. When the duration ends—like the "dissolving of atoms" at the end of her essay "The Moment: Summer's Night"—the breaking up of the moment (and of the love affair) is dramatized in the thaw and the breaking up of ice on the river. The "appalling race of waters" of the Thames to the sea is the speed of time which Virginia Woolf measures by emotional means—the emotions of the rejected Orlando.[8]

One of the many parables of *Orlando* is the lesson of how the mind can manipulate time, and Orlando's mastery of it (or is it that of the novelist, through his art?)[9] makes

[7] *Psychology*, pp. 160-61.

[8] Compare with the "cruel churning" of the Amazon in the jungle love-scene of *The Voyage Out*, p. 332.

[9] In Mrs. Woolf's diary (September 18, 1934), while writing *The Years*, she notes "the exalted sense of being above time and

him a questing hero in the realm of time, a role familiar to the reader since he himself has played it in his own development and utilized it in his dreams.[10] Even Orlando's extraordinary longevity has its human, if heroic, aspects; he may go to sleep in one century and wake up in another, his identity as Orlando unchanged (though his sex might be)[11] even as our own consciousness is the same in the morning as when we went to sleep the night before, in spite of the lapse of "horizontal" time.

Orlando's role as time—hero/heroine is accentuated in the opening paragraph of the novel through symbolic action: he is "slicing" at a severed Moor's head with his sword. The dried head, with its skull-like grin, is, in a sense, time (with its properties of death).[12] Orlando's father, "or perhaps his grandfather, had struck it from

---

death which comes from being again in a writing mood. And this is not an illusion, so far as I can tell."

[10] Freud comments on how "dream-work" can accelerate our thought-processes "to a remarkable degree," in the second part of *The Interpretation of Dreams* (V), p. 496.

[11] At the beginning of Chapter II, Orlando sleeps for "seven whole days" and wakes up, not in the sixteenth, but in the seventeenth century. In the eighteenth century (Chapter III) he sleeps again for seven days and wakes up a woman.

[12] Orlando does literally kill time by living several hundred years. In another sense, the symbolic action of the killing of time exhibits the individual's unconscious yearning for immortality, for no-time (compare with the reverse metaphor of Lady Bruton as a clock dial slicing away at Clarissa's life in *Mrs. Dalloway*). The Moor's head is only one of the severed-head images appearing throughout Mrs. Woolf's work. They appear in *The Voyage Out* in the beheaded chickens and the old women's heads which Rachel sees rolling in her delirium. They are also suggested in *Mrs. Dalloway* in the ancestor of Sally Seton beheaded in the French Revolution and in Sally's decapitating flowers. Freud sees decapitation in dreams as symbolizing castration (see my Chapter VIII, ii, n. 15), and so suggests yet another unconscious meaning of the severed Moor's head. Orlando *does* succeed in symbolic self-castration by changing his sex and becoming a woman. Yet this may symbolize the "castration" of the dynasty rather than the individual, since once the estates are in the hands of a woman, the dynasty ends.

the shoulders of a vast Pagan . . . and now it swung, gently, perpetually, in the breeze which never ceased blowing through the attic rooms of the gigantic house of the lord who had slain him."

The "attic rooms" are Orlando's brain in this monster metaphor; his father, or grandfather, his inherited past. The Moor's head as time, a pendulum "perpetually" swinging, clarifies the metaphor as that of a time-sense within Orlando's mind which he can manipulate himself. For it is swinging in Orlando's own house—the estate being a surrogate for Orlando himself, as is Appleton House for its owner, Lord Fairfax, in the poem by Marvell which supplies the parody-pattern for this section of the novel.[13] If Orlando's house is described as having 365 bedrooms and 52 staircases, it suggests not so much mere mechanical time as calendar or historical time. As several passages show, calendar or historical time is equally a part of the human personality and influences it collectively, as well as individually, in the "temper" of a people.[14]

The use of "Upon Appleton House" is not merely to incorporate into the novel a typical poetic genre of the seventeenth century with which the chapter deals. The poem suggests, within its microcosmic structure, a synthesis of history and British character in one person—a theme which *Orlando* develops to show that any individual is the sum not merely of his own lived moments, but of his historical and racial past. Leon Edel sees *Orlando* as illustrating this theme in two ways: first, as a fable for

[13] Each chapter of the novel contains parodies of literary genres or specific works belonging to the period with which the chapter deals. Chapter II, set in the seventeenth century, parodies Sir Thomas Browne and Bacon's essay on gardens in addition to "Upon Appleton House."

[14] Time races in the Elizabethan era (pp. 27-28), drags out in the Victorian (pp. 205-207). In both cases, time seems intimately connected with the entire psycho-physical make-up of a people or a "temper of the times" which instills its rhythms in the actions and thoughts of its individuals.

biographers who must recreate the individual "out of a total past and not merely out of the mechanical calendar present of their lives"; and, second, as an autobiography of the author's own artistic development, so that Virginia Woolf herself, steeped as she was in English literature and history, is seen as "England and all that it had been."[15] In this dual manner, Mrs. Woolf dramatized her concept of the intimate relationship between time and personality on the historical as well as the individual level.

CHANGING THE speed of the moment—making time go fast or slow—can likewise be described as *contraction* and *expansion*. If Virginia Woolf was "perpetually" in debt to De Quincey, as she states in her preface to *Orlando*, it is for this sense of time's elastic powers. "His most perfect passages," she wrote in her first essay on De Quincey when she was revising *To the Lighthouse*, with its contraction of ten years into a single night in "Time Passes," ". . . are descriptions of states of mind in which, often, time is miraculously prolonged and space miraculously expanded."[16] Sir Leslie Stephen, in *Hours in a Library*, had earlier commented on the openings of "vast perspectives" and "geological periods of time" in De Quincey's writings which convey to the reader emotions of melancholy, awe, or terror. "He seemed to live," con-

[15] *Literary Biography* (Toronto, 1957), p. 95.
[16] Mrs. Woolf's description of De Quincey's childhood, "far away on some island separated from us by a veil of blue," gives a hint as to the extent of the influence of De Quincey on this most fluid of Virginia Woolf's novels. (Significantly, the spring after she finished *Lighthouse* she began *Orlando* with its experiments in mind-time.) (*G.R.*), *Essays*, I, pp. 170-71.

156

tinued Leslie Stephen, "ninety or a hundred years in a night."[17]

This eerie quality of time-expansion, with its suggestion of infinite emotional pressures, forms part of the psychological effect of the Great Frost scene in *Orlando*, in which everything either moves with bewildering rapidity or else is frozen to stone by the cold. People and animals are "struck stark in the act of the moment," as in dreams we find ourselves frozen by fear and cannot move, trapped by an anxiety or a conflict of wills.[18] The ancient terrors of nightmare, in which the familiar features of time and space shift and change, are thereby evoked.

But other time-intuitions, equally startling in their effect, are conveyed by the complex of the Great Frost scene. Not only a microcosm of the moment—with time frozen below and, on the surface, all the passions of the moment burning, like the bonfires on the ice—the scene is also a metaphor of memory and past time. Through the ice on the river, "of singular transparency," one can look down into the deeps of time and see the memories—"here a porpoise, there a flounder"—imprisoned by the ice at varying depths. Entire "shoals of eels" lie in a state "of suspended animation which the warmth would revive," suggesting the ability of the mind to bring to life clusters of past memories. At the very bottom of the Thames, a sunken wherry boat is still visible, "lying on the bed of the river where it had sunk last autumn." The distance we

[17] *Hours in a Library*, I, pp. 333-34. A later essay of Virginia Woolf's on De Quincey describes how "he was capable of being transfixed by the mysterious solemnity of certain emotions; of realizing how one moment may transcend in value fifty years." (*C.R.II*), *Essays*, IV, pp. 5-6.

[18] "Motor paralysis" in dreams, Freud explains, may express a "volition which is opposed by a counter-volition"—in other words, a *"conflict of will"* within the dreamer. *Interpretation of Dreams* (IV), p. 337.

glimpse here is not twenty fathoms but the span from autumn to winter. As Milton measured Mulciber's fall by hours, so Virginia Woolf, reversing the procedure, measures time by space,[19] bringing past events near as a telescope reduces the time-distance of the stars.

This ability to bring the past into the visible and tangible present forms the second mode of time, what we may term, because of its spatial properties, the *time-dimension mode*. Here the terms of contraction and expansion can be used in their more literal sense. The moment is contracted to the present—a "flat" instant of time because the past does not create a sense of distance or proportion. Or it is expanded beyond the momentary aspect of duration to probe far into personal or racial memory. Virginia Woolf uses the contracted moment to bring the reader back to sudden conscious awareness, as Orlando, after looking down a "tunnel" into the past, sees things suddenly "as if she had a microscope stuck to her eye"—the mental field of vision, as it were, limited to here and now.[20]

The expanded moment, on the other hand, is used to suggest elements of the unconscious, the residual traces

[19] Consciously, horizontal or clock time is always measured as "a motion on a space." Benjamin Lee Whorf, *Language, Thought and Reality: Selected Writings*, ed. John B. Carroll (Cambridge, Mass., 1956), p. 151.

[20] Here, the flat instant of time is envisioned as a "microscope" in contrast to the "tunnel" into the past which suggests the telescope (*Orlando*, pp. 287-88). The actual "telescope" metaphor is used twice in "Time Passes" in *To the Lighthouse* when Mrs. McNab sees Mrs. and Mr. Ramsay as if a telescope were fitted to her eyes (pp. 211 and 216). Freud, in *New Introductory Lectures* (XXII), p. 26, shows how dream-work represents psychological time by space, changing "temporal relations into spatial ones. . . . In a dream, for instance, one may see a scene between two people who look very small and a long way off, as though one were seeing them through the wrong end of a pair of opera-glasses. Here, both the smallness and the remoteness in space have the same significance: what is meant is remoteness in *time* and we are to understand that the scene is from the remote past."

of instinct and memory which cluster at the edge of awareness. If the ordinary moment or duration carries within
it simultaneous levels of response, ranging from conscious
to mere biochemical reactions, expansion renders a different kind of simultaneity in which (as James Hafley says
of the novel *Orlando*) "the whole past . . . is charged into
the present moment."[21] This past is frequently historical,
as depicted in *Orlando* and *Between the Acts*. More often,
however, it involves racial memory which transcends that
of particular people, a cutting back through De Quincey's
"geological periods of time" to obscure beginnings. Bernard in *The Waves* asks himself:

> And, what is this moment of time, this particular day
> in which I have found myself caught? The growl of
> traffic might be any uproar—forest trees or the roar of
> wild beasts. Time has whizzed back an inch or two on
> its reel; our short progress has been cancelled. I think
> also that our bodies are in truth naked. We are only
> lightly covered with buttoned cloth; and beneath these
> pavements are shells, bones and silence.   (p. 81)

Virginia Woolf's novels have any number of references to
the human reservoirs of primitive energies, instincts, and
feelings which she may picture as "an ape-like, furry form,
crouching" in the human shape, or hear as "the primeval
voice sounding loud in the ear of the present moment."[22]
Influencing perception, these feelings sometimes superim-
pose a hallucinatory image over that of the present. Lucy
Swithin in *Between the Acts*, reading the Outline of History, sees the maid coming in as a "grunting monster" in
a steaming primeval forest; it takes Lucy "five seconds in

---

[21] *Glass Roof*, p. 143.
[22] *Night and Day*, p. 205 (image repeated in *The Waves*, pp.
205-206, and *The Years*, p. 203); *Acts*, p. 165. In the latter
novel the "id" seems specifically to be the cesspool with which the
book opens and which is referred to throughout.

actual time, in mind time ever so much longer," to separate the two. The maid, meanwhile, feels "on her face the divided glance that was half meant for a beast in a swamp, half for a maid in a print frock and white apron" (pp. 13-14). Through one eye on the present, the other fixed on pre-history, Virginia Woolf bifocally renders an eerie dimension: a converging of the conscious and unconscious with their different psychological times.

IF A PERSON *is* his past, if all of time—historical, racial, and personal—merges to create the person as he is at a single moment of being, then there exists a peculiarly intimate connection between time and personality, a relationship of such interdependency that the equation of time = personality can very nearly be made. David Daiches, in discussing *Mrs. Dalloway*, sees "personality rather than space as one dimension, with time as the other,"[23] but does not equate them. R. L. Chambers notes in Virginia Woolf's writing a desire to create a unity of "time, place, person, self and otherself,"[24] a concept which posits an imaginary rather than a real connection between them. James Hafley, in an analysis of *Orlando*, sees the self as the "moment at which Orlando's awareness becomes complete and one is actually a communication of innumerable other moments"[25]—thus moving closer to what seems to be Virginia Woolf's own concept of the personal self as a synthesis of psychic moments. The clearest definition of this concept is perhaps that given by a follower of the Whitehead school of philosophy: "I am my time, and the changes which take place 'in' me are discriminated as past, present, and future by virtue of my capacity for remember-

[23] Daiches, *The Novel, and the Modern World*, rev. edn. (Chicago, 1960), p. 203.
[24] R. L. Chambers, *The Novels of Virginia Woolf*, p. 7.
[25] *Glass Roof*, p. 98.

ing and organizing my experience, always in a present, as involving *a* past and anticipating a future."[26] In Virginia Woolf's words, from *Between the Acts*, "It was now. Ourselves" (p. 216).

If Virginia Woolf's use of *dimension* takes the form of the flat instant or the moment projected longitudinally into the past,[27] it also takes the round or global form, a graphic way of transmitting the microcosmic aspect of the moment which holds within it the entire world of the self. The image of the globe runs throughout *The Waves*, as the globe itself, as the "drop" ("time lets fall its drop"), as the bunch of grapes which represents an aggregate of round moments.[28] In *The Years*, Eleanor "held her hands hollowed; she felt that she wanted to enclose the present moment; to make it stay; to fill it fuller and fuller, with the past, the present and the future . . ." (pp. 461-62).

This presence of the future within the moment of being, a future portending change and movement, validates Virginia Woolf's use of the image of the globe. For the globe, whether world or water drop, is created by motion in space. It is poised in the present, and (like the water drop or world) about to fall or move into the future. Henri Bergson referred to "duration" as "the continuous progress of the past which gnaws into the future, and which swells as it advances."[29] This "fullness" of the moment led Alfred North Whitehead to speak of it as "pregnant," a quality of coming into being and preparing for the next moment's birth; while in Professor Bertocci's words, it is a felt change (within the original *"erlebt moment"*) that "we

[26] Peter A. Bertocci, "A Temporalistic View of Personal Mind," *Theories of the Mind*, ed. Jordan M. Scher (New York, 1962), pp. 398-420.

[27] Mrs. Woolf illustrates this graphically in *Mrs. Dalloway* when Rezia's mind goes back in time to Roman days as if following a shaft sunk into the earth (p. 28).

[28] *Waves*, pp. 178, 131, and 169 respectively.

[29] *Creative Evolution*, p. 7.

161

may describe as a thrust into a future 'emerging' from a present."[30] In *Mrs. Dalloway*, whose original title was *The Hours*[31] and which demonstrates that human life is not lived according to the hours of Big Ben or St. Margaret's but rather according to the emotional values of the moments of being, this sense of forward movement or "thrust" is plain. Beginning with the movement of the cavalcade, then of the airplane, each charged with its anticipatory emotion, the episodes of *Mrs. Dalloway* are carried forward on a crest of feeling.[32] In this manner, the "leaden circles," as Mrs. Woolf describes the bells of Big Ben or St. Margaret's—individual units of horizontal time —"dissolve" in the air, and the intensity and fluidity of the moment of becoming is more accurately implied.[33]

VIRGINIA WOOLF'S third way of conveying the experience of time is by the *mnemonic mode*,[34] which is concerned with memory, its mechanism of stimulus and

[30] Bertocci, "A Temporalistic View," p. 403.

[31] The maroon *Dalloway* notebook sketches out the novel in hourly episodes from 10 a.m. until 2 a.m. the following morning. See also *Diary*, June 19, 1923.

[32] Compare with what Virginia Woolf says of De Quincey's prose: "successive waves of emotion in the same mood." (*C.R.II*), *Essays*, IV, p. 2. In the earlier essay on De Quincey, "Impassioned Prose" (*G.R.*), *Essays*, I, p. 171, she speaks of "each paragraph flowing and following like the waves of the sea." This movement forward may be one of the meanings of the word "waves" in the later novel. Each episode, a filled moment of perception, rises and flows out of the past and pushes forward into the future with the weight of emotion and memory behind it.

[33] "The leaden circles dissolved in the air" runs as a leitmotif through the novel.

[34] I am indebted to Susanne K. Langer for this term, which she uses in Chapter 15, "Virtual Memory," in *Feeling and Form*. The phrase as used here is adapted and changed for the purposes of this study.

response, and its quality of constant accretion and change —a repetition and variation of our sense of the past which suggests the passage or transience of time. Some implication of this mode was given in the discussion of the *erlebt* moment which noted how part of the "fullness" of that moment consisted of past memories crowding in on it. Proust observed how "the moments of the past . . . retain in our memory the motion which drew them toward the future."[35] Not only is the past always with us,[36] but consciousness is forever changing,[37] and so our memories, redefined each moment by the present self and colored by fresh perceptions, are in a state of continuous alteration. By presenting the initial stimulus, the character's successive memories of it, and the means by which those memories are revived, the sense of internal change and motion which we feel as *living*, or *growing older*, can be expressed.

Part of Virginia Woolf's attention to the mechanisms of memory is certainly due to Proust's influence. Memory with its stimulus and response plays very little part in the three early novels. It is only with *Mrs. Dalloway*, with its caves of the past "tunnelled" out behind the characters,[38] that Virginia Woolf was forced to find a mode by which to bring emotions of the past into the present, making them felt with their original sharpness yet leaving that margin between present emotion and past recollection by which the years' changes could be perceived. As her novels

[35] *Remembrance of Things Past*, II, p. 726.

[36] Bergson, *Creative Evolution*, p. 7. In fact, memory images are part of the present process of perception, and so are indissolubly linked with the moment of now. *Matter and Memory*, pp. 69-71.

[37] "Consciousness cannot go through the same state twice," Bergson states in *Creative Evolution* (p. 7), echoing William James. The person remembering an incident from childhood at age twenty differs radically from the same person remembering it at fifty-five. Therefore, the memory itself will alter, due to intervening experience.

[38] See her diary entry of October 15, 1923.

163

proceed, the search for the past and its means of evocation becomes more intensive. The final section of *To the Lighthouse* is an exercise in memory which seeks, through emotion, to recreate the first part of the novel. *Orlando*, a sequence of successive memory-selves which add up to the present-time Orlando, constantly shows how the "seamstress" memory stitches together "by a single thread" the "rag-bag of odds and ends within us" (pp. 73-74), that single thread symbolizing the sensory connection between consciousness and recollection.

Before moving on to the more complicated mode of memory-release used in *The Waves* and *The Years*, mention should be made of Proust's distinction between voluntary and involuntary memory, both of which Virginia Woolf utilizes in these last two novels. Voluntary memory, for Proust, is mainly conscious, governed by the intellect and apt to be colored (or discolored) by the attitudes of the moment. The stimuli which release these "voluntary" memories tend to be visual and verbal associations, and so constitute a kind of game the mind plays, an exercise in imagination, rather than an unconscious calling forth of a past emotion. Involuntary memory, on the other hand, triggered by the stimuli of "the lower, more bodily senses, such as the feeling of his own body in a particular posture, the touch of a napkin, the smell and taste of a flavor, the hearing of a sound—noise or melody,"[39] bears the "stamp of authenticity" because the response comes directly from the unconscious. These memories "make us savor the same sensation under wholly different circumstances, they free it from all context, they give us the extra-temporal essence."[40]

[39] Ernest G. Schachtel, *Metamorphosis: On the Development of Affect, Perception, Attention, and Memory* (New York, 1959), p. 312.

[40] *Letters of Marcel Proust*, ed. Mina Curtiss (New York, 1949), pp. 226-27.

Virginia Woolf's use of voluntary and involuntary memory veers away from Proust's when the emotions she wishes to convey become complex. *Mrs. Dalloway* frequently uses sound as the stimulus which triggers memory-response, and once, in the manuscript version of the novel, has a bodily position revive a memory of Clarissa for Peter Walsh.[41] The narrator in *Orlando* carefully describes (p. 74) how the act of dipping a pen in ink can call up different memories, depending on the violence of the movement. James Ramsay, watching Cam in the boat on the way to the lighthouse, sees a look in her face which reminds him of his mother, a look combined with a movement of the head. The emotion of hatred for his father, who was so easily able to subdue his mother, flares again.

However effective it might be, the use of this process of stimulus and response, as Virginia Woolf was to discover when she began *The Waves*,[42] could become repetitious. Moreover, it could fail to convey the complexity of the emotion, rooted not in one memory only but in a combination. Pull one wire, and a whole series of connections might respond. When James felt the flash of hatred for his father, he "began to search among the infinite series of impressions which time had laid down, leaf upon leaf, fold upon fold softly, incessantly upon his brain; among scents, sounds; voices, harsh, hollow, sweet; and lights passing, and brooms tapping; and the wash and hush of the sea, how a man had marched up and down and stopped dead, upright, over them."[43] What Virginia Woolf seems to have searched for in later novels was a way in which

[41] *Dalloway Notebook III*, pp. 86-88 (November, 1924).

[42] Virginia Woolf's diary (October 11, 1929) notes that she was "not quite satisfied with this method of picking out things in the room and being reminded by them of other things." In other words, the process of memory through visual association did not allow for the transmission of any complexity of emotion. At the time this notation was made she had worked for several months on the first version of *The Waves*.

[43] *Lighthouse*, pp. 260-61.

these "infinite series of impressions" enfolded in memory might be simultaneously conveyed by a single image, a symbol which, even as James's knife in *To the Lighthouse* gathered about itself a host of related images, would abstract an intricately woven network of remembered relationships and feelings. In this manner whole worlds of past emotions might blossom from a single symbol as Combray unfolded from a madeleine dipped in a cup of tea. Proust used this image metaphorically. Virginia Woolf was to use it more literally, abstracting and condensing memories into symbols which, like Japanese paper flowers, would expand in the reader's mind,[44] evoking almost automatically an entire scene from the past.

This type of complex symbol is what Virginia Woolf uses throughout *The Waves* as a mode of memory release, not in the mind of the character but *in the mind of the reader*. The reader himself responds to the visual-emotional stimuli offered, calling up a past scene from the novel and, as the images repeat and vary, building up a fund of emotion around the remembered event. These symbols take the form of a single image, a leitmotif, or a refrain. The leitmotif or refrain rarely changes: "bright arrows of sensation," "the chained beast," "the nymph of the fountain always wet"—these recur with fairly constant phrasing whenever the memory of a particular character's emotion is to be recalled. The symbolic images, on the other hand, whether a phrase or a single noun or verb, undergo throughout the book a series of constant transformations, shifting either in the mind of the character or moving from one character to another with a change in meaning. For example, the image of the circle varies from

---

[44] *Remembrance of Things Past*, I, p. 36. Cf. "The Art of Fiction" (*M.*), *Essays*, II, p. 52: "Mr. Forster has the art of saying things which sink airily enough into the mind to stay there and unfurl like those Japanese flowers which open up in the depths of the water."

that of a globe to an air ball, a knotted handkerchief, a ball of string, a circle, a ring, a chain, a loop. A circle means an engagement ring for Bernard, desired unity for Rhoda, broken friendship for Neville. The globe is life or the full moment for Bernard, love for Neville, and so on. The variation in the images—all based on a single primary shape—makes each repetition trigger in the reader's mind a *multiple response*. It is not merely a single scene or emotion that is revived, but a synthesis of the characters' different feelings toward a single idea or emotion. Seen metaphorically, it symbolizes the changing attitudes toward a particular memory of our own which (as the incident in *To the Lighthouse* showed in its entirety) involves not only that individual memory but a related series. We might term this a *matrix of memory*, an extremely complicated nesting of schema which, lifted to consciousness, can revive forgotten complexities of feeling.

An example of the way memories grow and change can be seen in the repeated image of Susan's knotted handkerchief—an image given several times in the opening chapter to affix its particular emotion in the reader's mind:

"I will wrap my agony inside my pocket-handkerchief. It shall be screwed tight into a ball."

"Susan . . . has passed the tool-house door with her handkerchief screwed into a ball."

"Her nails meet in the ball of her pocket-handkerchief."

"I followed you, and saw you put down your handkerchief, screwed up, with its rage, with its hate, knotted in it.

". . . this knot of hardness, screwed in your pocket-handkerchief." (pp. 9-11)

Immediately following this final repetition by Bernard is Susan's speech with the leitmotif, " 'I love, I hate,' " epitomizing the violence of the double-edged emotion already implicit in the image and its related symbols of screw, tool, and nail. This image reappears in the next chapter when Susan, tearing sheets off the calendar, " 'screwed them up so that they no longer exist, save as a weight in my side' " (p. 38). The hardness of the emotion reappears in subsequent pages in connection with Susan as " 'something hard' " (p. 39), " 'some hard thing' " (p. 71), " 'my hardness' " (p. 153). Neville, speaking to Susan, says " 'love makes knots . . . I have been knotted' " (p. 152). The memory which began as one of *cause* (Susan's jealousy of Jinny kissing Louis) has now changed to one of *effect*—the "weight" or "knot" of "hardness" in her side (i.e., her heart)—and thus conveys the passage of time. From this central matrix of emotion other images radiate; the "nails" which clenched the pocket-handkerchief and suggest a crucifixion image appear in the first chapter in another phrase spoken by Bernard about himself and Susan fleeing the gardeners: " 'We should be nailed like stoats to the stable door' " (p. 12). In the farewell dinner for Percival, this nailed-to-the-door image appears in Louis' thoughts of Susan: " 'To be loved by Susan would be . . . to be nailed to a barnyard door' " (p. 86). There it conveys in a different way the force of Susan's emotion. This image is used twice in the same paragraph.[45] When the original childhood memory is later recalled by Susan— " 'we should be shot and nailed like stoats to the wall' " (p. 137)—it draws strength from the original nails-in-the-pocket-handkerchief image and Louis' subsequent feelings about her. The final variation (again revealing the effect of Susan's emotions on someone else and so changing our

[45] The paragraph which follows, still spoken by Louis, connects the nail-crucifixion image to Rhoda in the word "torture"; she pursues a "tortuous course" and it "tortured" by the cruelty of her friends. Susan's "square-tipped finger-nails" appear two paragraphs later.

apprehension of the original memory) occurs in the last chapter when Bernard, remembering his initial encounter with the weeping Susan, says that " 'her wet pocket-handkerchief . . . screwed my nerves up' " (p. 170). Changed, enlarged, and given new meanings through intervening experience, the image-memory is embedded in an ever-expanding matrix of emotion, with its linking threads. As we ourselves are involved with memories clinging to different aspects of our self, so in *The Waves* we become (as does Bernard himself in the final chapter) the repository of collective memory, looking back over the past with its lived connections.

This is only one illustration of the metamorphosis, growth, and change of a memory-image in *The Waves*; the entire novel is structured on just such image-symbols which enlarge into complex and intersecting matrices. The reader at the beginning of the novel is presented with the key images or motifs which will be used as memory stimuli. As the opening scene progresses, the images assume variations, and leitmotif is added to symbol. The " 'fling of seed' " mentioned by Rhoda will become a leitmotif of Bernard. The image of bubbles rising in a saucepan shifts from Jinny to Bernard in later chapters and assumes a host of meanings.[46] As the subsequent chapters progress, each with a formal recapitulation of memory at the chapter's opening, the sense of time's passage is evoked through variation of the image by word or meaning. A physical stimulus becomes an intellectualization (image of the sponge, p. 89), and we know that the child has become a man. The maggot runs in and out of philosophers' skulls instead of leaves (p. 51). The flowers that adolescent

---

[46] " 'Up they bubble—images' " (p. 27; varied pp. 35 and 61). Connected with "linked phrases" (p. 35), they later become "phrases," "faces," "words," and finally " 'the crystal, the globe of life' " with " 'walls of thinnest air . . . the walls of my bubble' " (p. 182).

Rhoda wishes to bind for someone (p. 41) are later flung into the river as an offering to Percival (p. 117). Echoing sometimes the exact tone of the scene's emotion, sometimes a similar yet changed feeling, these shifting images give a sense not only of time's passage but of its cyclical actions and occurrences—*the thing repeating but never quite the same*, a variation in feeling which conveys the sequence and movement of hours, days, and years. Both *The Waves* and *The Years* are filled with these echoes—a sense of *déjà vu*, which is certainly one of the most difficult phenomena to portray.

> Does everything then come over again a little differently? she thought. If so, is there a pattern; a theme, recurring, like music; half remembered, half foreseen?
> . . . a gigantic pattern, momentarily perceptible?

This passage could be spoken by Bernard of *The Waves* in regard to the three dinner scenes[47] in the novel which, seeking to explain the present in terms of past memories, exhibit a repetition and variation of the same experience. It belongs, however, to Eleanor Pargiter of *The Years* (p. 398). The two novels use the same modes of memory: the stimuli which call up individual recollections, the leitmotif, repetition, refrain, and hiatus which indicate a sense of the passage of time and the cyclical rhythm of experience. *The Years*, however, presents the modes with greater clarity. It is as if Mrs. Woolf, discouraged by the

[47] There are two actual dinner scenes, the dinner for Percival in Section IV and the recapitulation of that dinner some years later at Hampton Court in Section VIII. The third is what Mrs. Woolf termed "the phantom dinner party" in the final chapter when Bernard, eating alone, recalls the past gatherings of the six characters. *Small Waves Notebook* (1930-31).

170

bewilderment with which *The Waves* had been received, decided to show the mental operation of memory and time in a more simplified manner.

The most obvious difference between the two novels is that *The Years* appears to be lifted from the submerged world of *The Waves* into the sunlit atmosphere of the conscious. It seems a novel of fact, a family chronicle concerned with the Pargiters and their professions from "1880" until "Present Day." Yet if we examine the novel carefully, we see that the surface events are only part of *The Years*, just as the calendar is only a visible or social recording of lived time. Diary entries during the novel's genesis point to Mrs. Woolf's concern with the "external and internal," the "I and the not I," the "outer and the inner," and "layers" or "strata of being" which seem to be developed into "upper air scenes" or "submerged" ones.[48] It is more helpful, however, since we are discussing *The Years* from the viewpoint of the mnemonic mode, to see these opposites as the "hidden" or "unconscious" and the "surface" or "conscious." What is "surface" consists of everyday events; what is "unconscious" is the world of memory comprising those events which are constantly called up through the novel so that, through their repetition and variation, we get the same sense of perspective of the past which was presented in a less clarified manner in *The Waves*. The novel's long opening section, "1880," is, significantly, childhood at Abercorn Terrace. The following shorter chapters, composed of eight random years end-

[48] Diary entries of January 11, 1935; November 18, 1935; November 1, 1934 and October 16, 1935; June 13 and November 21, 1935. The different "layers" or "strata" Mrs. Woolf refers to seem to be scenes which echo different levels of consciousness, some of which are placed literally in the open air or in basements. An example of the latter is the air-raid-shelter scene in which the submerged emotions of Nicholas, Sara, and Renny are suggested. As the scene moves upstairs after the raid is over, we learn that Nicholas cannot love women, and so an area of repressed or tabooed emotion is brought to light. *Years*, pp. 311-24.

171

ing with 1918, recapitulate and add glosses to those early years which underlie the novel like the sound of the wood pigeons ("Take two coos, Taffy. Take two coos."), a leitmotif whose "interrupted lullaby" constantly reminds the reader of the Pargiters' childhood. The final chapter, "Present Day," which Mrs. Woolf noted in her diary must give the "submerged side" of the opening one,[49] is the longest of them all. The moment of *now* is expanded; the years between, and especially those of childhood, rise to the surface.[50] As the various leitmotifs are repeated,[51] and familiar sounds and gestures echoed, the reader experiences, almost as in a dream, the separate moments of the past which converge in the present reality.

A less complex use of leitmotif, as well as a continual employment of repetition, rhyme, and refrain throughout the novel, is another way in which Mrs. Woolf seems to have simplified and "pointed" her method of *The Waves*.[52] The leitmotif, rather than sounding merely the emotional "tone" of a particular character or situation,[53] revives a

[49] May 22, 1934. Pp. 45-46 of *The Years* repeat the phrase "suppressed emotion." In the final chapter (p. 450) Delia reveals that Abercorn Terrace had been "Hell." The reader's memories of the suppressed emotions of the opening chapter are reactivated and seen in a different light.

[50] Eleanor illustrates this surfacing of the past by thinking about Nicholas (i.e., reviving memories). Nicholas then walks in (i.e., memory becomes reality). " 'Just as I was thinking of you!' she repeated. Indeed it was like a part of her, a sunk part of her, coming to the surface" (p. 396).

[51] Specifically, those of "Red Rose, thorny Rose" and "Pargiter of Pargiter's Horse"; recurring motifs such as the *Antigone*, the "ink-corroded walrus," the Colonel's missing fingers; and phrases such as "a ripple of some disagreeable sensation went across his back as if a knife had sliced it," recalling similar sensations felt earlier by other characters (pp. 456-57; see also 321, 356, 362, and 437).

[52] As she was revising *The Years*, Mrs. Woolf noted in her diary: "I must still condense and point: give pauses their effect, and repetitions" (December 29, 1935).

[53] Mrs. Woolf appears to have followed Thomas Mann's use of leitmotif, especially that in "Tonio Kroeger," in which time past continually impinges upon time present. The phrase Delia repeats

matrix of memory embedded in childhood but bearing on the present moment. These leitmotifs are frequently enclosed in quotation marks as if they were parts of songs (some are, such as "Sur le Pont d'Avignon," whose "Ron ron ron et plon plon plon" calls up an unpleasant childish memory of a slimy piece of flannel),[54] emphasizing the fact that memory is a concrete "duration," by symbolizing it as a unit of music, or "heard time."[55] A similar function is served by repetition, rhyme, and refrain, which again act as units of "heard time" and transmit not only the virtual experience of the lived moment but the sense of time's transience, growth, and cyclic recurrence. All through the novel, spoken sentences and thoughts are repeated (Eleanor observes that "words went on repeating themselves in her mind—words and sights," p. 30); sometimes the repetitions pass from one character to another, so that additional movement is conveyed:

"Where am I?" she [Mrs Pargiter] cried. She was frightened and bewildered, as she often was on waking. She raised her hand; she seemed to appeal for help. "Where am I?" she repeated. For a moment Delia was bewildered too. Where was she?

---

in the opening of *The Years* (p. 22), "the man in the frock-coat with the flower in his buttonhole," recalls the leitmotif connected with Tonio Kroeger's father, "the tall, thoughtful man with the wildflower in his buttonhole."

[54] Other parts of songs include " 'Brandishing, flourishing my sword in my hand' " (p. 200), the words of "some pompous eighteenth century march," which is connected thematically with the leitmotif "Pargiter of Pargiter's Horse," " 'Count your blessings' " (p. 8), " 'This broken glass, this faded heart' " (p. 145). Street singers, barrel organ players, and trombone players add musical sounds throughout the book.

[55] The relation of music, or "heard time," to "pure duration" is discussed by Susanne K. Langer in *Feeling and Form*, pp. 112-29, and explains to a great extent the psychological novel's use of musical techniques to transmit the experience of the *lived time* so much a part of subjective reality.

"Here, Mama! Here!" she said wildly. "Here, in your own room."

She laid her hand on the counterpane. Mrs Pargiter clutched it nervously. She looked round the room as if she were seeking someone. She did not seem to recognize her daughter.

"What's happening?" she said. "Where am I?"[56]

In addition to such doublets, Mrs. Woolf also uses "triplets"—consisting of one- or two-syllable words struck, like tympani, three times: " 'Spoons! spoons! spoons!' "; "Hammer, hammer, hammer"—to transmit not only the pure emotional sense of "cry" referred to in the last chapter, but also progression and intensity. The startling incantatory effect of these several time-devices used together can be seen in the following passage:

"Maggie!" he exclaimed, pulling himself up. It was she who was sitting there, putting flowers into water. "Yes, it's Maggie's turn to speak," said Nicholas, putting his hand on her knee.

"Speak, speak!" Renny urged her.

But she shook her head. Laughter took her and shook her. She laughed, throwing her head back as if she were possessed by some genial spirit outside herself that made her bend and rise, as a tree, North thought, is tossed and bent by the wind. No idols, no idols, no idols, her laughter seemed to chime as if the tree were hung with innumerable bells, and he laughed too.

(p. 458)

[56] *Years*, p. 23. This technique is repeated over and over: " 'Captain Pargiter,' said North, touching his tie. 'And Captain Pargiter!' the maid called out." Or: " 'Your life,' said Sara. 'My life?' Eleanor repeated." The "doublets" frequently appear closer together. " 'Come along!' he said. 'Come along . . .' "; or " 'Don't mind it, don't mind it.' " In the novel's final section this technique appears exaggerated as if to show not only the way in which old people repeat themselves (the party is a gathering of "the old brothers and sisters") but the cyclic quality of experience as well.

Coming as this passage does in the center of Delia's party, at which the original generation of 1880 are present, the repetitions and variations, especially the word "idols," set up a vibration in which the very memories of the Pargiter clan seem to hang, simultaneously, in the air. The rhyme (took-shook) and the half-rhyme (idols-bells) express the sense of things repeating in variation[57]—just as certain figures reappear, slightly changed, throughout the novel (like the man in the "gold lace")[58]—and again suggest the quality of growth or accretion of memory.

A final way in which repetition stresses the quality of lived time is through the words or sentences which not only thread a scene together, giving the sense of a single duration (as the way "spoons," sounded at the opening of Delia's supper, unifies the sequence, pp. 428ff.), but also link one duration with another. In the first half of the opening chapter of *The Years*, for example, more than twenty-seven words and phrases are repeated, reappearing in the same or in a subsequent scene and giving the brief and seemingly random episodes the quality of connected experience.[59]

[57] Occasionally the rhyme carries one back to the nonsense rhymes of childhood, as on p. 410:

"I know," he said, stiffening the muscles of his face, "I'm like the picture of a Frenchman holding his hat."
"Holding his hat?" she asked.
"And getting fat," he added.

". . . Holding a hat . . . who's holding a hat?" said Eleanor, opening her eyes. . . .
"What nonsense are you talking?" she said. "North's not holding a hat! And he's not fat," she added.
[58] *Years*, p. 148. He reappears in a "gold coat," p. 182, and in "gold lace, with a star," p. 269. There is also a woman who eats ices, and various figures who gesture with sword, pistol, knife, or hand.
[59] These include the question "Where am I?"; the Colonel's fumbling hand with its missing fingers; the falling rain; "It's come," "I saw," etc. As noted in an earlier footnote, these motifs reappear in the final chapter and at other points in the novel.

A different technique of time (one also used in music), that of *hiatus*, gives not the connection but the gap between the episodes, each of which represents a distinct duration with its own emotional values. These gaps between episodes and chapters (in the sweep of the entire novel whole blocks of years are omitted) are also suggestive of the blanking-out of some events in the memory and the enduring vividness of others. Entire parts of life can disappear from view, like the Colonel's missing fingers.

This dramatization of the hidden, the repressed, the concealed—in order to show how the unconscious underlies the conscious and interfuses with it at every point[60]—is the third way in which Mrs. Woolf has simplified her method in *The Years*. The manner in which memory activates subterranean emotions was seen as one of the themes of *The Waves*, but it was nowhere given the sharp symbolization that Virginia Woolf achieves in the later novel. The Colonel's hidden mistress, the sexual pervert at the pillar-box, the wires and drains beneath church towers, the view of people from basement windows, the inability of the child Rose to communicate her hidden terror, the image of Antigone in her brick vault, North's question "Why do we hide all the things that matter?"[61]—all of these images and more, many of them repeated and varied throughout the novel, suggest that the most important part of our lives lies concealed in hidden memory and the un-

[60] "Who was it who said through the unconscious one comes to the conscious, and then again to the unconscious?" *Diary*, February 27, 1935. Mrs. Woolf was then rewriting *The Pargiters* (original title of *The Years*).

[61] For the image of drains beneath church towers, see *The Years*, pp. 107-108; view from basement, p. 311 and my Chapter VI, i; North's question, p. 445. The Antigone theme, introduced on p. 54, is elaborated on pp. 145-46 when Sara reads the *Antigone* which Edward has translated into English and then goes to sleep in "cold smooth sheets" and blanket "fitted softly round her" as the brick tomb around Antigone. Later references to "cubicles" and "cripples in a cave" (pp. 319-20) reinforce the image.

conscious. Hidden within us is all of time past, repressed for the large part,[62] yet called up at odd moments by a fume of wine, a word, a childhood song. It can here be noted again that Mrs. Woolf emphasizes infantile memories,[63] especially the childhood traumas which emotionally warp and cripple the character. The leitmotifs associated with Rose and her cousin Sara plunge back to childhood experience. Rose, who becomes a martyr for women's rights and never marries (her leitmotif changes from the masculine-toned motif of "Red rose, tawny rose . . . wild Rose, thorny rose" to "Rose of the flaming heart; Rose of the burning breast; Rose of the weary world," recalling Crashaw's poem to the martyred St. Theresa), has been emotionally maimed by her nurse's neglect: she has been allowed to go out alone at night and encounters a sexual pervert. The horrors of the encounter at the "pillar-box," and their subsequent effect on Rose, are recalled through this leitmotif and an associated one, "Pargiter of Pargiter's Horse."[64] Rose's cousin, Sara Pargiter, an invalid, who

---

[62] Freud, *New Introductory Lectures* (XXII), p. 74.

[63] Cf. the opening of the final section of *The Waves* (p. 169): "'In the beginning, there was the nursery, with windows opening on to a garden, and beyond that the sea.'" Jean Guiguet notes that "everything came from there, as from the Word, everything is rooted there, everything will return there." *Virginia Woolf*, p. 294.

[64] The motif of the *rose*, which runs through the book, is centered first in the theme of roses fading (brevity of life) connected with the death of the mother, Rose Pargiter senior; her red-haired portrait, with a basket of flowers in her lap, dominates the Pargiter living room. "I don't like to see your roses fade," her mother says to Kitty (also red-haired) just after Mrs. Pargiter dies. The second red-haired Rose, Rose Pargiter junior, is introduced with a song hummed by Sara (p. 175), "'Go search the valleys, pluck up every rose,'" which then concentrates on Rose herself, "'Red hair; red Rose'" (p. 177). The leitmotif variations, including "thorny Rose" and "spiky Rose," suggest the masculine drives which have pushed her to women's rights. Another variation, "brave Rose" (p. 453), links this aspect of Rose to the childhood encounter with the pervert, in which she bravely crossed the deserted streets to Lamley's store on a "desperate mission" to a besieged garrison to which she is carrying "a secret message."

177

THREE MODES OF TIME

becomes the Antigone of the book, entombed in her brick
house, is physically crippled as a result of having been
dropped by her parents as a child. Under the surface of
the outward actions of the novel lie the crippling horrors
of the past, entombed in memory.

A final symbolic image of memory and the unconscious
unfolds in the Round Pond scene (pp. 261-67) in a sequence which could be a rendering of a hypnagogic state.
The "round" pond itself is suggestive of sleep, the unconscious, the infant primordial world. Martin and Sara have
met Maggie there with her baby; the baby sleeps, then Sara
sleeps. The sounds of clocks striking, images of shut eyes,
the pond itself, and low voices, lull the reader. The voices
are those of memory; Martin talks to Maggie of the past
in low tones so as not to waken the sleepers. The manipula-
tion of time in the scene, with the suggestion of the no-
time of sleep and the unconscious, gives it an extraordinary dimension.[65] Martin tells of his father's mistress; we
see the novel's opening scene through a different lens; the
initial scene revives, yet changed. Martin's story of his own

---

(The "secret message" of the encounter remains secret—she is
never able to tell Eleanor about it.) Pretending to hold a pistol, she
claps imaginary spurs to her mount: " 'I am Pargiter of Pargiter's
Horse,' she said, flourishing her hand, 'riding to the rescue' " (p.
27). The luncheon scene with Sara and Maggie (pp. 177-82)
revives the scene with its images of spurs and horse. "Flourishing
the arm that held the pistol" (p. 28) is varied in the scene from
the opera *Siegfried* in which Siegfried "brandished the sword
over his head" (p. 199). On the next page Sara sings "the words
of some pompous eighteenth century march"; " 'Brandishing,
flourishing my sword in my hand' " (Sara has just been out with
Rose). On p. 449, in the final party scene, the reader learns that
there was a real "Pargiter of Pargiter's Horse"—an old uncle
who was a military man of whom Rose is the "very spit and
image." During the scene, Rose holds a knife erect (p. 449) and
brandishes it in someone's face. The "Pargiter's Horse" refrain
is repeated on p. 453.

[65] Cf. North's long hypnagogic reverie at the party in the
novel's final section (pp. 457-58) when he is drowsy with wine.

mistress adds a parallel scene which is grafted onto the original memory and adds still another perspective. In this small, quiet microcosm Mrs. Woolf has evoked the movement of the larger mnemonic modalities of the entire novel.

CHAPTER ELEVEN

The Shapes of Feeling

THE FINAL classification of subjective modes are those pictorial means of presenting emotion: image, metaphor, and symbol. They may be termed the "primitive" modes because the processes which convert feeling into image are generally considered to precede those of conceptual thought. They are also primitive in that they tend to explore basic instinctual areas—the suppressed regions of drives and desires which motivate thought and action. Reproducing the operation of the dreaming mind, which translates emotion directly into image, the primitive modes are able to compress vast areas of feeling, to suggest latent aspects of experience, and so form the psychological novelist's most graphic way of showing emotional reality. Because their meaning lies very close to the unconscious, and because a particular image or symbol may vary in meaning for the individual, they are of all the subjective modes the least susceptible to analysis.

Yet if we ignore their function in Virginia Woolf's novels, we are in danger of classing Mrs. Woolf as a mere impressionist who found it easier to work in pictures than through action. However we understand and respond to them, her images are not lyric excesses but rather units of subjectivity which she exploits deliberately for their emotional values and whose many modes of operation—abstraction and concretization, expansion and contraction, metamorphosis or transformation, and compression—she appears to have recognized. Indeed, three of her novels, *To the Lighthouse*, *Orlando*, and *The Waves*—the last novel

180

forming the climax of her concern with aspects of the creative mind—reveal her specific understanding of the workings of the primitive modes, and from them may be drawn conclusions regarding the principles which underlie her use of image. These principles are more complex than those of the modes of time, for they are involved in the very processes of perception and of thought. Furthermore, their functions appear to be governed by obscure urges—by human needs for energy, for relief of anxiety, for adaption to reality—all of which Virginia Woolf seems to have understood. Of these particular needs we can offer only a suggestion. It is the processes themselves (some of which parallel principles governing other modes of subjectivity) with which we are most concerned, for it is through them that we feel, see, and experience our relation to the world and self.

Our first consideration is the principle alluded to in Chapters V and VII on "seeing the object" and on "reflection": that we use image, i.e., the object, to explain and translate our feelings. In other words, the external world acts as metaphor for us: our feelings are "like" something, and we use an image as their objective correlative. Thus the external world—at least that external world of Virginia Woolf's novels—becomes *the medium through which we experience reality, rather than the reality itself*. It is for this reason that the primitive modes are so important, for they form the link between outer and inner so necessary to our visually-oriented thinking.

Let us see Mrs. Woolf's apprehension of how image "works" as shown in a particular passage from *To the Lighthouse*. In Section 8 of the final part James is sitting at the boat's tiller in a calm; old antagonisms stir in him. If his father were, at that moment, to "demand . . . something quite unreasonable," James thought he would "take a knife and strike him to the heart" (p. 282). At this point, while James sits "staring at his father in an impotent rage," he thinks about "this old symbol" of taking a knife. But it is not his father, he realizes, that he wishes to destroy; it is something else which he cannot name but which he visualizes (i.e., concretizes into an image) as "that fierce sudden black-winged harpy, with its talons and its beak all cold and hard, that struck and struck at you." He can still "feel the beak on his bare legs." What, he asks himself, after more analysis, "was this terror, this hatred?" And he looks for an image to translate this inner reality.

> Turning back among the many leaves which the past had folded in him, peering into the heart of that forest . . . , *he sought an image to cool and detach and round off his feeling in a concrete shape.* Suppose then that as a child sitting helpless in a perambulator, or on someone's knee, he had seen a waggon crush ignorantly and innocently, someone's foot? Suppose he had seen the foot first, in the grass, smooth, and whole; then the wheel; and the same foot, purple, crushed. But the wheel was innocent. So now, when his father came striding down the passage knocking them up early in the morning to go to the Lighthouse down it came over his foot. . . .[1]

As James searches for the specific memory from which this image sprang, he goes back to his childhood (perhaps to the scene on pages 61-63 where his father stands by his mother, "demanding sympathy" and disturbing the "perfect simplicity and good sense of his relations with his mother"):

> It was in this world that the wheel went over the person's foot. Something, he remembered, stayed and darkened over him; would not move; something flourished

[1] P. 284. Italics mine.

182

up in the air, something arid and sharp descended even there, like a blade, a scimitar, smiting through the leaves and flowers even of that happy world and making them shrivel and fall.　　　　　(p. 285)

The central image we are concerned with here is that of the wheel going over the foot, the image with which James "cools" and "detaches" his emotion, thus relieving himself of the anxiety which his father's presence raised in him.[2] Something of this relief is passed on to the reader. Meanwhile, we have seen the shape of the emotion. The violence of the image, however, has been carefully prepared for by the preceding pictures of James attacking his father with a knife and of the black-winged harpy. It has been further prepared for long before by the way in which James, as a little boy, felt "crushed" when his father announced bad weather and postponement of the trip to the lighthouse.

James's hatred for his father, his dislike of his father's unreasonable—crushing—ways, is compressed and concretized in the image of the wheel. This is what might be termed the manifest meaning[3] of the image, every facet of which has been explicitly given us by Virginia Woolf. But is there not "something beneath the surface, something left unsaid for us to find out for ourselves and think over"?[4] James's little reverie is very like a dream: it shows the process of *displacement*, a shifting or distortion of the

[2] The image externalizes and objectifies the emotion, thus enabling James to deal with it. See Simon Lesser's description of how the "language of fiction" serves a parallel purpose in "distancing" and "objectifying" the reader's own inner anxieties. *Fiction and the Unconscious*, pp. 150-52.

[3] Freud terms the "collection of sensory images and visual scenes" which appear in the dream "manifest" images. The hidden or "latent" dream-thoughts which produced them have been disguised and distorted by the "censor" into an acceptable image. *New Introductory Lectures* (XXII), p. 20.

[4] "Life and the Novelist" (*G.R.*), *Essays*, II, p. 135.

THE SHAPES OF FEELING

image for reasons of censorship.[5] Its latent meaning is likewise disguised by the censor. Here, in James's reverie, Mrs. Woolf seems to imply a hidden meaning with a cluster of what might be called parallel images which precede and follow the wheel image: the harpy with "its beak all cold and hard," the "arid . . . blade," the "scimitar," which, "smiting through the leaves and flowers," made them "shrivel and fall." Added to these images are James's manifest feelings of the way rage makes for impotence. In the boat, he is "in an impotent rage." He remembers himself as a child sitting on the floor, "impotent, ridiculous" (p. 287) after the scene with his father.

Whatever the reader's reactions may be to these private symbols, he is made to feel the surge of violent emotion in James and to know its genesis. James himself is aware of nothing beyond his hatred, nothing beyond the childhood experiences of the crushing absolutism of his father. But the reader has been made conscious of the depth of the feeling aroused in James by his father—a very complex relationship which Mrs. Woolf has conveyed with a minimum of space. "The writer's task is to take one thing and let it stand for twenty," she wrote.[6] Virginia Woolf's careful preparation of the image, seeding along its path the associative meanings which make it take root and grow in the reader's mind, ensures an apprehension of the basic emotional experiences of her characters.

This illustration from *To the Lighthouse* tells us a number of things about Virginia Woolf's use of image, metaphor, and symbol. It shows her principle of enriching and *expanding* the symbol (or image), building it up until its full energy potential is reached and it can stand not merely for a state of mind at a single moment but for a lifetime of psychic states. It tells how she *intensifies* the emotion

[5] *New Introductory Lectures* (XXII), pp. 20-21.
[6] "Life and the Novelist" (*G.R.*), *Essays*, II, p. 135.

184

(or energy) of the image through the dynamism of *motion* or action (i.e., the wheel moving over the foot and crushing it).[7] It shows her use of the principle of *compression* or *condensation*, the forcing of a powerful image or complex of images into a single phrase. It exhibits her attention to the *latent* meaning of an image (however personal that meaning may have been for Mrs. Woolf herself) so that the reader's mind can toy with it on two levels—that of the known, and that of the subliminal or unknown. And, finally, it points to the first of the basic principles of image, one which works in dreams as well as in conscious thought: that of presenting an abstract idea or feeling in a concrete shape. We call this *concretization*.

THE PRINCIPLE behind the process of *concretization* has been suggested earlier: a complex of emotions is externalized ("cooled" and "detached," to use James's words) into a transfiguring image. Thus, in the third part of *To the Lighthouse*, Lily Briscoe, trying to make conversation with Mr. Ramsay, praises his "beautiful boots" and finds him at last responsive. "They had reached, she felt, a sunny island where peace dwelt, sanity reigned and the sun for ever shone, the blessed isle of good boots" (p. 238). Here, the meaning of the metaphor of "the blessed isle of

---

[7] In experiments in parapsychology, it has been found that a moving image is more easily transferred from one person's mind to another's than a static one. Some examples of Virginia Woolf's use of motion in an image are: "Her sympathy seemed to fly back in her face, like a bramble sprung" (*Lighthouse*, p. 242); "Had he been a horse, the thin brown skin would have twitched, as if a fly had settled" (*Acts*, p. 70); the "brandishing of silver-flashing plumes like pampas grass in a tropic gale in her breast" (*Dalloway*, p. 52). Since motion is part of perception and of the moment of being, image is more easily visualized and emotion felt through its use.

good boots" has been practically explained beforehand. The reader has been crossing, with Lily, the barren seas of conversation; the relief of communication, of finding a sympathetic topic of talk, is implicit in the metaphor. The reader's experience is made richer by the concretization of Lily's desperate feeling and her final emotion of relief.

Both these images—or, more properly, metaphors—from *To the Lighthouse* appear to extract the *essence* of a complex emotional state. A similar effect is achieved through the metaphoric mode of *abstraction*, which likewise reduces a welter of sensory and mental stimuli into a clearly drawn image. But where concretization compresses emotion into a picture which may be taken literally as well as symbolically, abstraction gives us merely a hint of the meaning behind the shape. The "doodlings" of dots and flames in *Night and Day*, for example, are the correlatives of Ralph's "confused and emotional moments" (p. 522).[8] In *The Voyage Out*, the muddle of Rachel's rather adolescent mind is glimpsed in her attempt to see the world "as composed entirely of vast blocks of matter" and people as "patches of light" like "soft spots of sun"—a conversion of bewildering mental stimuli into pleasing and simple abstract shapes (p. 358). *To the Lighthouse*, however, offers us the best illustration of the abstractive process, for in it Virginia Woolf shows us, through Lily Briscoe's "painter's vision," how complex interrelationships and emotions may be expressed in geometric form.

Three particular moments serve to explain this principle which works in metaphor as it does in abstract art. In the canvas Lily is painting of the island house, with Mrs. Ramsay reading to James in the window, she uses a "triangular purple shape" which, "without irreverence," reduces the mother-child relationship to a shape we intuitively

[8] See my Chapter IV, iii.

understand.[9] When she simplifies Mr. Ramsay's philosophy into a "phantom kitchen table" which she then places upside down in the pear tree,[10] Lily reflects on "this seeing of angular essences, this reducing of lovely evenings . . . to a white deal four-legged table" (p. 41). In the last part of the novel, trying to reconstruct her memory of Mrs. Ramsay, she calls out to "that essence which sat by the boat, that abstract one made of her, that woman in grey" (p. 275).

These three abstracts, or "essences," are conceptual as well as visual. Sir Herbert Read, commenting on the word "abstract" as related to abstract art, noted that the abstract shape "drawn from the particular concrete object in front of the artist" forms "an *essence* . . . nearer to the truth than any mechanical representation of its appearance" and cited Kandinsky's feeling that the aim of these "precise forms" (abstract shapes) is to "express an inner emotional state— to find satisfaction for vague feelings."[11] *Essence*, if we pursue its dictionary meaning, is a "distillation," or, in philosophical terms, a permanent substance underlying "all outward manifestations."[12] The triangle, the table, the abstract of Mrs. Ramsay—all distill felt emotion. Lily, thinking later of "the scrubbed kitchen table," calls it a "symbol of her profound respect for Mr. Ramsay's mind" (p. 43), and so confirms the emotional quality of this abstraction. Farther on, in *The Waves*, Mrs. Woolf would use the image of "the square . . . upon the oblong" to illustrate the second aspect of essence as inner reality. Rhoda, listening to Mozart's music, strives to sort out and reduce the conflicting emotions created by Percival's death. Using

[9] Pp. 84-85. The triangle may symbolically include the father, Mr. Ramsay.

[10] Part of this image, in Lily Briscoe's thoughts, is quoted here in Chapter IV, i.

[11] Herbert Read, *Selected Writings* (New York, 1964), p. 285.

[12] *Webster's New Collegiate Dictionary*, 2nd edn.

images from the mythic transcription of the dinner for Percival (see Chapter VIII, iv), images of sacrifice and violence, she presents the shapes of memory, music, and emotion:

> " 'Like' and 'like' and 'like'—but what is the thing that lies beneath the semblance of the thing? Now that lightning has gashed the tree and the flowering branch has fallen and Percival, by his death, has made me this gift, let me see the thing. There is a square; there is an oblong. The players take the square and place it upon the oblong. They place it very accurately; they make a perfect dwelling-place. Very little is left outside. The structure is now visible; what is inchoate is here stated; we are not so various or so mean; we have made oblongs and stood them upon squares. This is our triumph; this is our consolation."　　　　　　　(p. 116)

It is concretization, however, with its hidden and overt meanings, which Virginia Woolf uses most often to hollow out the "caves of feeling" behind her characters, to show the submerged emotions which wrack and haunt them. And the images conveyed, to allow for a preparation and expansion of the symbol, tend to be generalized. Of De Quincey's writing she notes that his "power lay in suggesting large and generalized visions; landscapes in which nothing is seen in detail; faces without features; the stillness of midnight or summer . . . anguish that for ever falls and rises and casts its arms upwards in despair."[13]

Parenthetically, we might note that here Virginia Woolf almost seems to be describing her own use of image, especially in *Mrs. Dalloway* and *The Waves*. The pictures given are mere outlines;[14] we fill in the details, the

[13] See my Chapter VI, iii. "De Quincey's Autobiography" (*C.R.II*), *Essays*, IV, p. 3.
[14] The new novel, Mrs. Woolf writes in "The Narrow Bridge of Art," "will give, as poetry does, the outline rather than the detail.

features of the faces Mrs. Woolf never describes for us. Given the shape only, we are unhindered by externality; the object becomes more easily the envelope of our own subjective feelings. Two other ways in which "generalization" contributes to emotion might be mentioned. It suggests the vagueness of the dream-state, in which we see concrete forms thrown up from the unconscious and in which images carry not their overt meanings but deeper, hidden ones.[15] And it allows symbolism itself a freer play. All of Virginia Woolf's images may be said, in this sense, to be symbolic. The distant figure of the lighthouse, Rhoda's broken column, Jacob's slippers "like boats burnt to the water's rim,"[16] Orlando's oak tree, the great carp in Lucy Swithin's pool—none of these have a specific meaning to which we can point. They are bound up with the character's emotions and become a mode of explaining them. In *Orlando*, the same idea is stated in a reverse manner. Orlando finds the emotion of love "cumbered" with the objects which translate it "like the lump of glass which, after a year at the bottom of the sea, is grown about with bones and dragon-flies, and coins and the tresses of drowned women."[17]

However generalized the image, Virginia Woolf tends to make it specific with supporting symbols and metaphors.

It will make little use of the marvelous fact-recording power . . . of fiction." (*G.R.*), *Essays*, II, pp. 224-25.

[15] The passages to which Mrs. Woolf refers in the essay on De Quincey are those which describe visions and dreams.

[16] There is something extraordinarily moving about this image (*Jacob's Room*, p. 37). Energy is, of course, roused by the picture of boats burning which is linked with our own memories of conflagration and war. But beyond this, the emotion utterly eludes analysis.

[17] P. 94. Cf. the passage from De Quincey which Mrs. Woolf quotes: " 'Far more of our deepest thoughts and feelings pass to us through perplexed combinations of *concrete* objects . . . than ever reach us *directly* and in their own abstract shapes.' " "De Quincey's Autobiography" (*C.R.II*), *Essays*, IV, p. 6.

Clarissa Dalloway, just before her party, "felt herself a stake driven in at the top of her stairs" (p. 187). Three pages earlier, specific allusions to martyrdom, self-pity, self-punishment, and guilt are given: "Why seek pinnacles and stand drenched in fire? Might it consume her anyhow! Burn her to cinders!" With the image of the stake, the two passages connect and the emotion becomes clear. Similiar feelings contribute to the elaborate image of the monster in the forest which embodies Clarissa's feelings for Doris Kilman:

> It rasped her, though, to have stirring about in her this brutal monster! to hear twigs cracking and feel hooves planted down in the depths of that leaf-encumbered forest, the soul; never to be content quite, or quite secure, for at any moment the brute would be stirring, this hatred, which, especially since her illness, had power to make her feel scraped, hurt in her spine; gave her physical pain, and made all pleasure in beauty, in friendship, in being well, in being loved and making her home delightful, rock, quiver, and bend as if indeed there were a monster grubbing at the roots, as if the whole panoply of content were nothing but self love! this hatred!
>
> (p. 15)

Here, the image is expanded; we sense every reverberation of the emotion, as Mrs. Woolf moves the image here and there with action words so that its ambiguities can be felt. Part of its power, however, comes from the sheer strength of the animal image itself, and a glance through Virginia Woolf's work reveals many such images. Love may be a moon rising at Bourton, but more often it is a "great fish" which hooks man, a bird of paradise or a "dung-bedraggled fowl." Fear is a "dumb creature" which gallops to the end of a field. Sexual challenge changes Clarissa and Peter into two horses who "paw the ground" and "toss their heads" before a battle. Emotional triumph over conflicting elements is a mermaid, as Rachel swims about a room to escape Terence, or Clarissa, wearing a "silver-green mermaid's dress," is "lolloping on the waves" of her party's success.[18]

The latter images use the metaphoric mode which I have termed *metamorphosis* or transformation—the concretization of an emotion in an animal, vegetable, or mineral form. A metaphor in action, metamorphosis expresses a sudden psychic state or change of states, as Ovid's *Metamorphoses* pictures through the outer transformations of people the emotional changes within them. Of these transformation metaphors, the animal is the most vivid, both for its shock content and for the deeper levels of instinct which it may touch in us. *Mrs. Dalloway*, with its emphasis on deep unformulated emotions, has, as we have seen, a large share of these images; so has *The Waves*. The best novel in which to observe the principles of transformation, however, is *Orlando*, which overtly shows us every aspect of this mode—not only in metaphor but also in larger symbolic metamorphoses such as those of the Great Frost scene, Orlando's sexual change, or the transformations accompanying each "spirit of the age." Symbols themselves undergo subtle transformations to suggest linked emotional influences and urges. For example, the wild goose which springs up at the end of *Orlando* with Shelmerdine's arrival—almost as if it were an aspect of Shelmerdine himself—has been connected with Shakespeare and Orlando's search for poetry (pp. 281-82). It is also related to the "steel blue feather" of Shelmerdine's name, to the rook feathers on the moor before Shelmerdine's appearance (p. 223), to the "old

[18] *Dalloway*, p. 53; *Orlando*, p. 50 (cf. the image in *Jacob's Room*, p. 149: "the hook gave a great tug in his side"); *Orlando*, p. 109; *Dalloway*, p. 146; *ibid.*, p. 50; *Voyage*, p. 365; *Dalloway*, p. 191.

stained goose quill" with which Orlando writes his first poetry (p. 18) in imitation of his boyhood glimpse of Shakespeare writing. Changing and gathering meaning throughout the novel, linking the creative urge for literature and for love, the wild goose (and its single feather) is a teasing, suggestive symbol.[19]

Another type of metamorphosis exhibited in *Orlando* is change in size and shape, *contraction* and *expansion*, the fourth of the metaphoric modes. "To compare great things with small," *Orlando*'s narrator says, quoting Milton,[20] to alert the reader to one aspect of this mode as used throughout the novel. Contraction and expansion may be a transformation in the size and shape of an object to show a "state of mind": Orlando, weeping, sees a toy steamer on the waves of the Serpentine turn into her husband's brig in a "mountain of water off Cape Horn" (p. 258); and in a different state of mind (that of the twentieth century) she sees women narrow "like stalks of corn" (p. 267). Or the mode may exhibit a "change" of mind, as when, in *Mrs. Dalloway*, Clarissa finds her image of Doris Kilman "dwindling" from "some prehistoric monster armoured for primeval warfare" to "merely Miss Kilman, in a mackintosh" (p. 139). Often contraction (used again this time with metamorphosis) illuminates not only the

[19] Maud Bodkin calls the wild-goose symbol, "the haunting image of the poet, and the lover" (*Archetypal Patterns in Poetry*, p. 305). Another transformation of symbol in *Orlando* is that of Love, which changes before our eyes from a soft-plumed bird to a black and hairy vulture called Lust (pp. 107-108), suggesting the conflicting elements and ambiguities within that emotion.

[20] *Orlando*, p. 239. Milton, *Paradise Lost*, Bk. II, lines 921-22. Milton uses this mode of metaphor frequently as well as that of transformation, in which Satan changes shape and size to show the psychological change within. Both modes are in use when Satan dilates like *"Teneriff* or *Atlas"* (Bk. IV, lines 986-87) or squats small as a toad beside the sleeping Eve—a comparison of "great things with small" or small with great.

192

quality of the perceived but also that of the perceiver (i.e., reflection); in *To the Lighthouse* Mr. Ramsay seems to his son "like some old stone lying on the sand" (p. 311) or to Mrs. Ramsay like a "desolate sea-bird." "It was his power," Mrs. Ramsay thinks, to "shed all superfluities, to shrink and diminish" so that, finally, he appears as a stake "marking the channel out there in the floods alone" (p. 72).

Virginia Woolf, in *Orlando* and elsewhere, appears to mean that, for the human mind, everything is not itself alone but is mingled with what it resembles. When Orlando tests the truth of the statement that "the sky is blue . . . the grass is green," he finds that, "on the contrary," the sky is like the veils of "a thousand Madonnas," the grass colored with the movement of nymphs fleeing satyrs (p. 94). Much later, as a woman, looking at the reflections in "the dark hollow at the back of the head," she sees the visible world changed by things that "dwell in darkness so deep that what they are we scarcely know." Everything in the world around her became "partly something else, and each gained an odd moving power from this union of itself and something not itself."[21] When Orlando tries for metaphors to describe Sasha, he can only think of things he had known or "liked the taste of as a boy": "a melon, a pineapple, an olive tree, an emerald, and a fox in the snow." Sensory experience intermingles with memory: "He did not know whether he had heard her, tasted her, seen her, or all three together" (pp. 36-37), a suggestion of synesthesia. Thus metaphor becomes yet another means of conveying emotional reality.

[21] P. 290. The last section of the sentence ("and each gained . . .") is deleted in the revised Uniform edition—a loss, considering the insight into her understanding of metaphor which it gives.

🐿 🐿 🐿

When young James at the opening of *To the Lighthouse* is cutting out pictures from the catalogue, he has already endowed them with meaning. Even the wheelbarrow or lawn mower "were so coloured and distinguished in his mind that he already had his private code, his secret language."[22] This secret language of childhood—in which image and metaphor reveal what transpires in the mind and eye of the beholder—is somewhat decoded for us in the opening chapter of *The Waves*. We mentioned earlier Virginia Woolf's original working plan for the novel as a reconstruction of the creation and development of man's mind and creative faculties, moving from the child's earliest awareness of the object to the complex abstractions of which the mature mind is capable.[23] Here, observing the way Mrs. Woolf shows us the child's early visual experience, we see that metaphor can be a primitive way of seeing and understanding the world and the self. As the metaphoric modes the child uses increase in complexity, so does our apprehension of the character's emotions.

In the beginning of Chapter VII on reflection, we quoted the opening passage of *The Waves* in which the children see or hear particular objects. They are in the garden (symbolic of their early childhood) and their comments are expressed in simple imitative images which appear to "fluctuate between 'active analogy' and simple

[22] Like the refrigerator, which James has endowed with "heavenly bliss" because of his happy emotions at the moment, these and other objects are colored by his feelings and as such achieve symbol-status, enabling him to use them as he wishes.

[23] See Chapter V, iv.

194

concrete comparison."[24] In general, these comparisons appear to be a way of *seeing* new objects by selecting features similar to those objects already known. This relationship between image and object is one "directly experienced by the mind of the individual";[25] abstraction (reduction of visual image to a few main lines) and memory join. Thus Bernard in the first sentence describes the handle of a cupboard[26] as a ring in " 'a loop of light' "; his eye has found points of analogy or comparison with the sun's luminous halo. Louis sees a shadow on the path " 'like an elbow bent.' " Susan, raised on a farm, perhaps thinks of an animal as she looks at leaves " 'like pointed ears.' " As the children grow older, their metaphors become more complex, the modes of perception more involved. Visually oriented, the children describe nonvisual sensations in terms of color and shape, utilizing synesthesia, which is believed to be not merely an exercise of metaphor but an actual experience of sensory interchange.[27] A metaphoric substitution similar to synesthesia is that of perceiving one element as another —for example, light as earth, or air as water—as primitives do. Rhoda sees patches of light like " 'islands . . . swimming on the grass' "; Bernard hears the cock crow " 'like a spurt of hard, red water in the white tide.' "[28]

[24] This is the way a child of nursery age naturally speaks. Jean Piaget, *Play, Dreams and Imitation in Childhood*, pp. 227-28.

[25] *Ibid.*, p. 169.

[26] So identified in the final chapter of the novel.

[27] Benjamin Lee Whorf believes that "metaphor arises from synesthesia and not the reverse." Part of this is due to the fact that our main sense being visual, we tend to describe nonspatial things in terms of the spatial; part is due to the "underlying unity behind the phenomena so variously reported by our sense channels." *Language, Thought and Reality*, pp. 155-56.

[28] Here sound is both color and water. This is an example of "color hearing" and actually occurs in "the perception of the tonal quality of colors and the chromatic quality of musical tones." Carl G. Jung, *Symbols of Transformation: An Analysis of the Prelude to a Case of Schizophrenia*, trans. R.F.C. Hull, Bollingen Series XX:5, 2nd edn. (Princeton, 1967), p. 165.

When he and Susan flee into the woods, the "waves" of the "green air of the leaves" close over them, and they sink through them like "swimmers."

The emotions conveyed so far by Mrs. Woolf's use of perceptual and metaphoric modes are mainly generalized —a child's spontaneous reaction to new stimuli. There is a suggestion that the use of a familiar object to describe a newly encountered one helps the child adapt or accommodate to reality by expressing the unknown in terms of the known.[29] In Bernard's swimming-through-air metaphor, a different kind of adaption is shown: the attempt to gain control over environment through magic play. In the scene in which Bernard and his friends change the garden into a "malarial jungle," seeing a worm as "a hooded cobra," or a hand "mottled" like "a snake's skin," they depend not on familiar objects for comparison but on unknown or dangerous ones, profiting by the thrill of terror—a raising of energy—which the alien images produce. For a further sense of mastery or power, the children contract and expand their view of themselves and their environment. " 'Things are huge and very small. The stalks of flowers are thick as oak trees. Leaves are high as the domes of vast cathedrals. We are giants, lying here, who can make forests quiver.' " They are already learning to shape their own mental and emotional world.

Yet however generalized these childhood emotions may be, the children's individual feelings have been differentiated for us from the beginning. Through their perception of external shapes, we feel Rhoda's fear, Bernard's adventurousness, Susan's stolidity, Jinny's responsive spirit.

[29] Thus Bernard formulates a phrase when he goes away to school: " 'Now the awful portals of the station gape; "the moon-faced clock regards me." I must make phrases and phrases and so interpose something hard between myself and the stare of housemaids, the stare of clocks, staring faces, indifferent faces, or I shall cry.' " *Waves*, pp. 21-22.

And, as in James's secret language, certain shapes or symbols have individual meanings. Mrs. Woolf introduces these specific images in the opening prologue describing a dawn landscape. The arcs and fans of the rising sun later take on the completed forms of the circle (rings, globes, chains, etc.) which will have a different meaning for each child; the birds which sing a "blank melody" will spell terror to Rhoda; the sound of the waves will, for Louis, become an elephant stamping; Jinny will assume the dawn colors of red and gold. Each child uses a particular image or symbol with which to express himself throughout the book.

As the complexity of the external world asserts itself, the metaphoric modes the children use appear to arrange and simplify the world around them. When the children leave the garden for the school, Bernard says that " 'the heat is going . . . from the Jungle,' " and we find ourselves in the cooler, more ordered atmosphere of the classroom. The children's observations are more exact. Louis sees Rhoda's shoulder blades meeting " 'across her back like the wings of a small butterfly' " (pp. 15-16). Susan, seeing the butler kiss the cook, notices that " 'his mouth was sucked like a purse in wrinkles' " (p. 18). As grammar and mathematics introduce their concepts of differentiated function and abstraction on the school blackboard, concretization and abstraction come into play. Rhoda, for example, uses both principles in a double allegory of her relationship to time. In the first metaphor, the fear is made concrete, with moving images; in the second, it is abstracted to a zero or "loop."

> "The figures mean nothing now. Meaning has gone. The clock ticks. The two hands are convoys marching through a desert. The black bars on the clock face are green oases. The long hand has marched ahead to find

197

water. The other, painfully stumbles among hot stones in the desert. It will die in the desert. The kitchen door slams. Wild dogs bark far away. Look, the loop of the figure is beginning to fill with time; it holds the world in it. I begin to draw a figure and the world is looped in it, and I myself am outside the loop; which I now join—so—and seal up, and make entire. The world is entire, and I am outside of it, crying, 'Oh save me, from being blown forever outside the loop of time!' "

(p. 15)

In these two metaphors, whose expansion into a moving image sequence resembles a brief but vivid nightmare, the principle of *condensation* appears to be at work. An examination of the metaphors, which use the same "dream-content" as do some successive dreams, reveals that they present variations on a "nesting" of images. The loop which is filled with time as with water is a variation of the oasis image. The distance between the two clock hands is repeated in Rhoda's separation from the "loop of time." Both express a sense of exclusion, of loneliness, of being "outside." Both suggest, as does her inability to cross the puddle of water, her difficulty in making moments of time fuse with one another.[30]

As *The Waves* progresses, the metaphors tend towards a condensed or "overdetermined"[31] type of image, and we

[30] See my Chapter VI, ii. On pp. 46 and 113 of *The Waves*, loss of identity is connected with crossing the puddle: " 'cadaverous, awful, lay the grey puddle . . . I could not cross it. Identity failed me. We are nothing, I said, and fell.' " (This is consistent with Rhoda's repeating that she has " 'no face.' ") Since time and self seem equated in Mrs. Woolf's writing, losing one's sense of time sequence would mean losing one's sense of self. Cf. *Diary*, September 30, 1926.

[31] "Over-determination" refers to the variety of meanings attached to a particular symbol (image). It differs from "condensation" which, as Susanne K. Langer explains, is "essentially a fusion . . . by intersection, contraction, elision, suppression, and many other devices. The effect is usually to intensify the created

feel unconsciously the subtle changes in thinking and emotion which they convey. We grow with the child. By rendering "translations" of perhaps originally unverbalized states of feeling, in the very modes the children would use were they to voice them for themselves, Virginia Woolf has conveyed with remarkable sensitiveness their evolving worlds. Here are grounded the emotional relationships which will surface in image, metaphor, and symbol throughout the remainder of the novel.

THE *condensation* of an image brings us to our final mode of operation, that of *compression*. One principle implies the other. Sometimes, in Mrs. Woolf's novels, we are given a suggestion of the background of the image; at other times, it is a single image whose strong emotional overtones convey a particular state of feeling or being. At still other times, it can sum up a lifetime of feeling— as does the image of the wheel going over the foot.

For these compressed images Mrs. Woolf tends to use a symbol—an image which has over the centuries collected about itself a variety of myth and meaning from whose vastness the reader is free to choose. Such an image is that of catching the salmon in *Between the Acts*:

> They had met first in Scotland, fishing—she from one rock, he from another. Her line had got tangled; she had given over, and had watched him with the stream rushing between his legs, casting, casting—until, like a thick ingot of silver bent in the middle, the salmon had leapt, had been caught, and she had loved him.
>
> (p. 60)

image, heighten the 'emotional quality'; often to make one aware of complexities of feeling." *Feeling and Form*, pp. 243-44.

Or it can be a phrase as compressed as "the great hand opened and shut" in the remarkable afternoon-tea scene in *Mrs. Dalloway*, when the compulsive needs of Doris Kilman are symbolized by this powerful and frightening image of the opening and closing of the hand.[32] Or it can be the use of one dominant symbol throughout a scene— like the knife which Peter Walsh is continually taking from his pocket (it is mentioned eleven times), snapping open the blade and shutting it again as he talks to Clarissa in the upstairs drawing room. Clarissa tells herself that it was an "extraordinary habit . . . making one feel, too, frivolous; empty-minded; a mere silly chatterbox" (p. 49). A manuscript version of this passage illuminates the symbol: "That knife! Always that knife! When he proposed to her, he had that knife!" And later: "It had always been the same. When he had asked her to marry him the same sort of repulsion had come over her."[33] In the published version, this scene, which takes place while Clarissa is mending her dress, opens with Peter Walsh's step on the stair and Clarissa's effort "to hide her dress, like a virgin protecting chastity." One of Peter's first gestures is to "tilt" his "pen-knife towards her green dress." As Clarissa opens her scissors, when Peter shuts his knife "with a snap," a duel of emotions seems to have been started between them which continues throughout the scene. The reader has had a glimpse—however subliminal—of the cutting edge. And we are reminded of what Virginia Woolf wrote about the way Proust builds up a scene "dominated by an emotion which has nothing to do with

---

[32] Other powerful images have been used to expand this symbol —the dropping of Elizabeth's white gloves under the table, the greedy gobbling of the chocolate éclair, the metaphor of Elizabeth's instinctive fright as a "dumb creature" which gallops "in terror" to the end of the field. The emotional sequence opens on page 145 with, "Her large hand opened and shut on the table" and ends, on the next page, with "the great hand opened and shut."

[33] *Dalloway Notebook I*, pp. 187, 191.

the eye" although "it is the eye which has fertilized . . . thought." As "images and comparisons" present the sensory scene, "our minds are tunnelling logically and intellectually into the obscurity of the young man's emotions . . . in flash after flash, metaphor after metaphor, the eye lights up that cave of darkness and we are shown the hard tangible material shapes of bodiless thoughts hanging like bats in the primeval darkness where light has never visited them before."[34]

The symbol clusters which appear and reappear in Mrs. Woolf's novels—the lighthouse, tower, and room; the knife, bird-beak, and severed head; the moth and the snail; the horse and the mermaid; the fountain, fish, and sun—form the center of matrices of emotion which, with supporting concrete images, flash for an instant in the "primeval darkness." We are shown the shapes of feeling which we only glimpsed before. A final quotation illustrates how Virginia Woolf gathers around one of these vague yet powerful symbols the secondary images which explain and expand it, giving us not only a state of mind but also the compression of a lifetime. Clarissa muses what "gaiety" would have been hers had she married Peter Walsh, and she is plunged into one of the moments of depression which assail her throughout the novel:

> It was all over for her. The sheet was stretched and the bed narrow. She had gone up into the tower alone and left them blackberrying in the sun. The door had shut, and there among the dust of fallen plaster and the litter of birds' nests how distant the view had looked, and the sounds came thin and chill (once on Leith Hill, she remembered), and Richard, Richard! she cried, as a sleeper in the night starts and stretches a hand in the dark for help. Lunching with Lady Bruton, it came

[34] "Pictures," *M.*, p. 141.

back to her. He has left me; I am alone for ever, she thought, folding her hands upon her knee.

(pp. 52-53)

In this small cosmos of feeling which Virginia Woolf has created, the images are arranged with extreme care: the bed in the foreground, the view from the tower, the sounds in the distance. The sleep-walking image with its irrational call for help balances the life-image of blackberrying in the sun. Each auxiliary image—the shut door, the birds' nests, the fallen plaster—multiplies with its own meanings of melancholy. Through a moment of Clarissa's thoughts as she is sitting with Peter Walsh and mending her dress, we are given the metaphor of her marriage—not a single emotion, but an emotional totality. Through one brief paragraph, dominated by the image of the lonely tower, we feel instinctively the quality of Clarissa's relationship to herself, Peter Walsh, her husband, Lady Bruton, and the friends of her childhood. The signal emotions of Clarissa's life—coldness, loneliness, jealousy, treachery, melancholy—are illuminated for us. We may never learn what happened on Leith Hill, but we know its emotional reality.

CHAPTER TWELVE

The Subjectivity of Form

THE WAYS IN which we see, feel, think, and experience time and personality—these, in their many phases, comprise the modes of subjectivity. Each mode exhibits one particular aspect of emotion. Reflection, for example, shows the character's emotion through his perception of an object. The primitive modes measure the energy content of the emotion. The modes of time tell us emotion's speed, quality, and relationship to the past. When we come to form, we approach still further aspects of feeling which, converted into such modalities as rhythm and pattern, comprise a largely unexamined area of Virginia Woolf's work.

The key to our understanding of Mrs. Woolf's concept of form is her belief that " 'the book itself' is not form which you see, but emotion which you feel."[1] The way we shall approach the question of form in her novels, and so try to grasp her particularly elusive vision, is two-fold. The first considers the over-all aspect of internal form, the gestalt which she achieved by trying to cast her later novels, particularly *The Years*, in "the dimensions of the human being."[2] The second deals with certain elements of outward form whose principles Mrs. Woolf internalized into structure by seeing their emotional equivalents and relationships. These elements are mass, connection, rhythm, pattern, and space. As in any consideration of a gestalt,[3]

---

[1] "On Re-reading Novels" (*M.*), *Essays*, II, p. 126.

[2] *Diary*, October 16, 1935.

[3] It is useful to remember that "gestalt" means *shape, form, configuration*, and that Gestalt psychology deals with the integrated and interdependent structures or patterns which make up

the elements must be seen as interdependent, and it is their mutual relationship which this chapter will attempt to explore.

The word which Virginia Woolf uses frequently to describe form in its total aspect is "mould." "Form" she finds confusing, not only because it derives from the visual arts, but also because it suggests something "interposed between us and the book as we know it."[4] "Scaffolding" and "plot" she also rejects as being too external.[5] "Mould," however, appears to suggest the impress of a totality of vision.[6] It is a container, a vessel in which something fluid or plastic can set and take shape. It also suggests a boundary, limits within which a particular vision and principle may operate.

What are the boundaries and limits which impose shape? In "The Narrow Bridge of Art" Virginia Woolf wrote that the future novel would "take the mould" of "the modern mind."[7] In *The Years*, which broke the "moulds" of her earlier novels,[8] she strove for the "dimensions of the human being" and concluded that "one should be able to feel a wall made out of all the influences."[9] Yet as early as *Jacob's Room* she was searching for a form to "enclose everything, everything," including "the human heart."[10] When we call up again the image of the semi-transparent envelope of consciousness, when we consider

---

experience and which form a reciprocal whole rather than a sum of the parts.

[4] "On Re-reading Novels" (*M.*), *Essays*, II, pp. 124 and 126.

[5] A diary note regarding *Jacob's Room* says, "no scaffolding; scarcely a brick to be seen" (January 26, 1920). In *Between the Acts*, Miss La Trobe thinks, "Don't bother about the plot: the plot's nothing" (p. 109).

[6] Cf. the description of newspapers in *Jacob's Room* like "thin sheets of gelatine pressed nightly over the brain and heart of the world" which "take the impression of the whole" (p. 97).

[7] (*G.R.*), *Essays*, II, p. 226.

[8] *Diary*, July 27, 1934.

[9] *Diary*, October 16, 1935.

[10] *Diary*, January 26, 1920.

the way in which Jacob's "room" (i.e., his personality or state of mind) was formed by the influences of Greek and English civilization, when we remember how the diners in *The Waves* were magnetized by the presence of Percival (the " 'moment . . . whose walls are made of Percival' "), we realize that the shape of Mrs. Woolf's novels, as her work progressed, moved steadily toward an attempt to convey the total aspect of man and his consciousness, walled in by the influences that control it.[11]

This is the general outline of the mould. Two particular essays by Mrs. Woolf cast a more specific light on its shape and reveal its outlines to be human. In her analysis of the appeal of Spenser's *The Faery Queen*, she notes how that poem touches "different layers" of the mind and gratifies as well "the desire of the body, desires for rhythm [and] movement," because the poet himself is "not merely a thinking brain" but "a feeling body . . . the whole being is drawn upon."[12] In her wise examination of D. H. Lawrence's *Sons and Lovers* she notes a certain "incandescence" of the flesh, a restless excitement and movement to the book like that of "the body of the hero."[13] What emerges from the sum of these many scattered comments throughout her work and her diary is her apprehension, however vague, of a mind-body-feeling gestalt, a vision of the novel as a living organism whose totality would embody certain recognizable human features. If her subjective modes themselves approached the many different ways in which man experiences life, would not a form approximating man himself be the logical extension, indeed the very envelope, of subjectivity?

This vision of the novel as a microcosm of man seems

---

[11] "The Narrow Bridge of Art" closes with a list of "those influences which play so large a part in life" which the new novelist of emotion will dramatize.

[12] (*M.*), *Essays*, I, p. 16.

[13] (*M.*), *Essays*, I, p. 354.

revolutionary, but it is not new. Joyce's *Ulysses*, although using a formal structure based on episodes from the *Odyssey*, attempts a human shape, that of a "living organism," as Stuart Gilbert reminds us in his study of *Ulysses*.[14] Each episode is governed by one organ of the human body which lends its symbolism to the imagery of that section and sometimes suggests its particular prose rhythm. Peristaltic rhythm, for example, governs the episode of the Lestrygonians, or an increasing flow of vitality and rhythm illustrates the growth of the embryo in the Oxen of the Sun episode.[15] The influences which wall in the consciousness of Leopold Bloom are those of a single day in Dublin; the impact of each visual association, each memory and emotion, is registered on it.

To embody so much of the human being as "shape" requires a long work, one encyclopedic in nature. Of the three novels which most nearly embody Virginia Woolf's vision of the mind-body-feeling gestalt—*Orlando*, *The Waves*, and *The Years*—the last is the longest and is the one which she hoped would correspond to the dimensions of the human being. Yet it appears less responsive to analysis than the others. In *Orlando*, the dimension seems that of time, which, as we noted earlier, is equated in Mrs. Woolf's work with personality and so achieves a certain human shape. In *The Waves*, the total aspect of man is perhaps the clearest, with different characters representing varying physical, biological, mental, intellectual, and spiritual elements (see the Appendix). The physical is especially stressed, the sensuous movement of Jinny lending

[14] Stuart Gilbert, *James Joyce's Ulysses: A Study*, 2nd rev. edn. (New York, 1952), p. 40, n. 1.

[15] *Ibid.*, pp. 40-42. With the exception of the first three episodes, each has an organ which, together, "compose the whole body, which is thus a symbol of the structure of *Ulysses* . . . and of the natural interdependence of the parts between themselves" (p. 40, n. 1).

a body-restlessness to the entire work. In *The Years*, this physical restlessness seems absent, save in the figure of Delia. There exist instead the larger outlines of birth and death, of crippling and of pain, of maimed sexual instincts, and the shaping of "upper" or "lower" scenes to suggest mental or bodily states.[16] As in *Orlando*, the most human dimension is that of time, which, we might be reminded, is the element in which man himself moves and takes shape and as such forms both the boundary and container for the being. Yet somehow, in this immense novel, which gives the time/memory experience of a full generation of Pargiters, the vision remains unfulfilled. Even as Mrs. Woolf was writing *The Years* she was groping for a still more satisfactory mould for her vision. Her diary notes: "New combination in psychology and body. . . . This will be the next novel, after *The Years*."[17]

MAN IS A feeling, thinking, moving whole, and the single most pervasive quality of that being may be said to be *emotional rhythm*: the fluctuations in mood, the increase and decrease in intensities of feeling, the motion inherent in the single duration or in the larger clusters of psychic states which compose the various scenes of her novels. *The Waves* especially seems sensitive to these curves or alternations of feeling. Virginia Woolf does not attempt to reproduce the specific biological rhythm of a part of the body as does Joyce; she is concerned instead with the rhythm of the body organism as a whole.[18] This

[16] See Chapter X, iv.

[17] November 18, 1935.

[18] In the "eating-house" monologue of Louis (pp. 67-68), Mrs. Woolf attempts to reproduce the rhythm of the entire scene which the diner shares—perhaps a conscious variation of the Lestrygonian episode:

Meanwhile the hats bob up and down; the door perpetually shuts and opens. I am conscious of flux, of disorder; of annihilation and despair. If this is all, this is worthless. Yet I feel, too,

inward movement of flow and ebb, of transition and change, carries us along the larger motions within the novel—the human cycle of "growth, expectation, fulfillment and frustration, decline"[19]—whose curves the nine chapters chart for us and whose larger emotional qualities are reflected in the sea and landscape descriptions which preface them. The flux and reflux of feeling, the sense of being carried along on a stream of currents and countercurrents, now on the crests, now in the troughs, is the rhythm of *The Waves*.

Like *The Waves*, each novel has its own governing cyclic or rhythmic pattern. *The Voyage Out* shows the larger rhythms of growth and change from adolescence to maturity, with movements outward (from England to South America, from villa to hotel) or inward (from house to ship, from Santa Marina to the jungle) which parallel the thrusts toward society and self which the maturing person essays. *Night and Day* abstracts the shift and interchange of feeling between the characters with the movement of sun and moon, stars and planets, as well as the polarization of the imaginative/dreaming and rational/waking personalities. This latter contrast is implicit in *To the Lighthouse* in the cyclic rhythm—light, dark, light—of the lighthouse beam, which suggests alternating influences or emotions and is externalized in the tripartite structure of the novel: the longest beam, with which Mrs. Ramsay identifies herself, being the first part, and the darkness "Time Passes."[20] In *Mrs. Dalloway*, the progres-

---

the rhythm of the eating-house. It is like a waltz tune, eddying in and out, round and round. The waitresses, balancing trays, swing in and out, round and round. . . . The circle is unbroken; the harmony complete. Here is the central rhythm; here the common mainspring. I watch it expand, contract; and then expand again.

[19] Dorothy Brewster, *Virginia Woolf*, p. 126.

[20] Joan Bennett, *Virginia Woolf: Her Art as a Novelist*, pp. 103-104.

sion of hours, 10 a.m. to 3 a.m., is counterpointed by the movements of sun and moon, of summer and winter,[21] which mirror Clarissa's mounting rhythms of tension. Critics have tended to see in Mrs. Woolf's novels a certain natural rhythm and organic growth.[22] As part of her apprehension of the novel as a highly complex and interrelated organism, her works reflect the influence of G. E. Moore's principle of organic unity and lead us to a further consideration of what we earlier called its aesthetic correlative, Clive Bell's concept of "significant form."

THE MEANING of "significant" in the term *significant form* lies in the response of the reader to certain emotional relationships within the work of art. Susanne K. Langer criticizes Clive Bell for stopping at the "aesthetic emotion" and not questioning what produces that emotion. Bell, she feels, "confusedly" identified " 'significant form' . . . with 'aesthetic quality' " instead of seeing this form as the "non-discursive but articulate symbol of feeling."[23] Roger Fry, however, who adopted Clive Bell's phrase, carried the concept of emotional relationship into the psychological realm. Form, he wrote in *Vision and*

---

[21] I.e., the leitmotif "the sun rose, the day sank," the rising of the moon at Bourton, the progression from summer into winter illustrated in the song from *Cymbeline*: "Fear no more the heat o' the sun/ Nor the furious winter's rages" (p. 12). The novel opens on a day in June, closes with Clarissa contemplating the winter of her old age.

[22] Bernard Blackstone speaks of the "organic life" of Mrs. Woolf's characters "spreading and growing," and observes that *Between the Acts* "has a natural rather than an artificial rhythm" (*Virginia Woolf: A Commentary*, pp. 10 and 241). Winifred Holtby is aware of "organic growth" in *The Voyage Out* and calls Rachel's reactions and moods "organic" (*Virginia Woolf*, p. 67).

[23] Langer, *Feeling and Form*, pp. 34 and 50.

Design, is "the direct outcome of an apprehension of some emotion of actual life" by the artist. For the viewer, "the graphic arts arouse emotions . . . by playing upon what one may call the overtones of some of our primary physical needs." Nearly all "the emotional elements of design," Fry continues, are connected with them—rhythm with our muscular activity, mass with the force of gravity, light with our sensitivity to its changes in intensity.[24]

As noted in Chapter II, J. K. Johnstone presents an extensive discussion of the relationship of Clive Bell's and Roger Fry's theories to Virginia Woolf's concept of form.[25] He does not, however, tell how "certain elements of natural form—mass, space, light and shade, color"— which Roger Fry arranges into a system of his own in *Transformations*,[26] are themselves transformed into elements of inward form which Virginia Woolf herself would use. The five main elements which Mrs. Woolf considers in her essays and fiction are those of mass, connection, rhythm, pattern, and space. They are not aspects of perception, as are color and light (see Chapter V, iii), but rather of our apprehension of total experience. Intensity, quality, the sense of succession, transition, periodicity, and change—all are characteristics which these subjective modes of form attempt to convey.

Mass. Nothing could seem more unlike our mental and emotional grasp of experience than this term, which suggests undifferentiated totalities. Yet in "The Narrow Bridge of Art," when Mrs. Woolf is forecasting what the future novelist will attempt to convey, she says that "his effort will be to generalize and split up. Instead of enumerating details he will *mould blocks.*"[27] We can remind

[24] Fry, *Vision and Design*, p. 294 and pp. 34-35.
[25] Johnstone, *The Bloomsbury Group*, pp. 46-95.
[26] *Ibid.*, p. 55.
[27] (*G.R.*), *Essays*, II, p. 228; italics mine.

ourselves at this moment that Proust's narrator, when he dipped the madeleine in the cup of lime-flower tea, saw not just a single memory but "the whole of Combray and its surroundings." Like the matrices of memory in *The Waves* or *To the Lighthouse*, his is a solid group of experiences and feelings. As Virginia Woolf, in an early *Lighthouse* manuscript, noted about Lily Briscoe's sense of Mrs. Ramsay's past, "all things at once came together —like an organic compound."[28] The final section of *To the Lighthouse* is conceived as a block of feeling about both Mr. and Mrs. Ramsay. All that has occurred in the first part, "The Window," has come together like "an organic compound." It is not there in detail, but *en masse*. Not until Lily Briscoe solidifies her feelings about the Ramsays, clarifying their emotional relationship with each other as well as hers with them both, can she solve the problem posed in her picture at the novel's beginning: "how to connect this mass on the right hand with that on the left" (p. 86). As suggested earlier,[29] the painting is an "abstract" of the worlds of wife and husband; as Lily says, it is a question "of the relations of masses, of lights and shadows." The room with the rectangular purple shadow at the window is the area of Mrs. Ramsay; the area of light is that of her husband sailing to the lighthouse in the noonday sun. The slanting lines which connect the masses are the Ramsays' relationship. Like the tripartite cycle of the lighthouse beam, Lily's painting represents another paradigm of the novel's structure, with "Time Passes" as the slanting lines linking the two areas of light and shadow—"The Lighthouse" and "The Window."

The quality of "mass" in blocks or matrices of memory is illustrated in James's analysis of the hatred he feels

[28] *Lighthouse Notebook III*, p. 213 (August 4, 1926).
[29] Chapter V, iii, n. 21.

toward his father at the end of the novel. His terror, as we showed in the last chapter, gives rise to a scene that springs into his mind entire, as did the houses and gardens of Combray: a "setting" with a garden, trees, flowers, "a few figures" (p. 285). Is it a symbolic memory of the past or the reality of that memory itself? The reader is not sure; he only feels the mass—weight, extent, intensity—of the emotion. James thinks of this emotion as "a world." Mrs. Woolf appears to suggest that we do not experience emotion as a single detail, or a serialized sequence of details, any more than we experience time by the sequential moments of the clock. A memory, or an emotional duration, with its interpenetration of psychic states (with perhaps, as Bergson suggests, their equivalent physical tensions),[30] has a magnitude and unity hitherto unnoticed.

These, then, are the masses that form the aggregate of feelings at the dinner parties in *The Waves*; that compose the pure blocks of experience which, submerged in memory, rise to confront character and reader in the final chapter of *The Years*. *Orlando* presents blocks of historic or racial memory, as does *Between the Acts*; one feels their total impress, not their individual details. Like the modern composers' blocks of tone and rhythm, which substitute masses of sonority and durations for a melody line, Virginia Woolf exchanges blocks of emotion and feeling for the usual thread of plot.[31] Total man, massed influences, massed emotions, massed states of consciousness, the sense of life in its experiential totality—all compose this particular *felt* aspect of inward form.

[30] Henri Bergson, *Time and Free Will*, trans. F. L. Pogson (New York and London, 1910), pp. 27-29. Cf. Susanne K. Langer's statement in *Feeling and Form* that "feeling and emotion are really complexes of tension" (p. 373).

[31] In his discussion of *To the Lighthouse*, E. K. Brown observes that the "three parts of the novel are related somewhat as the three big blocks of sound in a sonata." *Rhythm in the Novel* (Toronto, 1950), pp. 69-70.

Connection. Like the slanting lines in Lily Briscoe's painting, the connection represents, on the larger level of form, the emotional linking between the parts. We have explained how this connection works in Chapter IV, where the transitions between sections of *Mrs. Dalloway* and *The Waves* were seen as a linking of emotional states. In *To the Lighthouse*, the connecting of the "mass" on the right with the mass on the left was accomplished in the novel's final section by Lily Briscoe's feelings for both Mr. and Mrs. Ramsay and by the reader's sense that the two worlds of Mr. and Mrs. Ramsay—sun and shadow, optimist and pessimist, intellect and intuition—are interdependent and form the two necessary halves of an enduring marriage relationship. In the central section, "Time Passes," these human conditions are allegorized and their universal counterparts presented. Instead of Mr. and Mrs. Ramsay we have the house or room, Virginia Woolf's favorite symbol of the personality or state of mind,[32] subject to the alternating influences which assail it. Near-destruction of the house by wind and weather, resurrection through the feminine creative process (Mrs. McNab and her helper)—this is the manner in which "Time Passes" "abstracts" the forces inherent in the human personality and connects them with the universal.

In still another sense, "Time Passes" is the night, the connecting link between the days, the "wedge of darkness" between the lighthouse strokes. It is our connection with the unconscious (where all connections are), with the very world of those mysterious forces humanized in

[32] The house/room image for a state of mind or personality is indicated in the titles of *Jacob's Room* and *A Room of One's Own*; in the essay on Henry James (*D.M., Essays*, I, p. 268); in the hotel rooms, which represent their occupants and which Rachel visits in Chapter XIX of *The Voyage Out*; in *Night and Day* (pp. 355 and 521); and in *The Waves* (" 'There are many rooms —many Bernards' "; p. 184). John Graham, in "Time in the Novels of Virginia Woolf," *UTQ*, January 1949, sees the room as the "selfhood formed in time."

the Ramsays. This human aspect is seen more clearly in the original manuscript where the phrase "the sleepers" is used continually (although only once in the published version) and recalls Whitman's poem "The Sleepers" with its similar dramatization of the transcending forces in the sleeping mind and its ubiquity in time and space.[33] It is a "collective mind" and in this sense is universal. Whitman's poem states that "I dream in my dream all the dreams of the other dreamers,/ and I become the other dreamers." Whitman's dreamer then becomes the "swimmer" moving through the waters of the unconscious, a giant in "red-trickled waves."[34] Images of sea and waves occur in the original *Lighthouse* manuscript. In the published version, Mrs. McNab "oars her way" through "sun-lanced waters." As the reader becomes both dreamer and sleeper, his identification with the deep unconscious forces at work in different sections of the novel is realized. The connection is made.

There is still one more aspect of connection which is clarified by the use of a traditional concept in the visual arts, that of *push-and-pull* or tension between masses, colors, and shapes. This is a tension which is perceptually experienced by the viewer, although it appears to take place only on the canvas. Just as various intensities of relationship are set up between the colors, masses, and

---

[33] *Lighthouse Notebook II* (April-May, 1926). The original version is more clearly seen to be in the form of a dream, dominated by the figures of "the sleepers" who see, as in a vision, the death and rebirth of the house over the ten-year period. In the published version, the allegorical sleepers are replaced by the characters in the novel who go to bed and wake up ten years later. Yet the section still seems a communal dream: the trees and flowers watching, "eyeless and thus terrible," like figures in dreams; the metamorphosis of the house; the strange spirit-like beings of chaos and night who move through it; the sense of expansion and contraction of space and time.

[34] *The Poetry and Prose of Walt Whitman*, ed. Louis Untermeyer (New York, 1949), parts 1 and 3, pp. 390-91.

shapes in art (some repel or attract, for example; others come forth or recede), so tensions, which form part of her novels' patterns, are set up between Mrs. Woolf's characters. These tensions, or connections, we emotionally feel. Lily Briscoe of *To the Lighthouse* and Septimus Smith of *Mrs. Dalloway* yearn for connection with people. Lily, sitting by Mrs. Ramsay's knee, desires emotional unity. Septimus, cut off from all feeling, yearns for connection with the world. It is not Lily's desire for unity which moves us, it is the force of the tension between her skimpy yet honest self and the vast maternal powers of Mrs. Ramsay who has "knowledge and wisdom . . . stored" in her heart. When, at the book's closing, Lily has her vision of Mrs. Ramsay at the window, we feel the desired connection to be complete. Likewise the closeness achieved between Septimus and Rezia before his suicide is felt all the stronger because of his previous failure to connect.

Rhythm. In her diary, while she was writing *The Waves*, Virginia Woolf expressed the feeling that the connections or transitions between the dramatic soliloquies (as she then envisioned them) were to be made by rhythm: "The thing is to keep them running homogeneously in and out, in the rhythm of the waves."[35] Later she asked herself, "Suppose I could run all the scenes together more?—by rhythms chiefly. So as to avoid those cuts; so as to make the blood run like a torrent from end to end."[36]

Actually, as we have suggested, the idea of connection via emotional rhythm had been achieved earlier in *Mrs. Dalloway*, where, one might say, the bloodstreams of Clarissa and Septimus Smith, her double, join in one torrential flow. We shall discuss these particular rhythms a little later. Now, however, it is useful to examine what

[35] *Diary*, August 20, 1930.
[36] *Diary*, December 30, 1930.

Mrs. Woolf says, in a letter to Vita Sackville-West, about the rhythm which she tried to achieve in *To the Lighthouse*:

> Now this is very profound, what rhythm is, and goes far deeper than words. A sight, an emotion, creates this wave in the mind, long before it makes words to get it; and in writing (such is my belief) one has to recapture this, and set this working (which has nothing apparently to do with words) and then, as it breaks and tumbles in the mind, it makes words to fit it.[37]

This suggests that, for Virginia Woolf, rhythm was a synthesis of emotion and style, *a way of thinking in which the rhythms of thought carry the overtones of the emotions which prompt them.* In *The Waves*, Bernard says of a page from Byron, " 'Now I am getting his beat into my brain (the rhythm is the main thing in writing)' " (p. 57). In her diary, Mrs. Woolf speaks of the "obsessive" rhythm of Pointz Hall (*Between the Acts*) which she heard and used "in every sentence I spoke."[38] As it is handled in her novels, rhythm becomes far more than mere prose rhythm; it is a dynamic pattern of feeling to which the reader responds emotionally as his inner ear does to the different voices of subjectivity. Like the wave's rise and fall, its curves of emotion carry the reader with it.

The "wave in the mind"—its cresting and diminution— sets the pattern for Virginia Woolf's use of rhythm, one which she may employ for a general sense of emotion or for a specific feeling such as yearning or despair. Her early novels depend on image rather than rhythm for emotion. It is in *Mrs. Dalloway*, whose opening page presents the image of a wave, that the first conscious attempt is made to convey a specific pattern of rising and falling

[37] Pippett, *Moth and Star*, p. 225.
[38] November 17, 1940.

216

movement which would reflect the characters' feelings. The technique is perhaps too artificial; leitmotifs and phrases constantly draw the reader's attention to the rise-fall motion.[39] But the rhythm is sustained, and Clarissa Dalloway becomes the first character in Mrs. Woolf's fiction into whose emotions we can enter completely.

More specifically, the rhythm in *Mrs. Dalloway* is based on the alternation of the two emotions of vitality, or euphoria, and despair. Each character, to a certain extent, exhibits these cycles of feeling which may last but a moment or carry through an entire scene. For the sense of vitality, the motion is an upward or rising one; for despair, it is a falling or downward one. Virginia Woolf accents these downward motions by literary allusions to Alice's falling down the corridor,[40] the plunge of Icarus,[41] the fall of Satan into flames.[42] The rising motion is suggested in images of birth or emergence,[43] pinnacles,[44] staircases. In the main, Clarissa exhibits the rising emotion, the cresting of the "wave of divine vitality" that carries her

[39] The words "rising" and "falling" themselves recur. Suggestive leitmotifs are the earlier cited "the sun rose, the day sank," the song from *Cymbeline*, and the ambiguities of "If it were now to die, 'twere now to be most happy." The wave image is repeated in "So on a summer's day waves collect, overbalance, and fall; collect and fall" (pp. 44-45).

[40] " 'Down, down, down, would the fall *never* come to an end?' " Mrs. Woolf quotes from *Alice in Wonderland* in her essay on Lewis Carroll (*M., Essays*, I, p. 255). This forms the pattern for such sentences as "Turning, the shelf fell; down, down she dropped" (Rezia thinking, p. 28).

[41] Septimus is thought of as a "young hawk" by Rezia which may suggest Icarus, whose wax wings melted from the "heat o' the sun"—a leitmotif connected with both Septimus and Clarissa. Stephen Dedalus in *Portrait of the Artist* thinks of Dedalus as the "hawklike man."

[42] "Falling down, down . . . into the flames" (p. 74); repeated pp. 155 and 157; on p. 98 he is reading Dante's *Inferno* which Rezia makes him put down.

[43] The doors "taken off their hinges," the plunge "into open air" (p. 5); London in the early morning (p. 7).

[44] "Why seek pinnacles and stand drenched in fire?" (p. 184).

triumphantly to the conclusion of her party in her upstairs rooms. Septimus, her double, exhibits the negative of this emotion, a despair which finally drives him to plunge to his death on the area railing. Yet throughout, Clarissa moves in cycles of her own: from exaltation to anxiety over her party; from joy at seeing Peter Walsh to anguish at realizing what their marriage might have been; from a high crest of hate for the "odious Kilman" "down, down" to an "ordinary" level of peace at seeing an elderly neighbor in the window.[45] Septimus moves from despair to peace or euphoria as his schizoid visions shift and change:

> But he himself remained high on his rock, like a drowned sailor on a rock. I leant over the edge of the boat and fell down, he thought. I went under the sea. I have been dead, and yet am now alive . . . and as . . . the sleeper feels himself drawing to the shores of life, so he felt himself drawing toward life, the sun growing hotter, cries sounding louder, something tremendous about to happen. (p. 77)

Yet for all the individual cycles of feeling, the novel conveys a general sense of mounting tension which increases until the moment at her party when Clarissa hears of Septimus' death and the double climaxes interpenetrate. In the maroon leather *Dalloway* notebook, Mrs. Woolf noted: "This is to be psychology. Gradually increasing in tension all through the day." Contracting and expanding its sense of tension—Peter Walsh thinks, on the way to Clarissa's party, "The brain must wake now. The body must contract"—the novel exhibits on a mass scale the tension-release pattern of the moment of being.[46]

[45] "Down, down, into the midst of ordinary things the finger fell, making the moment solemn" (p. 140).

[46] Peter Walsh, for example, opens and closes his pocket knife throughout the novel, which suggests not only the advance and recession of feeling but also a certain sexual tension. The sexual

THE SUBJECTIVITY OF FORM

When Virginia Woolf started her next novel, *To the Lighthouse*, the rhythm of rise and fall appears to have been firmly ingrained in her mind. As we noted earlier, its use in *Mrs. Dalloway* tends to be artificial; the images which control the rhythms reflect the feeling rather than exhibit the motion intrinsic to them. In *To the Lighthouse*, image, character, rhythm, and emotion seem fused; the movement is more subtle, more interior, more organic. Indeed, until one carefully analyzes the images, wording, and rhythm of the novel, one is scarcely aware that Virginia Woolf has consciously worked in this particular mode of feeling.

The basic emotion behind the rhythm in *To the Lighthouse* is that of yearning, expectation; or, on a more explicit level, a search for energy, alleviation, sympathy, a "balm" for some wound. In early notes for "The Window," Mrs. Woolf planned "an impression . . . of waiting, of expectation."[47] The expectation is on several levels: the yearning of Lily for Mrs. Ramsay; the personal, indefinable needs to be satisfied by a wife or husband; Mr. Ramsay's struggle to reach "beyond Q"; James's wish for the lighthouse journey; Mrs. Ramsay's desire to make something of her life; Tansley's urge to assert himself and "relieve the thigh bones, the ribs" of "his urgent desire" (p. 142). These are some of the individual longings embodying the general emotion whose fulfillment, in some mysterious way, seems symbolized by the final landing on the lighthouse rock.

The particular rhythm of yearning or expectation is

---

imagery is more explicit in the passage ending with the metaphor of the "match burning in a crocus" (p. 36); there it is based on a sexual translation of the moment of exaltation which relaxes and heals what has been tensed and hardened. The passage, nearly a half-page long, attempts to render psychologically "what men felt" physically.

[47] *Lighthouse Notebook I*, August 6, 1925.

worked out in the novel's final section in a mounting sequence of rising and falling tensions which build up and subside again until they are resolved, for Lily in a vision of Mrs. Ramsay at the window, for Cam and James by the landing at the lighthouse. The rhythm of Lily's yearning is illustrated by a long passage in which she thinks of Mrs. Ramsay:

> To want and not to have, sent all up her body a hardness, a hollowness, a strain. And then to want and not to have—to want and want—how that wrung the heart, and wrung it again and again! Oh Mrs. Ramsay! she called out silently, to that essence. . . . It had seemed so safe, thinking of her. Ghost, air, nothingness, a thing you could play with easily and safely at any time of day or night, she had been that, and then suddenly she put her hand out and wrung the heart thus. Suddenly, the empty drawing-room steps, the frill of the chair inside, the puppy tumbling on the terrace, the whole wave and whisper of the garden became like curves and arabesques flourishing round a centre of complete emptiness. (p. 275)

The "curves and arabesques" of Lily's own emotion turn downward; she weeps. With the tears comes relief. But then the cycle starts anew. "The pain increased. That anguish could reduce one to such a pitch of imbecility, she thought!" (She had cried out Mrs. Ramsay's name.) Then the cycle subsides once more and leaves, "as antidote, a relief that was balm in itself."[48]

---

[48] P. 278. On pp. 274-75, Lily has described her feelings as "emotions of the body": "It was one's body feeling, not one's mind. The physical sensations that went with the bare look of the steps [i.e., bare without Mrs. Ramsay] had become suddenly extremely unpleasant" (p. 275). The "to want and not to have" passage follows immediately. Lily, of course, is overstating the case for effect: the emotion is one of both body and mind.

Yet throughout the novel this internal rhythm is sustained in a less exaggerated way. In Section 19 of "The Window," for example, when Mrs. Ramsay comes into the room "to get something she wanted" (it turns out to be partly an emotional settlement of the question of going to the lighthouse), she has a high feeling of elation at learning of Minta's and Paul's engagement. Then she "grew still like a tree which has been tossing and quivering and now, when the breeze falls, settles, leaf by leaf, into quiet." She begins to read, unable to talk to her husband, and her emotions fall, then rise, in a variation of the tree image, "zigzagging" from branch to branch, from one feeling to another, in the remarkable passage quoted and analyzed in Chapter IV. As she sat there, "something seemed . . . to go from him to her," and we find ourselves in a parallel cycle of feeling as Mr. Ramsay reads Sir Walter Scott. At the scene's end it is he who wants something—"the thing she always found it so difficult to give him . . . to tell him that she loved him." By a simple agreement on her part— "Yes, you were right. It's going to be wet to-morrow"— the separate tensions are resolved.

What are the images which control this emotion of yearning, this sense of "there is something I want—something I have come to get"? They are associated with Mrs. Ramsay, from whom everyone in the novel "wants" something, whether it is love, approval, sympathy, emotional satisfaction, or the mysterious energy which her son James feels she sends forth "like a fountain of spray."[49] The images are the fountain itself, the lighthouse beam, the

---

[49] See p. 54 re the children coming to her, "one wanting this; another that . . . she often felt she was nothing but a sponge sopped full of human emotions." Mrs. Ramsay also has needs of her own, as Lily senses on p. 143: " 'I am drowning, my dear, in seas of fire. Unless you apply some balm to the anguish of this hour and say something nice to that young man there, life will run upon the rocks. . . . My nerves are taut as fiddle strings.' "

tree. Each has the same rising-falling or alternating rhythm. The fountain is the primary image, however, and its first appearance occurs toward the beginning of the book when it is seen as rising at sunset from the ocean:

> They came there regularly every evening *drawn by some need*. It was as if the water floated off and set sailing thoughts which had grown stagnant on dry land, and gave to their bodies even some sort of *physical relief*. First, the pulse of colour *flooded* the bay with blue, and the heart *expanded* with it and the body swam, only the next instant to be *checked* and chilled by the prickly blackness on the ruffled waves. Then, up behind the great black rock, almost every evening spurted irregularly, so that one had to watch for it and it was a delight when it came, *a fountain of white water*. . . .[50]

Here, the fact of psychic or physical need is stressed—together with images of tension and release, of rise and fall—as it is in James's vision of his mother as a fountain, supplying his father who stands by, "demanding sympathy":

> Mrs. Ramsay, who had been sitting loosely, folding her son in her arm, braced herself, and, half-turning, seemed to raise herself with an effort, and at once to pour erect into the air a *rain of energy*, a *column of spray*, looking at the same time animated and alive as if all her energies were being fused into force, burning and illuminating (quietly though she sat, taking up her stocking again), and into this delicious fecundity, this *fountain and spray*

[50] P. 36. Italics mine. The fountain, later associated with Mrs. Ramsay, is close by the rock whose image appears linked with Mr. Ramsay (see esp. p. 58). The fountain-rock image is repeated at the end of the novel: "on one, a higher rock, a wave incessantly broke and spurted a little column of drops that fell down in a shower" (p. 317).

of life, the fatal sterility of the male plunged itself, like a beak of brass, barren and bare.[51]

The image is repeated on the next page when "James felt all her strength flaring up to be drunk and quenched by the beak of brass," and is varied in the following pages as the rising and rosy-flowering fruit tree which folds its petals "in exhaustion" and as the "pulse in a spring which has expanded to its full width and now gently ceases to beat."[52]

Is this central symbol related, however subtly, to the image of Henry James's *The Sacred Fount*—an image of psychic springs of energy being fed or depleted by someone so that the health or personality of another is increased or diminished, perhaps even led to death? Mrs. Ramsay herself dies in "Time Passes"; images of depletion or exhaustion occur throughout the novel or appear in Lily's memories of her.[53] It is an interesting conjecture, especially since Henry James would be associated in Virginia Woolf's mind with St. Ives in Cornwall, where she spent her childhood summers.[54] What we do know is that, while Mrs. Woolf was sketching a plan for *Mrs. Dalloway*, which directly preceded *To the Lighthouse*, she was reading *The Sacred Fount*, a review of which is drafted in the earliest *Dalloway* notebook.[55] A fountain appears in the beginning of the finished novel—broken, we find out later,

---

[51] Pp. 61-62. Italics mine.

[52] Cf. the tree image previously quoted (*Lighthouse*, p. 182).

[53] Particularly, pp. 64, 131-32, 306.

[54] The island in the Hebrides, Mrs. Woolf admits in her diary (May 14, 1925), is to be based on St. Ives. For Henry James in Cornwall, see Leon Edel's *Henry James: The Middle Years: 1882-1895* (New York, 1962), p. 380 and photograph facing p. 353.

[55] If the review of "Maud Evelyn & The Sacred Fount of Henry James" (so titled in *Dalloway Notebook I*, late 1922) was published, it has not been recorded in the Soho bibliography and is probably one of her many unsigned "lost" reviews.

223

perhaps to suggest some lack of feminine fullness in Clarissa.[56] The image, however, is not pursued nor is the rhythm of rise-fall overtly connected with it. It is in *To the Lighthouse* (which curiously opens with a child named James!) that rhythm and symbol converge with character to convey a complexity and depth of emotion unequalled in her other novels.

But it is with *Mrs. Dalloway* that, for the first time, Virginia Woolf depends entirely upon the pattern and movement of psychological relationships for the design; there is no other. Might not this new design have been influenced by *The Sacred Fount*?[57] It is the only one of Henry James's novels to base its design upon an emotional "figure in the carpet," a pattern which consists of the varying psychological relationships (however hypothetical) of certain pairs of characters with each other and with the narrator—not surface relationships but deep emotional tensions which could affect the physical or mental being and whose true pattern the narrator is trying to trace for himself.[58] With the exception of *Orlando*, Mrs. Woolf's subsequent novels would utilize this concept of interior emotional design.

[56] See *Dalloway*, pp. 10 and 71; Peter, in his memory, is aware of the broken spout, Clarissa not.

[57] In his introduction to the Grove Press edition of *The Sacred Fount* (New York, 1953), Leon Edel notes R. P. Blackmur's observation that *The Sacred Fount* was "closer to Joyce and Proust, Virginia Woolf and Franz Kafka, than to nineteenth-century fiction" (p. vii). The central figure, May Server, in James's novel is seen by the narrator to be depleted by husband, children, and a lover; Mrs. Ramsay in *To the Lighthouse* is depleted by husband, children, and friends. Both "serve." See the introd. to *The Sacred Fount*, p. xxvi.

[58] Lily Briscoe, too, is trying to figure out the exact emotional relationships of the Ramsays and of Minta and Paul Rayley. Like Henry James's narrator, she builds up "a whole structure of imagination," which has very little truth in it. *Lighthouse*, p. 267. Cf. the narrator's similar phrase, "palace of thought," in *The Sacred Fount*, p. 311.

Pattern. In the essay in which Mrs. Woolf declares that "the 'book itself' is not form which you see, but emotion which you feel," she suggests that form consists of "emotions which we feel naturally, and name simply, and *range in final order by feeling their right relations to each other.*"[59] In *A Room of One's Own* she expands upon this concept of the right relation of emotions by saying that the shape of the novel "starts in one the kind of emotion that is appropriate to it. But that emotion at once blends itself with others, for the 'shape' is not made by the relation of stone to stone, but by the relation of human being to human being. . . . The whole structure . . . is one of infinite complexity, because it is thus made up of . . . so many different kinds of emotion."[60]

This complex of emotional relationships we may term "pattern" as it appears in Mrs. Woolf's work. We have referred to it tangentially in our consideration of mass and connection. We have suggested the way it functions in *To the Lighthouse* in our discussion of rhythm. Now, it is our task to see pattern as composed not only of the relation between emotions, but also of their "kind" or quality and their mode of operation. Mrs. Woolf's awareness of the "different kinds of emotion" out of which this aspect of structure is made can be seen in manuscript notes on *To the Lighthouse* regarding Section 7 of "The Window," which opens with James's hatred of "the twang and twitter of his father's emotion" (p. 61):

> James hated him
> felt the vibration in the air
> felt the emotion
> a bad emotion?
> All emotion is bad

[59] "On Re-reading Novels" (*M.*), *Essays*, II, p. 126. Italics mine.
[60] *A Room*, pp. 107-108.

felt his mother's emotion
what her emotion was[61]

As hatred for his father governs the passages in the novel concerning James, creating what we might call a wire of tension between the two, so a particular emotion governs the relation of each character to each of the others, forming a criss-crossing of strands whose effect would seem quite tangled were it not that Mrs. Woolf gives us the relationships one at a time. The famous dinner scene, with its recessions and advances of feeling, its demands and surrenders of sovereignty, shows the "infinite complexity" of these "different kinds" of emotion. Shifting, changing, bringing forth now Charles Tansley's aggressiveness and the final relief of "his egotism"; now William Bankes's annoyance with Mrs. Ramsay, resolved to love; now Mrs. Ramsay's own despair followed by her rising sense of "relief and pleasure" at the dinner's climax (p. 172)—the scene is a brilliant example of the way pattern functions on the larger scale of the novel itself. We feel, as the dinner progresses, the right ranging of emotions in their natural order. We sense the way the emotions rise and fall, creating their own cycles of tension and relief. And we know the intensity and quality of each emotion. As we "trace the pattern" with its constant shift and change, we are brought to an apprehension of what Mrs. Woolf is attempting to accomplish—the presentation in its natural state of the flux and flow of the emotions.

The pattern of *Mrs. Dalloway* is more rigid and formal than that of *To the Lighthouse* and so more easily analyzed. Notes for "a possible revision of this book" in its earliest stages show her concern with inner form:

> At any rate, very careful composition.
> The contrast must be arranged. . . .

[61] *Lighthouse Notebook I*, January 31, 1926.

The pace is to be given by the gradual
increase of S's insanity on the one side;
by the approach of the party on the other.
The design is extremely complicated.
The balance must be very finely considered.[62]

As we suggested earlier, the pattern is based on the alternating movements of two basic emotions: an upward movement to convey a feeling of vitality, a downward or falling movement to show despair. The increase in Clarissa's excitement builds up slowly throughout the novel (although with its small reverses), matched by a corresponding increase in Septimus' despair. The very opening suggests the two alternate motions:

What a lark! What a plunge!

The word "lark" suggests a rising of joy (or of a bird in the skies), the "plunge," a fall into an atmosphere "chill and sharp" with "something awful . . . about to happen." The rooks are "rising, falling"; life and the moment are "building . . . tumbling." Yet the dominant emotion is one of emergence, joy, birth, creation. Clarissa's sense of the vitality of the London morning takes the upward movement of Milton's creation scene in *Paradise Lost*:[63] the "whirling young men, and laughing girls," the "bouncing ponies" who spring up from the ground, seem born from the morning itself. But hardly twenty pages later the images of falling begin—of trapdoors opening, of falling into flames or to the ocean depths—images associated with Septimus and Rezia, his wife.[64] Spaced throughout the book, they are counter-balanced by three rising sequences

---

[62] *Dalloway Notebook I*, October 16, 1922.

[63] In Book VII of *Paradise Lost*, the movement of the animals, "upspringing" from the earth, conveys the emotional tone of the entire scene of creation.

[64] *Dalloway*, pp. 28, 74, 77, 155, 157. Septimus' actual fall: p. 164.

of Clarissa on the staircase: the first when she reaches the landing and assembles "that diamond shape, that single person" (p. 43), the second when she reaches her upstairs drawing room to mend her green dress (pp. 44-45), and the third when she comes up the stairs to the party, seeking "pinnacles," then feeling herself "a stake driven in at the top of her stairs" (pp. 182-87). Mrs. Woolf's diary describes this "last lap of *Mrs. D.* There I am now—at last at the party, which is to begin in the kitchen, and climb slowly upstairs. It is to be a most complicated . . . piece, knitting together everything and ending on three notes, at different stages of the staircase."[65] At the novel's end, the two movements are brought dramatically together when, at the very climax of her party's triumph, she feels the "plunge" of Septimus' body as her own, sees the ground flashing "up." On the final page, Peter's thoughts reveal the alternation of "ecstasy" and "terror" which the two main characters experience and which the movements themselves express:

> "I will come," said Peter, but he sat on for a moment. What is this terror? what is this ecstasy? he thought to himself. What is it that fills me with extraordinary excitement?
> It is Clarissa, he said.
> For there she was.

Space. In a diary note concerning *The Years,* Virginia Woolf wrote: "I think I see how I can bring in interludes— I mean spaces of silence."[66] Regarding a short story of Turgenev, she wrote that "all round are the silent spaces."[67] The conjunction of "space" with "silence" suggests that she approached this aspect of form in the same way as does

[65] *Diary,* September 7, 1924.
[66] *Diary,* July 17, 1935.
[67] "A Glance at Turgenev," *TLS,* December 8, 1921, p. 813.

an architect, painter, or composer—to use negative "blank spaces" or "intervals" in a positive way so as to make them contribute to subjective feeling.

Virginia Woolf's conception of silence as space in which the reader's own personal emotions are freed to move and expand, grew and changed from *The Voyage Out*, in which Hewet states that he is writing "a novel about Silence," to her final book, *Between the Acts*, which seems the novel, however altered, which Hewet foretold. In *The Voyage Out*, Terence Hewet explains "Silence" as "the things people don't say," a silence which, as a later conversation seems to point out, indicates "feeling";[68] the second half of the novel, with its long tracts of verbalized inner thought, seems to illustrate just that. In *The Waves*, this verbalization is not in thought-patterns or reveries but in highly imagistic soliloquies whose movement, color, and imagery pantomime the inner tensions of the psyche; the voice is silent, the attitudes and emotions speak. By the time Virginia Woolf wrote *Between the Acts*, the concept became refined so that silence appears to mean that which is felt but not explicitly expressed, that which transpires literally between the acts of spoken thought.[69]

Several quotations from the early version of *Between the Acts* appear to illustrate this concept:

That feeling slipped between the space that separates one word from another; like a blue flower between two stones.

What breadth of time; what river of people feeling . . . ran between those islands of speech; leaving the old man high and dry on his; them on theirs?[70]

[68] *Voyage*, p. 262. On p. 364, Rachel asks Terence " 'Why don't people write about the things they do feel?' "
[69] Cf. "The Anatomy of Fiction" (*G.R.*), *Essays*, II, p. 138: "Between the sentences . . . a little shape of some kind builds itself up."
[70] *Pointz Hall Typescript*, pp. 5 and 12 (April, 1938).

In the published version Mrs. Swithin admits that " 'We haven't the words—we haven't the words. . . . Behind the eyes; not on the lips; that's all' " (p. 68).

What is sensed "behind the eyes" is the final meaning of silence as Virginia Woolf shows it in *Between the Acts*. The word "silence" itself occurs innumerable times in the novel,[71] as if to tell the reader to pause and let himself feel what Virginia Woolf has suggested, not through words, but by such means as symbolic action (see Chapter IV, iii), the poetry that Isa hums beneath her breath, or conversation so condensed it is scarcely dialogue at all:

> Nothing whatever appeared on the stage.
>
> Darts of red and green light flashed from the rings on Mrs. Manresa's fingers. He [Giles] looked from them at Aunt Lucy. From her to William Dodge. From him to Isa. She refused to meet his eyes. And he looked down at his blood-stained tennis shoes.
>
> He said (without words), "I'm damnably unhappy."
>
> "So am I," Dodge echoed.
>
> "And I too," Isa thought.
>
> They were all caught and caged; prisoners; watching a spectacle. Nothing happened.   (p. 205)

Here the conversation is not even spoken, only thought. There is very little movement in the scene save the flash of Mrs. Manresa's rings and Giles's shifting eyes. Nothing is happening, either, on the stage. But set in the context of the entire novel, the scene is rich in its suggestion of emotional relationships and their complexity which form the real spectacle or pageant of the novel.

Throughout *Between the Acts* spaces such as this are

[71] For example: "and in his silence, passion" (p. 9); a painting leads the eye of the beholder "into silence" (p. 46); Mrs. Manresa "making silence add its unmistakable contribution to talk" (p. 50); "drew them down the paths of silence" (p. 57); "the heart of silence" (p. 63).

utilized for brief interludes of emotional awareness that glimmer, like the flash of Mrs. Manresa's rings, at the edge of our introspective screen. Very little appears on paper. The book grows and grows in our minds. We might say of it what Virginia Woolf wrote of a scene in Turgenev's novel *Rudin*, that it has "a size out of all proportion to its length. It expands in the mind and lies there giving off fresh ideas, emotions, and pictures much as a moment in real life will sometimes only yield its meaning long after it has passed . . . we are surrounded on all sides . . . by the silence, by the look of things. The scene is extraordinarily complete."[72] Finally, we might see this mode of space, or silence, not as peculiar to Virginia Woolf but as part of the machinery necessary to transfer our interest "from the outer to the inner," as she says of the method of Laurence Sterne. In her essay on *Sentimental Journey* she names Sterne as "the forerunner of the moderns" because of his "interest in silence rather than in speech." He makes us "consult our own minds."[73] That, in effect, is what the many subjective modes of form invite the reader to do.

※ ※ ※

WITH THESE five aspects of inward form—mass, connection, rhythm, pattern, and space—we have attempted to illustrate Virginia Woolf's method of defining certain qualities of felt experience, life in its experiential totality rather than in its single state of being. To recapitulate, the sense of *mass* is the way we experience the impact, the density, the interpenetration of a series of emotional states. *Connection* is our relationship with what produces that emotion. *Rhythm* is the way we experience that emotion's

[72] "The Novels of Turgenev" (*C.D.B.*), *Essays*, I, pp. 247-48.
[73] (*C.R.II*), *Essays*, I, pp. 97-98.

fluctuations and intensities. *Pattern* is the ordering or harmonizing of the plexus of emotions so that we can more easily understand and feel them. And, finally, *space* is the means by which, with our own subjective sense, we can enter more fully the house of fiction which Mrs. Woolf has prepared for us, inhabit its rooms, move freely about it, and furnish it with emotional associations of our own. Thus we are able to do what Mrs. Woolf suggests is the reader's responsibility, to make of "these multitudinous impressions . . . these fleeting shapes one that is hard and lasting."[74]

This underlying shape, the shape we feel rather than see, is postulated three times by Lily Briscoe in *To the Lighthouse*. "Beneath the colour there was the shape," she first observes (p. 34). Later, and more explicitly, she sees "the colour burning on a framework of steel; the light of a butterfly's wing lying upon the arches of a cathedral" (p. 78). Still later, looking at her picture (which, we must remember, is an abstract of the novel), she thinks:

> Beautiful and bright it should be on the surface, feathery and evanescent, one colour melting into another like the colours on a butterfly's wing; but beneath the fabric must be clamped together with bolts of iron. It was to be a thing you could ruffle with your breath; and a thing you could not dislodge with a team of horses.
>
> (p. 264)

Might we not say, for the purpose of our discussion, that the steel framework is composed of the principles of inward form—of the many modes of subjectivity by which we can enter the cathedral, the great structure of man himself?[75] Mrs. Woolf seems to imply an infinite possibility of

[74] "How Should One Read a Book?" (*C.R.II*), *Essays*, II, p. 8.
[75] In *To the Lighthouse* Mrs. Woolf uses time-honored images of man such as "the tombs of kings," the "sanctuary," or the "dome" (pp. 81-83) connected with Mrs. Ramsay. The latter image suggests St. Peter's, which may be the "church in Rome" referred

interpretations and all of them lead to the heart of her work. For it is the totality of experience, the dimensions of the human being, which she wishes to show us—what shimmers on the surface and what is hidden and therefore can be merely glimpsed or felt. Indeed, we might say that the subliminal, the sensed, the guessed at—the entire underground world of the emotions to which she is constantly giving us the connections—constitute for her the larger part, the steel structure, of the reality of the self. In *To the Lighthouse*, the image of a boat sunk perhaps by a warship—"the silent apparition of an ashen-coloured ship . . . a purplish stain upon the bland surface of the sea as if something had boiled and bled, invisibly, beneath"[76]—points to the forces and emotions beneath the bland appearance of the conscious. What causes this "boiling" and "bleeding" may be glimpsed only as an "apparition." What we see is merely a stain upon the waters. But what has transpired below the surface—the sailors wounded and drowned, the attacks of the sharks (as suggested in the manuscript version), all the activity and pain going on *invisibly*—takes place in ways the reader cannot see but only feel, responding as does the nervous system to certain high-decibel sounds which the ear does not consciously hear.[77]

All this, of course, demands a great deal of the reader. The substance of these demands, the establishing of a right relationship between reader and writer, is the concern of the following chapter.

---

to on p. 100. See also the "shape" of a book as a "cathedral" in "How Should One Read a Book?" (*C.R.II*), *Essays*, II, p. 8.

[76] P. 207. The sinking is suggested in the original ship image in the manuscript: "a murderous looking ship; leaden, ashen, sinister; or, a little froth & stain upon the bland surface of the sea, as if something were foaming or ["being bitten by sharks" is crossed out] boiling beneath." *Lighthouse Notebook II*, p. 172 (May 14, 1926).

[77] Alfred North Whitehead, *Symbolism: Its Meaning and Effect* (New York, 1927), p. 85.

CHAPTER THIRTEEN

The Creative Reader

VIRGINIA WOOLF'S vision of the novel as a microcosm of man, with its very modes drawing upon the subjective experience and responses of the reader, implies an unusually close relationship between the reader and the work. The "new criticism," by calling any discussion of the reader the "affective fallacy," has closed most eyes to this significant, indeed integral, aspect of Mrs. Woolf's fiction. Although this study has continually stressed the collaborative role the reader plays in the subjective modes, it is useful to examine the meaning of that role and see what Virginia Woolf herself assigned to it.

The concept of a reader who would take an active part in the experience of the book may have had its origins not only in the exigencies of the methods, which demanded just such a reader, but also in Virginia Woolf's own urge for communication—an anxiety which, it must be fairly said, obsesses every writer but seems to have been unusually strong in Mrs. Woolf. "Communication is health," thinks Septimus Smith (who may have been patterned after his author),[1] and the inability to communicate on different levels forms one of the themes of *Mrs. Dalloway*.[2] Communication implies, of course, a receptive hearer. And we know from her diaries and Leonard Woolf's volumes of autobiography that the completion or publication of a novel brought nervous exhaustion or mental illness in

---

[1] *Maroon Dalloway Notebook*, November 19, 1922.
[2] See Chapter IV, i, n. 24. Characters in other novels, like Lily Briscoe in *To the Lighthouse* or Miss La Trobe in *Between the Acts*, share Septimus' anxiety and further the theme.

its wake. Fears of exposure,[3] the remorseless call of any new book for response on the part of critics and readers,[4] seemed to exert their psychological pressures.

It is this intuitive need for response which may have occasioned Virginia Woolf to choose Samuel Johnson's phrase, "the common reader," and adapt it for her personal needs into the empathic, if imaginary, audience for her essays—and, ultimately, her novels.[5] Isolated in a closed intellectual circle, she leaned toward a broader, more catholic audience as the Woolfs leaned politically toward the Fabians. The word "common," not derogatory but rather universal in its connotations, suggests a common ground on which writer and reader can meet and emotions be shared. Mrs. Woolf envisions people "reading for the love of reading, slowly and unprofessionally."[6] Her definition of the "lowbrow," filled with vitality, riding his body at a "gallop across life" (in contrast to the highbrow riding his mind in pursuit of ideas),[7] fits with her concept of the novel as communicating not abstract theory but lived experience.

Whatever Mrs. Woolf hoped for from her audience— and T. S. Eliot remarked that only in the England of her time was it possible for "the producer and the consumer of art" to be "on an equal footing"[8]—the demands she

[3] Conversation with May Sarton, autumn 1964. See also *Diary*, March 18, 1935.

[4] Cf. *Jacob's Room*, p. 92, re letter-writers who "addressed themselves to the task of reaching, touching, penetrating the individual heart. Were it possible!" Lily Briscoe's fears that her work may be hung in attics, or Rachel's encounter with a dry inkwell and pen with a broken nib (*Voyage*, pp. 314-15) may express fears of inability to communicate. See *Diary* September 13, 1926; October 23, 1929; September 22, 1931.

[5] Although she poses herself as the "common reader" in the brief essay prefacing *C.R.I*, the term seems to embrace the entire reading audience.

[6] "How Should One Read a Book?" (*C.R.II*), *Essays*, II, p. 11.

[7] "Middlebrow" (*D.M.*), *Essays*, II, pp. 196-97.

[8] T. S. Eliot, "Virginia Woolf," *Horizon*, III, no. 17 (May 1941), 315-16.

placed upon that audience were severe. Some of these demands are voiced in her essay-query "How Should One Read a Book?" which appropriately closes *The Common Reader: Second Series.* The reader must be capable of "great fineness of perception . . . of great boldness of imagination." He must "open the mind wide to the fast flocking of innumerable impressions."[9] And, finally, as "fellow-worker and accomplice" of the writer, he must "refresh and exercise" his own "creative powers." "Do not dictate to your author," she admonishes the reader; "try to become him." It is no wonder that she describes reading as "a difficult and complex art." If the reader is to achieve a "grasp upon the emotion" (for a novel "is not form which you see, but emotion which you feel"), he must be, as was Virginia Woolf, both actor and spectator.[10]

Such demands for full participation in the work may create problems for even the most cooperative reader. The first problem is that posed by the subjective modes themselves: the initial confusion of finding oneself within a mind, or a series of minds; of mastering the ability to sort out the "scrambled" and often seemingly random data into a meaningful and patterned whole; of utilizing to the full the modes of experience offered. A sense of the intensity of identification with the character which Mrs. Woolf herself felt, and which she probably hoped to pass on to her reader, may be glimpsed in a harrowing paragraph in "An Unwritten Novel." There Mrs. Woolf as narrator describes the irresistible urge "to lodge myself somewhere on the firm flesh, in the robust spine, wherever I can penetrate or find foothold on the person, in the soul,"

[9] See Chapter I, iii, re the atoms of sensation which she felt the new novelist must describe. Cf. also "the true reader" in "Hours in a Library" (*G.R.*), *Essays*, II, p. 34.

[10] *Essays*, II, pp. 2, 3, 5, and 9. Cf. characters who "make creators of us, and not merely readers and spectators." "David Copperfield" (*M.*), *Essays*, I, p. 193.

until, finally inside the character she is creating, she can recount the very feeling of being inside the flesh itself: "the ribs radiating branches; the flesh taut tarpaulin; the red hollows; the suck and regurgitation of the heart . . . and so we reach the eyes."[11]

What happens when those eyes are reached, that view from inside the flesh finally achieved, may create another problem for the reader. " 'Reality too strong,' " mutters Miss La Trobe when her audience at the pageant, exposed to "present-time reality," fidgets with irritation.[12] Part of the discomfort may come from repressed areas probed by the modes of subjectivity: the uncovering, in the reader himself, of "monstrous" and "unmanageable emotions," of "obscure terrors and hatreds"[13] which have been kept submerged. Other problems may arise out of an unwillingness to become, even for that moment of "suspension of disbelief," characters one may instinctively dislike, or to take part in situations which may repel—Doris Kilman wolfing her last inch of éclair at the tea-table, Clarissa in the garden with Sally Seton, Delia Pargiter wishing her mother would die. The role of voyeur has become one of participator. Persuaded to experience emotions which for a variety of reasons he may not enjoy, the reader may feel that the last protective barrier—his emotional anonymity —has been snatched away.

This possible invasion of a reader's privacy is related to a final problem which he may encounter: the pervasive presence of Virginia Woolf herself in her works. An anxiety for communication necessarily implies a desire to communicate one's self. And the various characters

---

[11] *Haunted House*, pp. 22-23. Something of this is communicated to the reader in the description of Rachel's illness in *The Voyage Out*. The "suck and regurgitation of the heart" is part of the body rhythm described in the section on rhythm, Chapter XII.

[12] *Acts*, p. 209.

[13] "The Narrow Bridge of Art" (*G.R.*), *Essays*, II, pp. 219, 229.

throughout her novels, both men and women, who exhibit in part certain facets of Mrs. Woolf's personality and feelings, are channels for this communication. The voice which seems at times to be the reader's own voice talking to himself is that of Virginia Woolf, however impersonal, however universal that voice may be. "I, I, I—how we have lost the secret of saying that!" she laments.[14] But no matter by what name we call it—*Je est*, the "indivisible 'I,'" the voice of subjectivity—that perpendicular pronoun is always present in her work, with a ubiquity perhaps guaranteed by the very function of the subjective modes. For if a reader is made to see and feel through the very eyes and mind of a character, and that character resembles the author, he may be said to experience that author as well.[15] For those charmed by the personality of Mrs. Woolf and attracted by the brilliance of her mind, this sense of identification offers no difficulties. Indeed, it can extend the emotional reach of fiction to the further dimension of autobiography. This is perhaps the closest communication which can be achieved between the reader and a work of fiction.

🙦 🙦

THE MOST graphic exposition of Mrs. Woolf's concept of the creative reader can be seen in her final novel, *Between the Acts*, a paradigm not only of the interdependence of author, work, and audience/reader, but also of certain principles basic to the subjective modes. By parabolic scene or brief allusion the novel shows the audience/

[14] "Reading" (*C.D.B.*), *Essays*, II, p. 29.
[15] Cf. Terence Hewet: " 'All you read a novel for is to see what sort of person the writer is' " (*Voyage*, p. 262). Or in *Orlando*: "In short, every secret of a writer's soul, every experience of his life, every quality of his mind is written large in his works" (pp. 189-90).

reader as participator; the work of art as a mirror in which the reader views himself;[16] the superiority of experience over formal plot; and the importance of the "act" itself—not as history or drama would see it, but as the person himself experiences it, a "living" or a "doing" rather than a dead *fait accompli*.

This concept of the act as a "becoming" or a "doing"——indicating still another meaning of the novel's title—serves to define the area within which the subjective modes may be said to operate. An expansion of her earlier concept of the moment of being (a vertical slice of emotional life), it presents a larger movement within reality whose greater potential brings it even closer to what we know as life. It is not merely the "act" or "moment" but also the "before" and "after"; its shape evolves in time; it has its own psychological history. Like the "daily drama of the body" which Mrs. Woolf describes, with its fluctuations in fever, its aches and tensions, its cycles of energy and fatigue,[17] the act has its own story. If the form which contains it is that of the human being, as the last chapter suggests, its "story" must be the very act and process of living.

The importance of the act as opposed to the artificially controlled event ("Don't bother about the plot: the plot's nothing," Miss La Trobe thinks in vexation)[18] can be seen in a brief scenario of "a new kind of play" which Mrs. Woolf toys with in her diary:

> Woman thinks . . .
> He does.
> Organ plays.
> She writes.

[16] This is a working-out of the principle of the object acting as mirror-image for the subject (see Chapter V, i).

[17] "On Being Ill" (*M.*), *Essays*, IV, p. 194.

[18] *Acts*, p. 109.

> They say:
> She sings.
> Night speaks
> They miss[19]

With its economy of subject and active verb, this "new kind of play" is a parable of the concentration on the act itself and participation in it. The act itself suffices, and it is this exclusive focus on it that allows full play of the subjective modes. As the pageant's audience in *Between the Acts* is asked to imagine entire sequences omitted from the sketches (or acts) presented on-stage,[20] as it is forced to be made aware of "present-time reality"—of the cows, the rain, the swallows—so the reader's attention is engaged in hitherto unnoticed or unrecorded processes of life. " 'What a small part I've had to play!' " Lucy Swithin tells Miss La Trobe, the pageant's creator, in acknowledging the audience's own creative role. " 'But you've made me feel I could have played . . . Cleopatra!' "[21]

Cleopatra—is the name not perhaps symbolic of the infinite variety of emotional response which can be activated in the reader; or, more specifically, the various means by which he himself aids in the creation of the work? He does not merely, as Louis phrases it in *The Waves*, " 'give out a sound like a beaten gong as one sensation strikes and then another.' "[22] He is part of the gestalt of the work itself, which, like the carnation, " 'a whole flower,' " seven-petalled, representing Percival and his friends, is whole only because " 'every eye brings its own contribution.' "[23]

The contribution of the eye, all the facets of the per-

---

[19] *Diary*, February 21, 1927.   [20] *Acts*, p. 166.
[21] *Acts*, p. 179.
[22] *Waves*, p. 28. This follows the statement that the soliloquies will some day be shared, presumably by the reader.
[23] *Waves*, p. 91. Cf., " 'I need an audience. . . . To be myself (I note) I need the illumination of other people's eyes' " (p. 83).

ceptive process—from the angle of vision through which Mrs. Woolf makes the reader view the object, to the creation of the image itself through a complexity of physical and psychical phases—are perhaps the most consciously realized means by which the reader participates. He sees only what the character selects, visually and mentally, from the scene about him; he contributes spontaneously from his own fund of knowledge and memory-association to the image thus presented and thereby offers a unique and wholly individual element to the work.[24]

In the same manner, the patterns of the character's thoughts—whether those of reverie, phantasy, or logical thought—place the reader within a particular ambience of feeling which is then augmented by memories of similar thought patterns of his own, contributing, perhaps, different shadings of mood. The rhythms of these patterns, as well as the sentence and word cadences themselves, are likewise reflected in the reader's own flux and flow of emotion or his biological rhythms, unconscious though these rhythms may be.[25] Thus, for example, the lullaby sequence in *The Waves* (" 'sleep, sleep' "—pp. 121-23) seems to echo not only the relaxed breathing of the infant, but also rhythms of rocking, which are cradled in childhood memory with their concomitant emotions. It is perhaps significant that the rhythm of the waves—up and down, to and fro—is that universal pattern of systole and diastole which finds its rhythmic analogies in so many aspects of our emotional, biological, and physical life.

The reader's response to these rhythms, as to certain images and symbols,[26] occurs mainly below the threshold of awareness, a psychic activity which results in the arousal of energies cathected with the personal emotions which the rhythms (or images) evoke. We may call this principle

[24] See Chapters III, iii; V; VI; VII, iii; VIII, i.
[25] See Chapters IX, v; X, iv; XII, i and ii.
[26] See Chapter XI, i.

"energy release"; and it is the second major way in which the reader may be said to contribute to the work. For if the reader is to experience the novel, he must feel the emotions of the character, and we tend to forget that emotions carry with them their own charges of energy, their own cycles of tension and release. These emotions, and their particular quality, may at first appear to be communicated wholly by the author; actually, they have their origin in us. Only the agent of stimulus is given. As we learn to know the character through the various modes of perception and mentation, so we participate emotionally in his life by means of the energy thus activated within our own complex being.

This is true to some degree of the relationship of the reader to any work of fiction. Deep anxieties may be raised or recalled, and energy momentarily stimulated; or guilts and fears may be lulled and energy thereby released. In either case, the energy is used in one's enjoyment of, or engagement with, the book.[27] Little is understood of this activity. What we do know is that certain passages in novels raise within us emotions of fright, pleasure, satisfaction. We seem to be relaxed by some scenes, agitated by others. Freud called the reservoir of instinctual energy thus tapped the *libido*; Jung identified "psychic energy" with the libido and posited a theory of energy release through the making of analogies with an archetypal or universal image.[28] Whatever the *modus operandi*, Mrs. Woolf appears to have utilized, through her subjective modes, an extraordinary variety of images and patterns of feeling—whether as a simple picture or elaborate met-

[27] Simon Lesser in *Fiction and the Unconscious* discusses the minimization or relief of anxiety as "an important objective of form," in Chapters VI, VII, and X. See esp. p. 257.

[28] The archetype, according to Jung, has specific energy stored with it which is released through the symbol of analogy. *Symbols of Transformation*, I, pp. 139-41, 158, 232.

aphor, a brief scene or longer passage (the word "passage" itself suggesting a sequence of felt emotion, as in a "passage" of music)—which arouse emotion and hence initiate an energy-cycle within the reader, or which imitate various biological patterns of rhythm that, because of our unconscious identification with them, our recognition of something familiar and reassuring, give a sense of pleasure or a momentary freedom from anxiety.

In certain of Mrs. Woolf's novels, an archetypal pattern of feeling appears to serve as the emotional form for the entire work. The elaborate fairy-tale phantasy of the awakening of the feminine instinct in *Orlando*, as well as the realization of its potentialities,[29] may touch a hidden area of response in women readers. The seeking of parental love and approbation in *To the Lighthouse* (in psychological terms, a search for the father- and mother-imago), and the myth of the "night journey" in *The Voyage Out* (with its descent into the self,[30] its repeating motifs of frustration and suffocation), are patterns of feeling which, evoking universal aspects of experience, seem to possess the power to touch deep reservoirs of energy. The reader is led to feel a catharsis of relief when Rachel dies, after her duplicate journeys into the jungles of love and fever. A similar resolution of conflict is achieved in *To the Lighthouse* when the related principles of father and mother, of *Logos* and *Eros*,[31] are reached as the children

[29] Maud Bodkin, *Archetypal Patterns in Poetry*, pp. 300-303.

[30] See Miss Bodkin's reference to Jung's theory of the "night journey," *ibid.*, pp. 52-54, and her application of it to the Book of Jonah and *The Ancient Mariner*.

[31] Mr. Ramsay, the philosopher, implies a universal masculine principle; Mrs. Ramsay, the creative mother, the feminine. As she is the wedge of darkness between the lighthouse beams, so he is associated with light (wisdom); and the qualities of yang and yin, the light and the dark, the masculine and feminine, are seen as a unity. In a parallel way, the children come to terms with their father on the journey; Lily, who is described as having a father but no mother, glimpses her mother-surrogate.

243

finally land at the lighthouse and Lily has her glimpse of Mrs. Ramsay. However complex the patterns of feeling, in each of Mrs. Woolf's novels a sequence of tensions is built up which, when the climax occurs, is suddenly resolved, and the reader seems to be bathed in a flood of peace.[32] St. John feels "a strange sense of quiet and relief." Lily has her vision. The sun rises over the Pargiters' London with "extraordinary beauty, simplicity and peace." Peter Walsh experiences joy at Clarissa's coming. Night falls on Giles and Isa—the tensions of hate are resolved in love. None of the novels' climaxes is concerned with overt action; rather they are the externalized or symbolized representations of internal conflicts. In *The Waves*, after the ride into the battle with death, carried on the image of an arching wave, the novel and tension end with the simple phrase *"The waves broke on the shore."* Whatever the reader feels at the climax, through his long internal participation in the novel, has been accomplished not by one mode of subjectivity only but by the working together of the modes—an organic response which is often unconscious or perhaps only partly realized.

🐦 🐦 🐦

AN UNDERSTANDING of Mrs. Woolf's concept of the creative reader brings to light more sharply the contemporary nature of her work. She died in 1941. Nearly thirty years later, ideas and trends whose shape could be glimpsed in her novels have become visible, not only in fiction—as in the *nouveau roman* of Nathalie Sarraute or Alain Robbe-Grillet, which carries subjectivity to its outermost limits—but also in music and especially in the the-

---

[32] Cf. Maud Bodkin's discussion of *The Ancient Mariner*, in *Archetypal Patterns*, pp. 37-60 (esp. p. 48), 308-309.

atre of the absurd. The participating audience, the random act; the emphasis on the global rather than the linear, on the kinetic instead of the static; experiments with mass, rhythm, and space—all suggest a creative and innovating intellect whose ideas fit intuitively into emerging patterns of artistic thought.

Her approach to certain philosophical and psychological problems was also far ahead of her time. One may be reminded of Bergson, William James, and Freud in reading her novels. But contemporaries like Edmund Husserl's disciple Merleau-Ponty, the Swiss psychologist Jean Piaget (whose studies of the child mind bear out many of Mrs. Woolf's own observations), the school of Cassirer, Whitehead, and Susanne K. Langer, seem just as pertinent. Indeed—and every generation approaches a great writer from its own perspective—Virginia Woolf belongs to the moment of now. On her work, as in her concept of the moment, the future already lay "like a piece of glass, making it tremble and quiver"[33]—by which she meant that the immanence of the future in the present brings it vitally alive.

This is not to imply, however, that Mrs. Woolf conforms to this or that current mode of thought. One does not draw a particular philosophy or discipline from her work. One can only conclude that her examination of her own encounter with lived experience was transmuted into the novel's form: modes of life became modes of fiction. And since a writer's apprehension of his methods, as Virginia Woolf was only too ready to admit, is apt to be mainly unconscious,[34] so is the reader's participation in

[33] (M.), Essays, II, p. 293.
[34] In "The Art of Fiction" (M.), Essays, II, p. 51, Mrs. Woolf notes that E. M. Forster "knows from experience what a muddled and illogical machine the brain of a writer is . . . how little they think about methods . . . how absorbed they tend to become in some vision of their own."

them. The purpose of this study has been to illuminate these methods, to alert the reader to them, and so enable him more easily to "refresh and exercise" his own "creative powers." For this reader, uncommon though he may be, Virginia Woolf's work remains a unique experience and a constant challenge.

Appendix

BERNARD AS THE COMPLETE ANDROGYNOUS PERSONALITY[1]

Mental and physical aspects drawn from a study of major symbols, images, and leitmotifs in *The Waves*

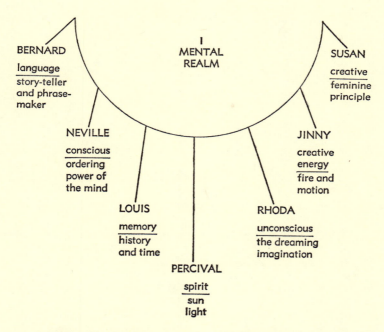

---

[1] Bernard: " 'I am many people; I do not altogether know who I am—Jinny, Susan, Neville, Rhoda, or Louis; or how to distinguish my life from theirs' " (*Waves*, p. 196).

" 'There are . . . many Bernards' " (p. 184).
" '. . . nor do I always know if I am man or woman' "
(p. 199)

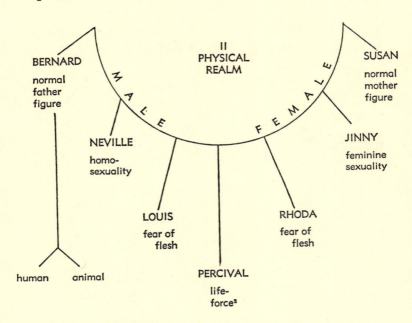

2 "The flower stands before us
the flower with six
sides; the flower
sun simultaneously:

. . . .
when we dined with Percival;
the flower is now . . .
something made of life."

From *Notebook VI* of *The Waves*, opp. p. 111. Correlative passage in the Uniform edn., p. 91: " 'There is a red carnation. . . .' "

A Selected Bibliography

THE FOLLOWING list is comprised of works consulted which proved of particular value to this study. For a complete guide to Mrs. Woolf's writings the reader is referred to B. J. Kirkpatrick's *A Bibliography of Virginia Woolf* (London: Rupert Hart-Davis, rev. edn., 1967), one of the Soho Bibliographies. The exhaustive critical comment compiled by Jean Guiguet for *Virginia Woolf and Her Works* is likewise suggested for more generalized reference.

ORIGINAL MANUSCRIPTS from the Berg Collection at the New York Public Library (in chronological order).

The Voyage Out. Two notebooks (hand-written), two typescripts.
    Typescript I. Early undated script, briefer than Typescript II. Appears to predate notebooks.
    March Notebook, 1912.
    December Notebook, 1912.
    Typescript II. Undated, but appears to follow the 1912 notebooks.

Jacob's Room. Three bound notebooks.
    Notebook I. April 15 to November 24, 1920.
    Notebook II. November 26, 1920, to May 6 (1921?).
    Notebook III. March 12 to October 16, 1922. Corrections for *Jacob's Room*; notes for *Mrs. Dalloway* and chapter "The Prime Minister"; book reviews including those on Henry James's *The Sacred Fount* and Dorothy Richardson's *Revolving Lights*; essays including "On Re-reading Novels."

Mrs. Dalloway. Four bound notebooks.
    Notebook I. Same as *J. R. Notebook III.* Entries on

Dalloway begin October 6, 1922. Last entry: scene of Clarissa and Peter Walsh.

Notebook II. Cover: "Reviews, 1924." January 7 to October 5, 1924. Reviews and essays; five pages of *Mrs. Dalloway.*

Notebook III. Cover: "Reviews, 1924." November 22, 1924. Corrections for *Dalloway*, story "The New Dress," notes and corrections for articles in *Common Reader.*

Maroon Leather Notebook (small). November 9, 1922, to August 2, 1923. Working notes for *Dalloway* and jottings on the *Choephori.*

To the Lighthouse. Three notebooks, two bound, one loose-leaf.

Notebook I (bound). August 6, 1925, to March 5, 1926. Notes and draft of novel's first section; notes on "Time Passes"; essay "Robinson Crusoe."

Notebook II (bound). March 17, 1926. Section later titled "Time Passes."

Notebook III (loose-leaf). May 27 to September 15, 1926. Final section of novel and revisions.

The Waves. Seven bound notebooks, one loose-leaf.

Notebook I. July 2 to October 28, 1929. Beginnings. Second chapter entitled "The Mind."

Notebook II. October 29, 1929, to January 18, 1930.

Notebook III. January 19 to April 12, 1930.

Notebook IV. April 13 to August 4, 1930.

Notebook V. August 5, 1930.

Notebook VI. November 5, 1930.

Notebook VII. February 2, 1931.

Small Waves Notebook (loose-leaf). June 15, 1930, to January 30, 1931. Ideas for revision.

Pointz Hall (*Between the Acts*). Three bound notebooks, one typescript.

Notebook I. 1938-39. Articles, essays, reviews, sequences of novel (December 14, 1938).

Notebook II. Early version of novel's second half. No date.

Small Pointz Hall Notebook. August 23, 1938(?). Random notes.

Typescript I. Earliest dated draft. Pp. 1 to 189 dated April 2, 1938 to July 30, 1939.

EDITIONS (in chronological order) of Virginia Woolf's works mentioned in this study. The Uniform edition has been used wherever available.

The Voyage Out. London: Duckworth, 1915; Hogarth Press, Uniform edn., 1929.

Night and Day. London: Duckworth, 1919; Hogarth Press, Uniform edn., 1930.

Jacob's Room. Richmond: Hogarth Press, 1922; second Uniform edn., 1945.

The Common Reader (First Series). London: Hogarth Press, 1925; Uniform edn., 1929.

Mrs. Dalloway. London: Hogarth Press, 1925; second Uniform edn., 1942.

Mrs. Dalloway. Introd. by Virginia Woolf. New York: Modern Library, 1928.

Mrs. Dalloway. New York: Harbrace Modern Classics, 1949.

To the Lighthouse. London: Hogarth Press, 1927; Uniform edn., 1930.

To the Lighthouse. New York: Modern Library, 1927.

Orlando. London: Hogarth Press, 1928; Uniform edn., 1933 (illustrations omitted).

Orlando. Afterword by Elizabeth Bowen. New York: New American Library, 1960 (illustrations).

A Room of One's Own. London: Hogarth Press, 1929; Uniform edn., 1931.

The Waves. London: Hogarth Press, 1931; second Uniform edn., 1943.

The Common Reader: Second Series. London: Hogarth Press, 1932; Uniform edn., 1935.

Flush: A Biography. London: Hogarth Press, October 1933; Uniform edn., November 1933.

The Years. London: Hogarth Press, 1937; Uniform edn., 1940.

Roger Fry: A Biography. London: Hogarth Press, 1940.

Between the Acts. London: Hogarth Press, 1941; Uniform edn., 1953.

The Death of the Moth and Other Essays. London: Hogarth Press, 1942.

A Haunted House and Other Short Stories. London: Hogarth Press, 1943; Uniform edn., 1953.

The Moment and Other Essays. London: Hogarth Press, 1947; Uniform edn., 1952.

The Captain's Death Bed and Other Essays. London: Hogarth Press, 1950. Uniform edn., 1955.

A Writer's Diary. London: Hogarth Press, 1953.

Virginia Woolf and Lytton Strachey: Letters, ed. Leonard Woolf and James Strachey. London: Hogarth Press and Chatto & Windus, 1956.

Granite and Rainbow: Essays. London: Hogarth Press, 1958.

Contemporary Writers (essays) ed. Jean Guiguet. London: Hogarth Press, 1965.

Collected Essays, 4 vols. London: Hogarth Press, 1966-67.

TRANSLATIONS AND CONTRIBUTIONS

Maitland, Frederic William. *The Life and Letters of Leslie Stephen*. London: Duckworth, 1906. Pages 474-76: impressions by "one of his daughters," i.e., Virginia Stephen.

Dostoevsky, F. M. *Stavrogin's Confession and The Plan of The Life of a Great Sinner*, trans. S. S. Koteliansky and Virginia Woolf. Richmond: Hogarth Press, 1922.

Goldenveizer, A. B. *Talks with Tolstoi*, trans. S. S. Koteliansky and Virginia Woolf. Richmond: Hogarth Press, 1923.

BOOKS, ARTICLES, and books with chapters specifically about Virginia Woolf and her work.

Auerbach, Erich. *Mimesis: The Representation of Reality in Western Literature*, trans. Willard R. Trask. Princeton: Princeton University Press, 1953.

Bell, Clive. *Old Friends: Personal Recollections*. New York: Harcourt, Brace, 1957.

―――. "Virginia Woolf," *Dial*, LXXVII (December 1924), 451-65.

Bennett, Joan. *Virginia Woolf: Her Art as a Novelist*. 2nd edn. Cambridge, England: Cambridge University Press, 1964.

Blackstone, Bernard. *Virginia Woolf: A Commentary*. New York: Harcourt, Brace, 1949.

Brewster, Dorothy. *Virginia Woolf*. New York: New York University Press, 1962.

Chambers, R. L. *The Novels of Virginia Woolf*. Edinburgh: Oliver and Boyd, 1947.

Chastaing, Maxime. *La Philosophie de Virginia Woolf*. Paris: Presses Universitaires de France, 1951.

Daiches, David. *The Novel and the Modern World*. Rev. edn. Chicago: University of Chicago Press, 1960.

―――. *Virginia Woolf*. Norfolk, Conn.: New Directions, 1942.

Delattre, Floris. *Le Roman Psychologique de Virginia Woolf*. Paris: J. Vrin, 1932.

Edel, Leon. *Literary Biography*. Toronto: University of Toronto Press, 1957.

BIBLIOGRAPHY

Edel, Leon. *The Modern Psychological Novel*. Rev. edn. New York: Grosset & Dunlap, 1964.

Eliot, T. S. "Virginia Woolf" (part 1 of a series of reminiscences), *Horizon*, III (May 1941), 313-16.

Forster, E. M. *Virginia Woolf*. New York: Harcourt, Brace, 1942.

Freedman, Ralph. *The Lyrical Novel: Studies in Hermann Hesse, André Gide, and Virginia Woolf*. Princeton: Princeton University Press, 1963.

Graham, John. "Time in the Novels of Virginia Woolf," *University of Toronto Quarterly*, XVIII (January 1949), 186-201.

Grant, Duncan. "Virginia Woolf," *Horizon*, III (June 1941), 402-406.

Gruber, Ruth. *Virginia Woolf: A Study*. Leipzig: Verlag von Bernhard Tauchnitz, 1935.

Guiguet, Jean. *Virginia Woolf and Her Works*, trans. Jean Stewart. London: Hogarth Press, 1965.

Hafley, James. *The Glass Roof: Virginia Woolf as Novelist*. Berkeley: University of California Press, 1954.

Holtby, Winifred. *Virginia Woolf*. London: Wishart and Co., 1932.

Isherwood, Christopher. "Virginia Woolf," *Decision*, I (May 1941), 36-38.

Johnstone, J. K. *The Bloomsbury Group: A Study of E. M. Forster, Lytton Strachey, Virginia Woolf, and their Circle*. London: Secker and Warburg, 1954.

Macaulay, Rose. "Virginia Woolf" (part 2), *Horizon*, III (May 1941), 316-18.

Nathan, Monique. *Virginia Woolf*, trans. Herma Briffault. New York: Grove Press; London: Evergreen Books, Ltd., 1961.

Overcarsh, F. L. "The Lighthouse, Face to Face," *Accent* (Winter 1950), 107-23.

254

Pippett, Aileen. *The Moth and the Star*. Boston: Little, Brown, 1955.

Plomer, William. "Virginia Woolf" (part 4), *Horizon*, III (May 1941), 323-27.

Rantavaara, Irma. *Virginia Woolf and Bloomsbury*. Helsinki: Annales Academiae Scientiarum Fennicae, 1953.

Sackville-West, V[ictoria]. "Virginia Woolf" (part 3), *Horizon*, III (May 1941), 318-23.

Thakur, N. C. *The Symbolism of Virginia Woolf*. New York: Oxford University Press, 1965.

Troy, William. "Virginia Woolf: The Poetic Method" (part 1), *Symposium*, III (January 1932), 53-63.

———. "Virginia Woolf: The Poetic Style" (part 2), *Symposium*, III (April 1932), 153-66.

Verga, Ines. *Virginia Woolf's Novels and their Analogy to Music*. English Pamphlet Series, No. 11. Buenos Aires: Argentine Association of English Culture, 1945.

Books, pamphlets, and introductions containing biographical or critical reference to Virginia Woolf, quotations from her letters, or extracts from her writings.

Allen, Walter. *The English Novel: A Short Critical History*. London: Phoenix House, 1954.

———. *The Modern Novel in Britain and the United States*. New York: Dutton, 1964.

Annan, Noel. *Leslie Stephen: His Thought and Character in Relation to His Time*. London: MacGibbon and Kee, 1951.

Bartlett, Sir Frederic. *Thinking: An Experimental and Social Study*. New York: Basic Books, 1958.

Beach, Joseph Warren. *The Twentieth Century Novel: Studies in Technique*. New York: Appleton-Century-Crofts, 1932.

Bodkin, Maud. *Archetypal Patterns in Poetry: Psychological Studies of Imagination.* London: Oxford University Press, 1934.

Brown, E. K. *Rhythm in the Novel.* Toronto: University of Toronto Press, 1950.

Edel, Leon. *Henry James: The Middle Years: 1882-1895.* Philadelphia and New York: Lippincott, 1962.

————. Introduction to *The Sacred Fount* by Henry James. New York: Grove Press, 1963.

————. Introduction to *We'll to the Woods No More* by Edouard Dujardin. New York: New Directions, 1957.

Forster, E. M. *Aspects of the Novel.* New York: Harcourt, Brace, 1927.

Frierson, W. C. *The English Novel in Transition: 1885-1940.* Norman: University of Oklahoma Press, 1942.

Frye, Northrop. *Anatomy of Criticism.* Princeton: Princeton University Press, 1957.

Garnett, David. *The Flowers of the Forest.* London: Chatto & Windus, 1955.

Gregory, Horace. *Dorothy Richardson: An Adventure in Self-Discovery.* New York: Holt, Rinehart and Winston, 1967.

Hoops, Reinald. "Der Einfluss der Psychoanalyse auf die Englische Literatur," *Anglistische Forschungen*, Vol. 77, ed. Dr. J. Hoops. Heidelberg: Carl Winter's Universitätsbuchhandlung, 1934.

Humphrey, Robert. *Stream of Consciousness in the Modern Novel.* Berkeley: University of California Press, 1954.

Isaacs, J[acob]. *An Assessment of Twentieth-Century Literature.* New York: Noonday Press, 1951.

Kris, Ernst. *Psychoanalytic Explorations in Art.* New York: International Universities Press, 1952.

Pritchett, V. W. *The Living Novel.* New York: Reynal and Hitchcock, 1947.

Sarton, May. *I Knew a Phoenix*. New York: Rinehart, 1959.

Stephen, Adrian. *The Dreadnought Hoax*. London: Hogarth Press, 1936.

Tindall, William York. *Forces in Modern British Literature: 1885-1946*. New York: A. Knopf, 1947.

———. *The Literary Symbol*. Bloomington: Indiana University Press, 1955.

Wilson, Edmund. *Axel's Castle*. New York: Scribner's, 1948.

Woolf, Leonard. *Sowing: An Autobiography of the Years 1880 to 1904*. London: Hogarth Press, 1960.

———. *Growing: An Autobiography of the Years 1904 to 1911*. London: Hogarth Press, 1961.

———. *Beginning Again: An Autobiography of the Years 1911 to 1918*. New York: Harcourt, Brace, 1964.

———. *Downhill all the Way: An Autobiography of the Years 1919 to 1939*. London: Hogarth Press, 1967.

GENERAL BOOKS AND ARTICLES on literature, art, philosophy, psychology, and related subjects.

Barfield, Owen. *Poetic Diction: A Study in Meaning*. 2nd edn. London: Faber and Faber, 1952.

Bell, Clive. *An Account of French Painting*. London: Chatto & Windus, 1922.

———. *Proust*. New York: Harcourt, Brace, 1929.

———. *Since Cézanne*. London: Chatto & Windus, 1922.

Bellak, Leopold, M.D., ed. *Schizophrenia: A Review of the Syndrome*. New York: Logos Press, 1958.

Bergson, Henri. *Creative Evolution*, ed. Irwin Edman, trans. Arthur Mitchell. New York: Modern Library, 1944.

———. *Matter and Memory*, trans. Nancy Margaret

Paul and W. Scott Palmer. London: Allen & Unwin; New York: Macmillan, 1911.

––––––––. *Time and Free Will*, trans. F. L. Pogson. London: Allen & Unwin; New York: Macmillan, 1910.

Bertocci, Peter A. "A Temporalistic View of Personal Mind" in *Theories of the Mind*, ed. Jordan Scher. New York: Macmillan, 1962.

Cassirer, Ernst. *Language and Myth*, trans. Susanne K. Langer. New York: Harper & Brothers, 1946.

––––––––. *The Philosophy of Symbolic Forms*, ed. Charles W. Hendel, trans. Ralph Manheim. 3 vols.; New Haven: Yale University Press, 1953-57.

Church, Joseph. *Language and the Discovery of Reality: A Developmental Psychology of Cognition*. New York: Random House, 1961.

Ehrenzweig, Anton. *The Psychoanalysis of Artistic Vision and Hearing*. London: Routledge and Kegan Paul, 1953.

Eliot, T. S. *On Poetry and Poets*. New York: Farrar, Straus and Cudahy, 1957.

Frazer, Sir James G. *The Golden Bough*. 1 vol., abr. edn. New York: Macmillan, 1951.

Freud, Sigmund. "The Relation of the Poet to Day-Dreaming," in *Collected Papers*, ed. Ernest Jones, trans. Joan Riviere. Vol. IV. London: Hogarth Press and the Institute of Psycho-Analysis, 1925.

––––––––. *The Standard Edition of the Complete Psychological Works of Sigmund Freud*, ed. and trans. James Strachey, Anna Freud, et al. Vols. IV, V, XIV, XV, XXII. London: Hogarth Press and the Institute of Psycho-Analysis, 1953-64.

Fry, Roger. *The Artist and Psycho-Analysis*. London: Hogarth Press, 1924.

––––––––. *Transformations: Critical and Speculative Essays on Art*. New York: Brentano's, n.d. (1926?).

258

————. *Vision and Design*. London: Chatto & Windus, 1920.

Gibson, James J. *The Perception of the Visual World*. Cambridge, Mass.: Houghton Mifflin, 1950.

Gilbert, Stuart. *James Joyce's Ulysses: A Study*. 2nd rev. edn. New York: A. Knopf, 1952.

Husserl, Edmund. *The Phenomenology of Internal Time-Consciousness*, ed. Martin Heidegger, trans. James S. Churchhill. Bloomington: Indiana University Press, 1964.

James, Henry. *The Art of Fiction and Other Essays*, ed. Morris Roberts. New York: Oxford University Press, 1948.

————. *The Art of the Novel: Critical Prefaces*, ed. R. P. Blackmur. New York: Scribner's, 1934.

James, William. *Psychology: Briefer Course*. New York: Henry Holt and Co., 1892.

Jung, C. G. *Symbols of Transformation: An Analysis of the Prelude to A Case of Schizophrenia*, trans. R.F.C. Hull. *The Collected Works of C. G. Jung*, Vol. 5, Bollingen Series XX. 2nd edn., Princeton: Princeton University Press, 1967.

Jung, C. G. and C. Kerényi. *Essays on a Science of Mythology: The Myths of the Divine Child and the Divine Maiden*, trans. R.F.C. Hull, rev. edn. Bollingen Series XXII. Princeton: Princeton University Press, 1969.

Koestler, Arthur. *The Act of Creation*. New York: Macmillan, 1964.

Langer, Susanne K. *Feeling and Form*. New York: Scribner's, 1953.

————. *Mind: An Essay on Human Feeling*. Vol. I. Baltimore: Johns Hopkins Press, 1967.

————. *Philosophical Sketches*. Baltimore: Johns Hopkins Press, 1962.

Langer, Susanne K. *Philosophy in a New Key.* 3rd edn. Cambridge, Mass.: Harvard University Press, 1957.

Lesser, Simon. *Fiction and the Unconscious.* Boston: Beacon Press, 1957.

Lewis, Wyndham. *Time and Western Man.* London: Chatto & Windus, 1927.

Lubbock, Percy. *The Craft of Fiction.* New York: Scribner's, 1921.

Moore, George Edward. *Philosophical Studies.* New York: Harcourt, Brace, 1922.

————. *Principia Ethica.* Cambridge, England: Cambridge University Press, 1903.

Piaget, Jean. *The Construction of Reality in the Child,* trans. Margaret Cook. New York: Basic Books, 1954.

————. *Play, Dreams and Imitation in Childhood,* trans. C. Gattegno and F. M. Hodgson. New York: W. W. Norton, n.d.

Piaget, Jean, and Bärbel Inhelder. *The Child's Conception of Space,* trans. F. J. Langdon and J. L. Lunzer. London: Routledge and Kegan Paul, 1956.

Read, Herbert. *Selected Writings.* New York: Horizon Press, 1964.

Schachtel, Ernest G. *Metamorphosis: On the Development of Affect, Perception, Attention, and Memory.* New York: Basic Books, 1959.

Stephen, Leslie. *Hours in a Library.* 4 vols. New York: G. P. Putnam's Sons, 1904.

Trilling, Lionel. *The Liberal Imagination.* New York: Viking, 1950.

Varendonck, J. *The Psychology of Daydreams.* London: Allen & Unwin, 1921.

Weston, Jessie L. *From Ritual to Romance.* New York: Anchor Books, 1957.

Whitehead, Alfred North. *Symbolism: Its Meaning and Effect.* New York: Macmillan, 1927.

Whorf, Benjamin Lee. *Language, Thought, and Reality: Selected Writings*, ed. John B. Carroll. Cambridge, Mass.: M.I.T. Press; London: John Wiley and Sons, 1956.

MISCELLANY

De Quincey, Thomas. *Confessions of an English Opium-Eater and Suspiria de Profundis*. Boston: Ticknor and Fields, 1855.

Durrell, Lawrence. *Justine*. New York: Dutton, 1957.

Joyce, James. *A Portrait of the Artist as a Young Man*. New York: Modern Library, 1928.

Keynes, John Maynard. *Two Memoirs*. London: Rupert Hart-Davis, 1949.

Milton, John. *John Milton: Complete Poems and Major Prose*, ed. Merritt Y. Hughes. New York: Odyssey Press, 1957.

Proust, Marcel. *Letters of Marcel Proust*, ed. and trans. Mina Curtiss. New York: Random House, 1949.

———. *Remembrance of Things Past*, trans. C. K. Scott Moncrieff and Frederick A. Blossom. 2 vols. New York: Modern Library, 1934.

Whitman, Walt. *The Poetry and Prose of Walt Whitman*, ed. Louis Untermeyer. New York: Simon and Schuster, 1949.

Index

abstraction: of emotion, 54, 55, 60, 187, 188; as essence, 186, 187; process of, 21, 36, 37, 180, 186-88, 195, 197; of novel, Lily's painting as, 78n, 211, 232; of shapes, 74, 76, 77, 186; technique of, in *Jacob's Room*, 108

Aeschylus, *Choephori*, 139

Alice in Wonderland, see Lewis Carroll

"Anatomy of Fiction, The," 229n

angle of vision, 21, 83-98; physical, 83-87, 94; psychological, 87-96. *See also* distortion, object

anxiety, 89, 97, 152, 157, 218, 234, 242; relief from, 181, 183, 242n, 243

archetype, 123, 126, 127, 242, 243

"Art of Fiction, The," 166n, 245n

Auerbach, Erich, 137

Austen, Jane, 144n. *See also* "Jane Austen"

Bacon, Francis, 155n

Balzac, Honoré De, 12

Bell, Clive, 19n, 20, 37n, 74, 75, 209, 210

Bell, Vanessa (Mrs. Clive), 19n, 74

Bennett, Arnold, 3, 5, 9. *See also* "Mr. Bennett and Mrs. Brown"

Bennett, Joan, 128n

Bergson, Henri, 37, 38n, 39, 149, 161, 163n, 212, 245

Bertocci, Peter, 161, 162

Between the Acts, 34, 56, 60-63, 79, 81, 82, 99, 112, 113, 115n, 129, 137, 143, 144, 148, 159-61, 189, 199, 204n, 209n, 212, 229-31, 237-40, 244

Blackstone, Bernard, 74, 88, 209n

Bloomsbury, 14, 19-22, 63

Bodkin, Maud, 32, 243n, 244n

body, xi, 12, 28, 29, 151, 205-207; emotions of, 220n; position and memory release, 164, 165; rhythms, 206, 207, 215, 222; states of, 92, 239; -subject or -self, xii, 115

Brontë, Emily, 23

Browne, Sir Thomas, 155n

Carroll, Lewis, 5, 45, 54, 57, 217n

Cassirer, Ernst, 245

Chambers, R. L., 160

change, 211; awareness of, 163; within consciousness, 127, 150, 163, 167, 191; cyclical, 28; emotional, 106, 107, 226; within memories, 167-70; within time and the moment, 29, 39, 142. *See also* time

character: motivation of, 17; mystery of, 25, 136, 137. *See also* leitmotif, personality

Chastaing, Maxime, 145

childhood, 64, 156n; memories of, 182-84, 241; secret language of, 194, 196; traumas of, 17, 177, 178; in *The Waves*, 69, 101, 102, 168, 169; in *The Years*, 171-73, 177, 178. *See also* perception

Coleridge, Samuel T., 122n; *The Ancient Mariner*, 243n, 244n

color, 74-77, 96, 98, 105, 106, 195, 210; abnormal experience of, 90; "color hearing," 195n; emotional values of, 105, 106; perception of, 76; response to, 102, 105, 106;

INDEX

hero, *see* poet, quest
Holtby, Winifred, 25, 209n
Hoops, Reinald, 63, 64
"Hours in a Library" (essay),
xi, 236n
Hours in a Library, see Sir Les-
lie Stephen
"How it Strikes a Contempo-
rary," 14
"How Should One Read a
Book?" 232, 233n, 235, 236
Hume, David, 67
Husserl, Edmund, 38n, 245
hypnagogic state, 35, 37, 178

image, 180-202, 241, 242; generalized, 188, 189; intensi-
fication of, 184, 185; latent
or secret meaning of, 183-85,
189, 194, 197; manifest
meaning of, 183; as organizing agent, 45, 71-73; preparation of, 183, 184, 188;
repetition of, 91, 92, 166-68;
of rising and falling, 216,
217, 227; shift in, 92, 166-
70, 175, 183, 184; thought
or feeling rendered through,
42, 58-60, 90, 91, 133, 134,
167-70, 180ff; transformation of, 166, 191. *See also*
object, symbol
imagination, 36, 74, 90n, 133;
child's, 82, 196; dreaming,
247; structure of, 55, 224n.
See also creative process,
games, phantasy
"Impassioned Prose," 58n, 156,
162n
internal monologue, 42-44, 129,
130, 133; definition of, 43n;
entrance into, 43, 129, 130;
in *The Waves*, 42, 58-60,
132-34, 229. *See also* thought

Jacob's Room, 18, 34, 35n,
45n, 46n, 48n, 76, 77, 79,
81, 83-86, 87n, 97, 98, 107-
10, 126n, 131, 133n, 136,
140, 146, 148, 189, 191n,

204, 205, 213n, 235n
James, Henry, 14n, 22n, 73,
128, 213n; *The Sacred Fount*,
223, 224
James, William, 9, 10, 21, 33,
37, 47, 50, 153, 163n, 245
"Jane Austen," 13, 15
Johnson, Samuel, 235
Johnstone, J. K., 19, 20
Joyce, James, 12, 15, 16, 42,
43, 50, 224n; *Finnegans
Wake*, 8, 142n, 144; *A Por-
trait of the Artist as a Young
Man*, 83, 94, 217n; *Ulysses*,
11, 53n, 144, 149, 206
Jung, C. G., 5, 123n, 195n, 242

Kafka, Franz, 224n
Kandinsky, Wassily, 187
"Kew Gardens," 46, 85
Keynes, J. M., 19, 67n
kinetic mode, *see* time
Koteliansky, S. S., 132
Kris, Ernst, 63, 64

"Lady in the Looking-Glass,
The," 100n
Langer, Susanne K., 31, 32,
35n, 36, 146n, 148, 162n,
173n, 198n, 199n, 209,
212n, 245
language: "of fiction," 183n;
sexual quality of, 147; universal, 144; as verbalization
of feeling, 32, 133, 134, 145,
148; as "verbal noise," 134n;
Vico's theory of, 133n. *See
also* style, words
"Lappin and Lapinova," 56
Lawrence, D. H., 12; *Sons and
Lovers*, 205
"Leaning Tower, The," 55n,
89
leitmotif, 53, 125, 162n, 166,
167, 170, 172, 173, 177,
178n, 209n, 217
"Letter to a Young Poet, A," 11
"Lewis Carroll," 54n, 217n
"Life and the Novelist," 183n,
184n

266

pattern: archetypal, 243; as element of internal form, 203, 210, 225-28, 232; of emotional relationships, 78n, 224, 225; of feeling, 243, 244; and movement, 227, 228; of rise and fall, 227; of tensions, 31, 224, 226; of plot vs experience, 239. *See also* thought

perception (visual/mental), 21, 22, 35, 36, 65, 82, 86, 89, 99, 133, 181, 240, 241; abnormal, 88-95; depth, 77; child's visual, 79-82, 194-96; influences on, 29, 35, 36, 87-90, 92, 96, 159; peripheral awareness in, 87; principles of, 20-22, 65; processes of, 21, 35, 36, 70. *See also* abstraction, color, focus, perspective, vision, visual

personality, 111, 113, 114; androgynous, 12, 18, 119n, 121-23, 247, 248; discontinuity of, 5, 6, 115; dissociation of, 41, 67, 88, 93; divided or double, 113, 117-23, 127, 135, 215, 218; historical, 143, 160; modes of, 113-23; multiple, 4, 53, 114, 117, 118, 120-28, 132; repressed elements of, 118. *See also* mythic double, self, time

perspective, 28, 74, 75, 83

phantasy, 49, 55, 56; in daydreams, 54, 64, 89; of disturbed mind, 56, 88; as fairy tale, 56, 68, 70n, 106, 243. *See also* thought

"Phases of Fiction," 15, 144

Piaget, Jean, 35n, 245

"Pictures," 75n, 201

poet: creation of fictive world by, 70, 73; as hero, 68, 191; methods of, in novel, 23. *See also*, object, reality

point of view, 29, 32, 42, 54, 58, 66, 129; transitions in, 52, 53. *See also* internal monologue, narrator, voice

Pointz Hall, see *Between the Acts*, notebooks

Post-Impressionists, 4, 75

primitive modes, 34, 37, 180, 181. *See also* image, metaphor, symbol

"Professions for Women," 12

projection, 89, 91

Proust, Marcel, 15, 16, 30, 36, 37, 54, 111, 113, 115, 116, 149, 163-66, 200, 211, 224n

psychological novel, 14, 23, 24, 173n

psychology, 4, 37, 63-65, 218, 243; Gestalt, 203n, 204n

quest: in *Orlando*, 154, 191; in *To the Lighthouse*, 219, 243; in *The Waves*, 125

Read, Herbert, 187

reader: "common," 235; creative role of, 134, 137, 234, 236, 240; memory release in, 166, 167; placed in consciousness of character, 29, 33, 66, 90, 127, 128, 140, 144, 217, 237, 238; problems of, 11, 236-38; relation of, to author, 235, 237, 238; relation of, to narrator, 129, 238; relation of, to work, 11, 105, 229, 231-33, 236-44; satisfaction of, 57

"Reading," 238

reality, 19, 20, 66, 140n, 149; of child, 82, 195, 196; distortion of, 88, 89, 93; emotion as, 30, 31, 66, 180, 201, 202, 233; of inner experience, 92, 95, 182, 187; Isa's poetry as accommodation to, 61; metaphor as, 88, 181; mirror world as, 100; of self, 115, 233; tonal sense of, 131n

reflection, 34, 55, 97-113, 181, 193, 194. *See also* mirror techniques